The Secret Science *of* Numerology

The Hidden Meaning of Numbers and Letters

By

Shirley Blackwell Lawrence Msc.D

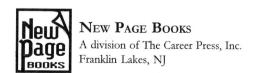

NEW PAGE BOOKS
A division of The Career Press, Inc.
Franklin Lakes, NJ

The Secret Science of Numerology
Edited by Kristen Mohn, Robert M. Brink
Typeset by Eileen Munson
Cover design by Foster & Foster
Printed in the U.S.A. by Book-mart Press

To order this title, please call toll-free 1-800-CAREER-1 (NJ and Canada: 201-848-0310) to order using VISA or MasterCard, or for further information on books from Career Press.

The Career Press, Inc., 3 Tice Road, PO Box 687
Franklin Lakes, NJ 07417
www.careerpress.com
www.newpagebooks.com

Library of Congress Cataloging-in-Publication Data

Lawrence, Shirley Blackwell.
    The secret science of numerology : the hidden meaning of numbers and letters / by Shirley Blackwell Lawrence.
        p. cm.
    Includes bibliographical references and indexes.
    ISBN 1-56414-529-8 (pbk.)
        1. Numerology. I. Title.

BF1623.P9 L38 2001
133.3'35—dc21   00-065376

*This book is dedicated to
all who seek more than
blind faith.*

*May they find in these pages,
answers.*

Acknowledgments

I wish to acknowledge with heartfelt thanks the following people who have made this book possible:

My husband, Jeff Lawrence, and children, Jennifer, David, and Julianne, for their understanding and encouragement during the years of research and writing this book;

My parents, Lloyd and Astrid Blackwell, for a wonder-filled childhood and for instilling in me a deep sense of spirituality;

Dr. Jack Ensign Addington, a true friend of many years who encouraged my writing and gave me professional advice;

Matthew Oliver Goodwin, numerologist/writer, who saw something of value in my book;

Ronald Fry of Career Press, who offered to republish this work when Newcastle Publishing ceased to be;

And finally, I would like to express my appreciation to Kristen Mohn, Editor, for her valuable input and communication during the republication of this book.

Contents

Part Three
Mystical Letters

Part Four
Number Groups and Numbers

Part Five
Keys To Self-Knowledge and Word Analysis

Part Six
The New Age Inner Guidance Number

Charts and Figures

Quest for Truth, Search for Knowledge

Have you ever wondered how some people can think so differently from you? Does it seem impossible to understand why others are so sure they are right when you know they are wrong? How can people be so opposite?

That had me puzzled for years, and the only thing that ever helped me to understand these differences was the study of numerology. I have researched and pondered the subject for years because this science is deep and much can be understood only by meditation on symbols.

As I researched I found answers to unusual phenomena that I had experienced and some I had heard about. I never expected to find answers to explain them, but I did; answers that are scientific and logical.

I eventually found these answers only because I had begun having vivid dreams with numbers in them. I wondered what they meant.

People began asking me if I knew what numbers meant. Why do they ask me? I wondered. Maybe I'm supposed to know.

A friend gave me a quarterly list of events at the Philosophical Research Society in Los Angeles, and I saw there was going to be a seminar on numerology. I had to go.

At that seminar I learned the basic meanings of numbers and how to analyze my own name. I was stunned. The vowels told me my innermost desires; the consonants, my personality. My whole birth name told me my talents and destiny, while my birth date told me what I'm supposed to do with those talents. This would have been invaluable information for me when I was deciding on a major in college. But what was most interesting was how true the information was.

I set about analyzing the charts of my husband and children, and what I learned answered a lot of questions. I wished I had known these things about us years ago—we could have made some better decisions. What I learned was incredible.

I read every book on numerology that was available and compared texts. They all agreed on the basic meanings of numbers and how they apply to the birth name and date. I studied every day. It was too interesting to stop. All these books were right on.

I was lucky in the sense that I could further verify the accuracy of these books by doing charts for many people. In my professional life in the film industry, I worked with different people on different sets every day, and they were all eager to hear what their names had to say about them.

All I did was tell them the positive and negative aspects of each number according to the position in which it appeared in their charts. Some people told me that I must have been using psychic power. They said, "You know more about me than my family. You told me things about myself that nobody knows."

I missed on a point only a couple times, but when they said what it was, I could spot it immediately in another part of the chart. On those occasions I had neglected to scan the entire chart before making a statement.

Sometimes there were newspaper stories about people in which the full name was printed. I would analyze those names to find how the story of their behavior fit with their name numbers. It was never hard to find. I learned that this study is an accurate character analysis. It helped me to understand people.

Numerology taught me that there are seven different ways of viewing things, and that all of mankind fits into one of these seven. There have always been seven schools of thought; every mind conforms to one of those seven. Through the centuries, the names of religions may change, but the seven basic thoughts remain. We are all on separate wavelengths, so to speak, and are most comfortable with those who are on our own.

Have you ever wondered what kind of world this would be if everyone in it were exactly like you? For that matter, do you really feel you know yourself? The most ancient axiom is "know thyself," and to do so is our greatest quest in life. If we can pinpoint the wavelength we are on, we are halfway there. Numerology gives us this information.

Many are happy with this knowledge alone. But knowing the basic meanings of numbers was not enough for me. There had to be a reason why they are so accurate in analysis. Some books mentioned it was because of number "vibration." But what did that mean?

I had to dig further. I had to know how this knowledge was originally conceived, who drew these conclusions. I reasoned that if names tell so much about a person and are so true, then words must also reveal their true import.

I analyzed every word that came to mind and was overwhelmed with the discovery that the numbers of a word explain its meaning perfectly. Furthermore, the shapes of letters that make up each word have a story to tell that is highly informative.

I learned that numbers are occult symbols. Occultism is the study of the hidden side of nature; it observes nature as a whole, rather than examining it in parts as science does. As William Eisen, a scientist by profession and author of *The English Cabalah*, said in one of his workshops:

> "Science has a lot of questions to which they are searching for answers, while the occult has all the answers and is waiting for the questions. When the day comes that the two meet, there will be greater strides in science than have ever been made before."

To me it proves that there is no way we can separate God from science. The bottom line is that they are one and the same.

This is what this book is about; the search for facts that explain the science behind number vibration and unraveling other mysteries on the way; discovering the thoughts of those who were most wise and how their beliefs have been and are being proved by science today. And most importantly, how we can use this science to discover hidden meanings in our everyday words, our names, and in character analysis. It is an accurate tool for understanding our children and for employing the right people for the job.

There are many fine books on numerology that cover name analysis well. This book is designed to provide background reference material that can be used with any one of them. It is a sourcebook of information that I found scattered throughout a great deal of literature, and through meditation.

I had a thirst for knowledge and a quest for truth. The study of numbers put me on the road to illumination. A whole world opened up to me and life took on new meaning. If this book proves to be as exciting and enlightening to anyone else who is sincerely seeking answers, then my work has been even more worthwhile.

"I prayed for wisdom and God gave me numbers."

Shirley Blackwell Lawrence
Palmdale, California

Introduction

Juno Jordan was in her late 90s when I heard her lecture at a conference sponsored by the now fondly remembered Numerology Association International. (Jordan, as you may know, died in 1984, less than two months short of her 100th birthday.) She was frail when I saw her but her voice was strong and her mental faculties still finely tuned. She spoke passionately of the need for numerologists to spend much more of their time in researching and studying the deeper meanings of the numbers. Jordan clearly felt that the symbolism of the numbers was at the very center of the ancient study of numerology.

In my experience, numerologists generally follow two chief avenues of study. One is to concentrate on finding and experimenting with new combinations of numbers and letters in search for new understandings. When a new book is published, for instance, many numerologists enjoy checking to see if there are any new configurations to test for accuracy and reliability. Less often, numerologists spend time researching, contemplating, or meditating on the symbolic meanings—and the extended meanings—of numbers and letters.

Some numerologists see, as I do, that the heart of the matter is to be found, simply enough, in these basic pieces. The more I understand about each number and letter, the more I can discern in the numerology charts I study and, in many ways, the more I also understand about myself and the world. I agree with Juno Jordan that the study of the symbolic meanings of the numbers—and their accompanying letters—is a vital place for numerologists to devote a considerable amount of their energies.

And Shirley Blackwell Lawrence has made that kind of study considerably easier by writing this book. In the substantial middle section, Lawrence gives the broadest contemporary analysis of this material that I've seen. It fills a vital need.

Though they're not as easy to read, I'll still enjoy browsing through three early books devoted to such symbolism, Harriette and F. Homer

Curtis's *The Key to the Universe* and *The Key of Destiny* (Newcastle Publishing) and Corinne Heline's intense *Sacred Science of Numbers* (DeVorss and Co.). Lawrence's modern presentation, though, includes some important additions. She provides in-depth information on the form of the symbols—and the derivations and meanings of these forms. She's also gone back to basic sources—the Bible, the Kabbalah, to name just two—to delve deeply into the symbolism.

In addition, there's some interesting commentary in Lawrence's book that you're not likely to find anywhere else. She writes in an enlightened manner. For instance, her recognition of the similarity between the look of the head of an ox and the uterus, along with their symbolic connections with beginnings, physical reproduction, the Hebrew letter Aleph, and the English letter A. I'd previously seen the oxhead mentioned with the Aleph, but hadn't been able to make any meaningful connection. Now, having digested Lawrence's commentary, I expect I'll remember the symbols—and the meanings—for the rest of my life.

Lawrence is often helpful in clarifying some meanings of the letters by discussing many words, which begin with the letter in question. She connects B to baby, M to mountain and magical, F to family and fatherhood. Her discussions of the numbers are equally enlightening and significant.

The beginning and ending sections of the book offer another wonderful treasure trove. They're overflowing with information that I expect will fill some important gaps in most numerologists' scientific and historical understandings. My favorites among the particular pieces of information are:

→ The discussion of scientific instruments—the eidophone, the psychograph, and the polygraph, among others—and numerology's tie-in to the world of sound and vibration.

→ The story of Pythagoras and his school. Since numerologists are always paying homage to Pythagoras, it's helpful to get a solid bearing on his life and accomplishments.

→ The history of the modern school of numerology. Lawrence suggests, as I have often thought, that although it's nice for numerologists to remember that the birth of their field was in distant antiquity, it's also more realistic to accept that the modern version of numerology—dealing particularly with character analysis—dates back only a little more than one hundred years or so. I'm delighted to see that numerologist Isidore Kominsky finally made it into a contemporary numerology text—along with L. Dow Balliet, Julia Seton, and the like. Thank you, Shirley, for helping to make the historical record a bit more accurate.

You will likely have your own favorites among the Lawrence treasures. But the section on letters and numbers is worth the lion's share of our attention. For me, that part of the book addresses one of the key areas in numerology, and is an especially valuable contribution.

Matthew Oliver Goodwin
Author, *Numerology: The Complete Guide*
Culver City, California

PART ONE

The Search *for the* Science Behind It All

CHAPTER 1

Unveiling the Secret Science

In *The Secret Doctrine,* Helen P. Blavatsky tells us that the secret laws were passed on orally from teacher to student for thousands of years, and that they were never written down. For centuries, the written divulgence of these secrets had been forbidden out of "necessity" because they could have been wrongly used by the profane and material-minded masses. She added that they would gradually be revealed to true and honest seekers of the New Age and that revelation would come when the time was right. At that time this information would be of use only to the enlightened minds of the day, for no one else would find sense in or use for it.

Certain mystic writers have been entrusted with part of the knowledge, and in the future there will be still others to reveal even more. I believe these ancient secrets are being made known now, in this New Age, or this small portion would not have been revealed to me. Why me? I'm as surprised as anyone. All I know is that I had a deep and honest desire to know and that something has been urging me in this direction all my life.

From the time I was a child I had a great interest in things of a spiritual nature. I thought ancient man must have been very fortunate to have been so close to his beginnings, and so close to nature. The stronghold of opinions had not yet begun to form. Ancient peoples did not have to go far to find forests and other natural scenes of beauty where they could feel the stillness of the environment, hear the song of birds and insects, and feel the strong aura of approaching animals. This was a time before men parroted other men's opinions; when they could learn no other way than by going within and meditating deeply; by joining their Higher Selves to the great consciousness of the Universe about them. I reasoned that in the very beginning there had to be only God, and that in order to create anything it had to come out of Himself. We are all divine substance— intelligent particles in the whole body of our creator.

I used to hear such wonderful lectures in my head that I wished someone would invent a machine that could capture every word that was spoken by that still, small voice. Eventually, I was able to write down some of these thoughts, until I had notebooks filled with them—thoughts that I later found written in other books. Where did these thoughts come from? At the time I believed that they were purely my imagination. But I did tune into something out there, or within, and it told no lies. I came to trust these inner monologues and in time learned to distinguish them from my own thoughts.

As I grew older I often thought I would like to study ancient Hebrew because it was the language from which all biblical translations originated. But I never expected this research to take me into the very heart of it. It is as though my Higher Self had been prompting me to do this since I was a child.

My research covered a vast number of books related to numerology —books that each held a key thought that struck a chord within me. Through meditation, deductive reasoning, and sudden insights, all of these key thoughts, like pieces of a jigsaw puzzle, fit together very neatly.

The secrets themselves have remained hidden by their very obviousness. The science is in the realm of physics, transcendental physics, and entwined with geometry and deep symbolism. Many of its truths are hidden in myths, math, and magic. A few key phrases led me to the unveiling of the secrets themselves, secrets that are described in Chapter 11 in "Prelude to Letters," and Chapter 22, "Prelude to Numbers."

In one source I read that all writers of the mysteries would never reveal these secrets clearly. Rather, they would surround a key idea with related material, which would draw attention away from the germ of the idea. Only the true seeker would understand it.

There were other key ideas that seemed to stand out for me in books I read. It was significant that Hebrew letters were also their numbers and that the two were completely interchangeable; that meanings were hidden in the shapes of the letters; and that these letter symbols were regarded as containers of, and manifestations of, concealed virtues. They represented arcane powers of a set and determinable nature which would reveal themselves to one who meditated on them.

It helps to know that when we meditate on any particular symbol it will reveal itself to us. You see, symbols are the universal language of the soul. This was why Pythagoras had those wishing to enter his school meditate on a given symbol and then share the meanings they derived from that meditation before they were accepted as students.

Then there was the fact that Pythagoras taught that a number is a living qualitative reality. It is not just representative of an amount, but a rate of vibration.

The Latin adage, "Omnia in numeris sita sunt" means: "Everything lies veiled in numbers." And Helen Blavatsky said, "number underlies form, and number guides sound. It lies at the root of the manifested Universe."

There was also the discovery by the turn-of-the-century piano-music composition teacher, Mrs. L. Dow Balliet, that the letter name of each note had the same vibration as its musical tone. It stood to reason that the sound of every letter in the English alphabet must therefore correspond to the vibration of its numbered place therein.

My subconscious was working on all this information, and I didn't really know that I understood exactly what it was all about until someone asked me why our letters are numbered as they are, and how we can know that their meanings are true. As I explained this, I heard myself giving the answer I had been looking for, and it became clear to me for the first time—but my subconscious had already known.

Then another puzzle was solved in a most unusual way. I read in several sources that Aleph (A) was called "oxhead" and its meaning was "physical generation." For months I pondered that. I could see no connection between an oxhead and reproduction. Then one day I noticed a man wearing a T-shirt with an unusual picture on it. At first glance it looked like the picture of a uterus. Curiosity made me take a closer look: It was an oxhead! The horns are the fallopian tubes. So that was it. The ancients knew anatomy. They knew what the uterus looked like and that it is in the shape of an oxhead. How very well matched it was after all! How ingenious! And how beautifully concealed the secret was in its obviousness. On January 22, 1989, I attended a lecture at the Philosophical Research Society by Manly P. Hall's wife, Marie Bauer Hall. I was amused to hear her say, "God made man to make secrets and he made woman to break all secrets wide open."

CHAPTER 2

The Power of a Name

A name creates an instant impression. Some of us love our names, while others are uncomfortable with theirs and change them. I noticed that the sounds of various names give us different feelings, as though they are energies.

Our youngest daughter let us know her own name soon after she was born. I cuddled her to me and softly spoke her name: "Kathryn." I recalled how our first two babies, Jennifer and David, had looked up at me and smiled at the sound of their names, but now I got no response. So I repeated, "Kathryn," and still no reaction. We had also been considering the name Julianne. So I said, "Julianne?" and she looked right at me and smiled.

I told my husband about it. He laughed and said it must be my imagination. The nurse overheard, and the next time he came in she said, "I want you to know it's true. I tried it when she was in the nursery and she did not respond to Kathryn. But when I said 'Julianne,' she turned her head to me and smiled. Your wife is right about that." So of course he had to try it, and when he got the same reaction there was no doubt about it— her name was Julianne.

It was interesting to us that she had made the final decision, for until then we had not been able to decide between the two names. Over 15 years later, through the study of numerology, I concluded that our names are not accidental, and that we choose the vibration that will help us fulfill our mission. Even if the birth registrar writes "Baby Girl" on the birth certificate, this is the incoming vibration that holds the clue to the child's talents and destiny.

When I first began working in the movie studios in the early 1960s, I met one of the main drivers on the Warner Bros. lot. He introduced himself, then immediately went into an explanation of his name.

"Now that's not my real name," he said. "I won't tell anyone my real name because it was made famous by a notorious outlaw years ago, and I don't want anybody to even think we are related. So I changed mine legally to the one I use now." No amount of coaxing would pry his natal name from his lips, and he never mentioned it again.

When I was in college, the Dean of Music used an initial for his first name, and his full middle and last names. There again, he would not reveal his real name. Now I notice that quite a few people prefer to use only their initials, or a nickname.

Some names are so common, and there are so many of them listed in phone books, that people have banded together and formed clubs for people with the same name. There are the "Mikes of America," "The Fred Society," the "Jim Smith Society," and a club of Susans called "Sic-M" who are all involved in communications and the media.

Experts say that when it comes to names, familiarity can breed contempt. For centuries people in crowded countries used formal names with titles before them because the titles generated respect. The act of saying Mister, Misses, or Miss helped people get along with one another.

We associate names with the persons we have come to know, and this makes them very personal. Often we also associate names with things, as in the Salk Vaccine, Disneyland, Steinway Pianos, and Bell Telephone. All these names seem to fit their inventions. Can you imagine a concert pianist playing Disney instead of Steinway? And instead of Disneyland, does it sound as much fun to go to Salkland?

In the advertising world, names are money. Corporations pay a great deal to find the right name for a product.

Even the name of a city can be important and affect an entire community. In January 1987, a portion of Los Angeles called Canoga Park was renamed West Hills. That name change made the value of the homes in the area appreciate $10,000 to $20,000—all because of a new name.

"A good name is better than a precious ointment"
(Ecclesiastes 7:1).

CHAPTER 3

The Power of the Word

"Here are the temples of his words," I heard, and I saw weird looking structures. Some were made of slime, while others were like crystalline palaces.

"Words?" I asked.

"Yes, words. Words are living entities. They are given birth through man's mouth and they continue to live in the fourth dimension, becoming his home at the crossover."

The sight of those structures never left me, even though it was in a dream, a vivid dream. That brief soul journey gave me valuable insight into the power of words and made clearer the meaning of such scriptural references as:

> "For I say unto you that for every foolish word which men speak, they will have to answer for it on the day of judgment. For by your words you shall be found guilty"
> (Matthew 12:34).

Then in my research I found the following statement in Eliphas Levi's *The Book of Splendours* (43):

> For in the world to come, all good words spoken in the world at hand will take on living forms, and you are creatures of goodness, you who manifest through the Word that which is true.

The spoken word is powerful because it brings forth a thought, and a thought is the start of every manifestation: "... for the mouth speaks from the fullness of the heart" (Matthew 12:34). This means that whatever appeals to you is where your consciousness lies, and that level of consciousness is revealed by the words you speak.

According to the Kabbalah, the name of God is found in the vowel sounds because they are the vibrations that form life. If you read this paragraph aloud without the vowel sounds, you will see why they are called "the animating spirit of the word."

The sound of the spoken word can be measured by its rate of vibration, and that vibration can create pictures visible to us on a device called an eidophone. This is a drum-like instrument with a rubbery material across the top. A mouthpiece extends from it that can be spoken into. Then a crystalline mixture is spread on the top, and as different words are spoken into the mouthpiece, the crystals form various shapes.

The vibrational effect of the word "butterfly" causes the crystals to take on a beautiful butterfly formation; "snowflake," the pattern of a snowflake. Such lovely words form lovely pictures. But harsh words do not form beautiful designs at all. Instead, they form haphazard, even grotesque forms as ugly to the eye as to the ear. The invisible takes form before our eyes, based on our words. How important, then, are the words we speak?

> "The words of a wise man's mouth are gracious; but the lips of a fool will ruin him" (Ecclesiastes 10:12).

CHAPTER 4

The Power of Thought

The spoken word is powerful because it brings forth a thought, and a thought is the start of every manifestation.

This was the subject of discussion in one of my science classes in college at San Diego State in 1957. We had been talking about thought forms and were wondering whether there was any scientific basis for them.

Our professor told us he was aware of a college that had an experimental group who gathered to concentrate their efforts on developing a thought form. First their teacher had them relax to bring their brain waves into the alpha state. He then proceeded to describe a dragon, and as he did so, all the students were to picture every detail as he described it. Once their concentration was unified, a mist began to form in the shape of a dragon, and held its shape until the students lost their power of concentration.

They concluded that thoughts are energy in a certain state of motion, and that collective thinking can be very powerful. Our discussion then shifted to the sensing of certain types of thought forms established in places where people of the same mind gather: shopping malls, bars, places of worship, etc. Obviously there is a different mood connected with each place. We sense the thought forms that have been built up by the mental atmosphere of the location.

Psychics, or sensitive people who may not realize they are psychic, pick up on these thought forms very clearly. Once understood, we see there is nothing supernatural about these things.

Our words leave a thought behind that continues to live. These words produce thought forms that become a part of our own personal energy field that creates a distinct vibration of its own. This vibration is like the kind sent out by a tuning fork and works on the same principle—when sound vibrations are projected on an object of the same natural frequency, the object will begin to vibrate with it. Objects of a different frequency remain untouched.

Dr. Baraduc of Bordeaux invented a machine that actually records the vibrations of thoughts. It registers a high speed, strong vibratory effect when an intelligent person approaches the instrument, and a feeble, slow rate when someone of low mentality comes near *(The Finding of the Third Eye*, 32). This shows how thoughts are energy in a certain state of motion. The more force, the higher the vibration. The slower the rate, the less force it contains and it becomes negative in action.

Our whole body goes into action when we think. Our muscles and larynx move, even if it seems undetectable. Scientists have discovered that chest movements are directly related to thoughts and even succeeded in recording them graphically. Each type of thought has a set wavelength!

In 1945, Sir Alexander Cannon, a professor and doctor, learned to compare types of thoughts at a glance by their mathematical interpretation from graphs. The graphs even showed the effects of different types of music on individuals *(The Power Within*, Chapter 8).

Such graphs show another amazing thing: The thoughts of one person actually influence another person by the mere mental atmosphere produced by these thoughts—and it is detectable by the respiration!

We can control our thoughts by taking deep, slow breaths. Some meditation techniques require deep breathing. This is good, for it keeps the mental state in balance and at the same time it is beneficial for the body.

It has been noted that mantras are effective aids in meditation. They are either spoken aloud, whispered, or thought upon, but the most powerful of the three are those repeated in thoughts. This is not surprising, for only in silence can we hear the inner voice.

By nurturing thoughts of contentment, disease can be cured. Likewise, inharmonious and worrisome thoughts filled with negativity can create disease. This is because our immune system is set up to release adrenaline when we are in danger. Stressful thoughts as well as other stress-filled stimuli, such as graphically violent movies, trigger the flow of adrenaline into the bloodstream. At the same time the heart beats faster and acid is released into the stomach.

Our body cannot tell the difference between actual bodily danger and the act of just "thinking" about a stressful situation. Even when it is only the mind that is occupied with these negations, the body prepares itself anyway.

If excessive production of hormones continues, it eventually debilitates the body, making it ripe for all kinds of physical problems. So gaining control of our thoughts and emotions is important for good health. People appear to be physically made of the same type of matter, but in reality, they are made of different chemical elements that correspond directly to their own level of consciousness. Have you ever wondered why you feel a kinship with some people at first meeting? Or why certain ones you haven't even met can repel you upon first sight?

It is their consciousness that sets up their personal vibratory rate. When we are of the same mind as someone else we say we are "in tune" with them, and we really are. We are like the object that vibrates with the tuning fork, and those of a completely different vibratory consciousness from our own may not seem as attractive to us.

Man's own growth vibration is recorded in his auric field. The more advanced a person is in his knowledge, the shorter the wavelength and the higher the frequency. That vibratory level is made manifest in the voice, so the tone of voice indicates the level of spiritual development *(The Key to the Universe*, 228).

This vibratory level is evident in our reading level as well. When we read with comprehension, we not only see the printed word, we see the form of it in our mind's eye and at the same time we are silently vocalizing the word and hearing it. Since each person comprehends at his own level of understanding, no two people can read the same passage and get the same meaning from it.

Thought always precedes action. The extent of our knowledge and all of our life's experiences arise from our thoughts. We draw our opinions, beliefs, actions, and reactions from this personal storehouse. The strongest influences are visual stimuli because they have an impact on our optic nerve, which stores them in our pictorial memory garden. Everything we see and hear is impressed on our brain cells, which are living tissue. Our thought forms appear in our sleep, in our daily life, and they color our reactions.

I once painted a thought form into a piece of furniture! While my husband and I were antiquing our dining room set we were watching *The Planet of the Apes* on television. To this day I see apes when I look at that furniture. Even pictures that artists paint include the astral and mental aspects of their conception as they paint. That remains as an influence on each viewer *(The Hidden Side of Things*, 400).

In a way we are all like computers—we cannot give out anything that has not been put in. Thus, our thought material has a profound effect on our life experiences.

Let pleasant thoughts mold your face.

CHAPTER 5

The Fourth Dimension

It was the day before Mother's Day in 1981 and my family had a large, beautifully wrapped present for me by the fireplace. Every time I walked by it I wondered what it could be. Then, all of a sudden, I saw it completely unwrapped and I knew what it was. I was stunned and quickly took a second look. This time it was completely gift-wrapped again.

I told my family I saw right through the gift-wrap and knew what it was. My husband laughed and said I couldn't know because it was something new on the market and he didn't think I even knew about it. The next day before I unwrapped it I said, "What I saw was a foot massager." My husband's jaw dropped. It was indeed a foot massager.

This experience, I knew, was called "clairvoyance," meaning, "clear seeing" into some fourth dimension. It happened to me, yet I could not do it at will. I wondered what caused it, and why it happens only occasionally, for I had other similar experiences.

As I reflected on this experience, it brought to mind times when I was equally perplexed by clairaudient (clear-hearing) experiences. When I was a child I heard both audible voices and music in my room at night that seemed to be coming from nowhere, well after my parents were asleep.

Once, when I was in my 20's, I heard a beautiful piano concerto coming from my living room in the middle of the night. I lay there enjoying it quite awhile before I woke up enough to realize it was coming out of nowhere and I felt frightened at the thought. "Oh, no," I said, "I'm scared. Please stop!" And at that I heard the conductor rap his baton on his stand, the music stopped, I heard all the music books shut, and there was silence.

I felt I was truly fortunate to hear such glorious music from another dimension. From then on I looked forward to such encounters. I could never experience them at will, but I did learn that I could communicate with the musicians by thought, and if I asked them to repeat any section, they would. I had been a music major in college, a singer and composer, so I began to memorize sections of music to write down, and I succeeded.

Probably the most outstanding example of such experiences was the time I heard the loveliest duet in a dream. A princess was having her hair brushed by a handmaiden and they were situated on a rock at the edge of a small lake in a great forest. A handsome prince approached, singing in his glorious baritone, "You are my music." The princess joined him in song and I was entranced by the scene as well as the music. I wanted to capture that music and asked them to repeat it. They did. I wrote it down, entered it in a composer's contest, and won first place in ballads.

It wasn't long afterward that I met the real prince of my dreams, and he had that same glorious baritone voice I had heard singing that song. Soon after we were married, the winning songs were to be performed in concert, and we sang "You Are My Music" together. The thrill cannot be described.

I knew there had to be an explanation for these experiences. It was only through my research to find the secret behind the accuracy of numerology that I learned the mystery behind these phenomena. Sometimes, for a moment, we are transported into the fourth dimension.

The physical plane about us is three-dimensional space of height, breadth, and thickness. We see the surface of all things but cannot perceive the hidden side, which is the interior from our exterior point of view. So this fourth dimension is the unseen of what we see, and it is also an aspect of mind and a dimension we experience in dreams.

Most of us at one time or another have experienced seeing something "out of the corner of the eye" and then realized that nothing is there. For a brief moment we may very well have seen something in the fourth dimension.

Where is it? The fourth dimension is in the astral plane that interpenetrates our physical plane, but which is usually invisible to us on our three-dimensional level. This is where thought forms exist. This "unseen side of things" is seen only with the mind's eye.

We tune into the fourth dimension when the sense organs of our astral or etheric body are awakened. The physical body is an exact copy of the etheric counterpart, which encircles us and extends several feet from the physical. It is the etheric body that determines the shape of the physical one by its lines of force. All through life it rebuilds and restores the physical. Any physical problems show up first in the etheric body. When they do, the etheric draws in closer to the physical. We sense this weakened energy field around those who are afflicted.

The reverse is also true: health can be accepted by the mind, and its healing effect restores the etheric first and then the physical. This is why affirmations, suggestion, and prayer are powerful aids in combating illnesses. The more faith and hope that can be instilled in the patient, the quicker the recovery. The stronger the life force, the further the etheric extends from the physical. The reason it is not seen on this dimension is because the molecules that compose it are much farther apart than those of the physical, which renders it invisible, though it is very real. "There is a natural body and there is a spiritual body" (1 Corinthians 15:44).

Anesthetics drive out the etheric body so the person is unaware of pain. The etheric body remains whole even if the physical has had an amputation. Amputees have attested that they are aware of their etheric counterpart when a limb is removed—they feel it as though it were still there *(The Rosicrucian Cosmo-Conception,* 60-66). Kirlian photography shows the etheric presence of such limbs, and parts of leaves that have been torn away.

It is not unusual to sense another person's etheric body. If you move your hand close to, but not touching, another person's hand, or even your own, you will feel a slight sensation as etheric touches etheric. This etheric body has its own set of sense organs, called chakras, which are the vehicles that attune us to the fourth dimension.

Chakra is a Sanskrit word for wheel, and the chakras appear to the seer as colored wheel-shaped objects. They are seven circular vortices, or force centers, which are connection points for the flow of energy from the Universe to our etheric counterpart, and then to us, supplying energy to our physical body.

There are three groups of chakras: the lower (physiological), middle (personal), and higher (spiritual) *(The Chakras, a Monograph,* 17). The physiological energize the desires of the flesh. Development of spiritual qualities activates the higher chakras. As a person grows spiritually, these chakras go into motion. They are like colored lotuses, with movement so slight as to be undetectable. But when activated, each petal opens as they vibrate. Through their unfolding comes the gift of seeing into the fourth dimension (clairvoyance), hearing in the fourth dimension (clairaudience), and a higher awareness.

Sometimes children are born with their chakras open and they can see and hear equally well in both worlds. They talk to and play with playmates who are unseen by us, but are very real to them.

When we understand the laws of vibration, we cannot help but realize the power we have in our thoughts. The ideas we entertain and create take form in the fourth-dimensional plane and will become realities here if we give them enough power. We give them that power when we think of them with such emotional intensity that it becomes ingrained in our soul. In a given amount of time, that "seed" will germinate into a force that will either spur us to action to accomplish, or, if a negative thought, will take hold in the etheric body, and then manifest itself in the physical body *(Knowledge of the Higher Worlds and its Attainment,* 62).

Another aspect of the fourth dimension is that of predictions. All through history people have wanted to know what the future has in store. Priests built high towers so that they could study the changing sky. They plotted the courses of the visible planets, drew up the zodiac, and related all the world's happenings to the stars. Astrology became a popular science, especially with regard to the forecasting of events. Today there are many seers who foresee that which takes place in the fourth dimension before it is manifested here. They must be careful not to make judgments and predict a negative event as a fact, for ultimately it is man who makes a choice that can change a course of events. Seers who do not make this distinction and foretell a negative event are as guilty of that event coming to pass as though it were planned and executed by them.

On the other hand, if the belief in their word is great, they could prevent a foreseen disaster by warning others to be cautious. They have an understanding of how present trends can lead to future results. Man has a power of choice and can change probable outcomes by taking the right action. The seers' power isn't so much just the fact that they can foresee future events, as it is a power to set an idea into the atmosphere that people will accept.

We find there is not that much difference between prediction and actuality when it is accepted in people's minds. That is proved over and over again in movies where the power of an idea is magnified to a living reality. Until Rod Serling wrote and filmed *The Hi-Jacking*, there had never been one. But less than one week after it ran on television, there was the first one in history. He said he often regretted deeply having filmed this idea, for he created a terrible monster and he realized it when it was too late.

Our thoughts—what we think about, read about, look at—are all fourth-dimensional, and all is initiated on that plane before it manifests on our third-dimensional physical plane.

This will be perfectly clear to the spiritual-minded, for the higher can understand the lower, but the lower cannot understand the higher.

According to Confucius, "Heaven sends down it's good and evil symbols, and wise men act accordingly."

This is potent stuff. We are working with the power of creation. We are able to draw from Eternal Mind, where all ideas exist, by tuning in with our higher mind to the fourth dimension, and beyond.

You have the power to love the world.

CHAPTER 6

As Above, So Below

The science behind numerology has given modern science great insight into the workings of nature. Numbers never fail. Numbers are law. There is nothing made that does not have size, shape, and dimension. The principle of the law is "As in the macrocosm (the Universe), so in the microcosm (man and nature)." By studying an atom or cell we can find the key to the functioning of a man, a planet, a galaxy. In other words, laws that are true to us on Earth are inevitably true in the Universe. The Hermetic aphorism is phrased simply: "As Above, So Below."

As an example of this truth, or law, there is a most striking demonstration that is found in the science of spectroscopy: the study and analysis of the phenomena observed with the spectroscope.

The spectroscope is an optical instrument that looks somewhat like a telescope. There is a prism in the middle. Light rays that enter are transformed into parallel rays, discrete colored lines that can be measured by their wavelengths and compared to known chemicals and elements.

Every element has its own pattern that never varies. According to the Hermetic law "As Above, So Below," the pattern will be the same on other planets: the above. The astronomers merely compare the picture presented with known elements on Earth: the below, and those that match up to a particular element will prove that element to be on that planet. Spectroscopic analysis shows that all elements known on Earth are found in the sun. So we see how it is true that as it is above, so it is below.

To get to the true nature of elements, we find that they are composed of basic molecules of energy. The ancients say this energy is made of God Himself: being the Creator of all there is, He had to create from the energy of His own ideas and the material of His own Being.

Even though we cannot see these molecules of energy with the naked eye, they nevertheless exist. And each invisible force has its own set of vibrations, starting with low frequency domestic electricity that has 50 to

60 vibrations per second. As the vibratory rate increases, there are sound, radio, television, and radar waves, microwaves, infrared rays, X-rays, and gamma rays, all invisible around us but powerful when harnessed.

There are only two kinds of matter: negative (electrons) and positive (protons), which are whirling bits of energy. The distance between them and their constant rate of vibration determine what form the matter takes: *solids* are close together and the rate is slow; *liquids* are further apart and move faster; and *gases* are the furthest apart and move the quickest.

Wavelengths affect form, color, sound, heat, light, and substance. All vibrate, and vibration has three factors: size, rate of oscillation, and its relation to fixed time.

Sound is produced by the vibrations of a body and is audible if the frequency lies between 20 and 20,000 vibrations per second. Loudness depends on the extent to which the sounding body vibrates. Above this range the vibration is called ultrasonic, and below, subsonic.

Light is a form of radiant energy transmitted in electromagnetic waves, which stimulate the organs of sight.

Heat consists of the kinetic energy of the vibrational motion of molecules. The more friction, the more heat. Friction and speed are the forces that form what appear to be different substances, yet there is only one substance. Everything breathes, even inanimate objects like metal. Solid matter, in its last analysis, is merely energy in a certain state of motion.

Color is simply a different rate of vibration in another octave. The color of an object depends upon the wavelength it reflects. Beyond the violet vibration the oscillation is so minute and rapid that it can interpenetrate solids, so we cannot see any further colors *(The Finding of the Third Eye,* 28-31). The principles that govern music apply to the vibratory rate of colors, and the same ratio exists between colors of the spectrum as between notes of the musical scale.

It was Sir Isaac Newton, the English philosopher and mathematician (1642-1727), who first described the mathematical synchronicity of color with music. It was he who discovered the dispersion of white light into the prism of seven colors and assigned each of them to its corresponding musical tone:

Red	Orange	Yellow	Green	Blue	Indigo	Violet
C	D	E	F	G	A	B

(Reader's Digest Great Encyclopedic Dictionary, 911)

Even disease has a distinct vibration. An American physician, Dr. Abrams, invented an instrument to measure all of the reactions to the human body and was able to assign a numerical value to each disease. He believed the remedy could also be figured out through numbers *(The Finding of the Third Eye,* 114).

Years later, in 1985, a woman named Karin Lee Abraham published a small book entitled, *Healing Through Numerology,* in which she furthers the idea that "disease" corresponds to certain vibrational rates. She shows how to construct an illness chart, and by using numerology, find the best medication. She stresses that a person's mental attitude is a major factor in overcoming any illness, that we are *mind* before we are body, and suggests that we can not only control the cure, but may certainly have created the illness in the first place *(Healing Through Numerology,* Introduction).

All of these studies bring me to the conclusion that the source of all color, sound, and vibration is in the spiritual plane, not the physical. "As Above, So Below." These are the tools for the making of the Universe.

According to Professor Jagadish Chandra Bose of Calcutta, who wrote the book, *Response in the Living and Non-Living,* there is some degree of life in the smallest grain of sand.

> ...not only the chemical compounds are the same, but the same infinitesimal invisible lives compose the atoms of the bodies of the mountain and the daisy, of man and the ant, of the elephant and of the tree which shelters it from the sun. Each particle, whether you call it organic or inorganic, is life.

His findings won him the highest scientific honors, for he proved that so-called inorganic matter responds to stimuli. He measured the reaction of different forms of life to different stimuli. When compared, he found that reactions were exactly alike *(The Secret Doctrine,* Vol. 1, 281).

> "The laws of reality cannot deviate from the ideal laws of mathematics" (Gottfried Wilhelm Leibniz, as quoted in Morris Klein's *Mathematics and the Search for Knowledge,* 213).

CHAPTER 7

The Influence
of Music

Can you picture anyone fighting to the gentle tune of "Love is a Many-Splendored Thing," or any other ballad of love?

I noticed many years ago that something wonderful happened when our choir sang in school. In those days music was a required subject, so we had quite a variety of students singing with us. Some were the macho guys who could be pretty rough. But when they sang, their countenances changed and the feeling around them became more genteel. I noticed something else. The students who tended to be difficult to get along with or the ones who were mad at each other would, after singing together, become renewed. The anger was gone.

In choir there was no intolerance or prejudice. We sang in harmony and we were as one harmonious chord, as people as well as musically. Music brought us together in a brotherly spirit. The right music, more than anything else, has the power to heal wounds, uplift us from this physical plane to the spiritual one. The human nervous system is so attuned to sound that our response is immediate.

Each person has a keynote. Max Heindel tells us in the *Rosicrucian Cosmo-Conception* that the medulla oblongata acts like a tuning fork when the right sympathetic tone is played. At that point it will vibrate along with the tone.

The medulla oblongata is the hindmost and lowest part of the brain, narrowing down into the spinal cord. It has a direct influence on breathing, for it controls the heartbeat. This explains why music has such influence on us. Some music can soothe and heal, while music that is antagonistic to our own vibratory nature makes us tense, uneasy, and even angry or ill (*The Sacred Word and Its Creative Overtones,* 143).

In music therapy, a person can be healed by soothing sounds of his own keynote, for the medulla oblongata will then vibrate in sympathy with the keynote and immediately get the heartbeat to normal and, like a relay station, the entire body will respond and adjust itself.

There are healthy and unhealthy sounds, and we take them in the same as food. Our minds learn to adjust to different sounds but our bodies can not. Musical passages have an effect on our muscles. To quote from *Sound Health* by Steven Halpern and Louis Savaryl (69, 70):

> One of the problems with much of rock and pop music is its standard rhythm called the "stopped anapestic rhythm"—a short-short-long-pause pattern. This rhythm tends to confuse the body and weaken the muscles. Among hundreds of persons tested by behavioral kinesiologist FDR. John Diamond, ninety percent registered an almost instantaneous loss of two-thirds of their muscle strength when they heard this beat. Interestingly, this often happens even when the listener likes the music. The end result is that the body's system is confused, the heart response is irregular, and the body gets weakened.

In the book, *The Secret Life of Plants* by Tompkins and Bird, an experiment is described in which plants, under controlled conditions, were tested in their reactions to different types of music. Beautiful music, both popular and classical, was beneficial to the plants. They grew toward the sound and tried to reach the speaker it came from. Where there was no sound at all, the plants grew straight up. But where there was abrasive music, the plants tried to move away from the sound and then died. Loud, dissonant music that makes repeated frictional air waves, is carried to the stems of the plants and kills them (*The Sacred Word and Its Creative Overtones*, 134). Gentle songs like "Love is a Many-Splendored Thing" are healthy for plants and promote kind feelings among people.

Every rate of vibration forms a different geometric figure. Ernst Florens Friedrish Chladni (1756-1828), a German physicist who analyzed sound waves mathematically, proved that sound can shape matter into forms. Because of this he became known as the "Father of Acoustics."

He formed sound pictures by placing sand over a thin metal plate. He changed the pitch by varying the position of his finger on the plate as though it was a violin's fingerboard. By doing so, the sand took on different geometric shapes according to pitch vibration that made the sound patterns visible. No two were alike unless their rate of vibration was the same. This was the forerunner to the eidophone (*The Sacred Word and Its Creative Overtones*, 74, 9).

Pictures have been taken of music with a device called a tonoscope where the vibrations make forms in a layer of fluid and are then photographed. Even a polygraph machine (lie detector) shows graphically the effect that music has.

But centuries before these machines existed, Pythagoras knew that form came about through vibration; that the world came into being out of chaos by sound and the intervals produced by that sound. Music was an important part of his school's curriculum.

This is one secret I had been searching for regarding the accuracy of numbers: everything that exists has vibration. The vibrational field of sound, music, color, matter, our words, thoughts, and names, all show form. All are vibrations. All vibrations are measurable. To measure vibration, we need numbers. Numbers are the basis of it all. Numbers are the keys to all mysteries. According to Helen P. Blavatsky (*E.S.T.*, 7):

"...number underlies form, and number guides sound.
Number lies at the root of the manifested universe..."

PART TWO

Tracing
the Roots

CHAPTER 8

Pythagoras
(582 B.C.–507 B.C.)

It is impossible to trace the roots of numerology without becoming entwined in a fascinating web of the Kabbalah, the Hebrew alphabet, biblical writings, the ancient wisdoms, and the background of the most famous proponent of numbers, Pythagoras. Here we find science interwoven with myths and philosophies, for the subject is not easily understood without them.

According to legend, Pythagoras's parents, Mnesarchus and Parthenis, were in Delphi on business and decided to ask the Oracle of Delphi if their journey home would be safe. Instead, the prophetess of Apollo informed them that the wife was pregnant with a boy-child who was to become handsome and wise and would impart of his wisdom to enrich and elevate mankind.

The child was born in Syria while his parents were there on a journey. He was named Pythagoras in honor of Pythasis, the oracle who foretold his birth. As a youth, Pythagoras studied in the temple of Melchizedek and became known as "the Son of God." Six centuries later Jesus of Nazareth studied in the same temple because his sect, the Essenes, embraced the teachings of Pythagoras (*The Secret Teachings of All Ages*, LXV).

Pythagoras lived a long life, nearly 100 years, and never looked aged but remained youthful, strong, and powerful. As a young man Pythagoras left his native Samos, and for the next 30 years he traveled and studied with various masters in surrounding countries. Rabbis taught him the secret traditions of Moses that had led to the laws of Israel. In Egypt he was given instruction by the priests of Thebes in the mysteries of Isis, and studied there for 22 years. Their central doctrine was that divine power dwelt within every man no matter how low he might be; that this divine power was in the form of a light they called "The Hidden Light." The Pharaoh's motto was "Look for the light," meaning there is good to be found in everyone and it is everyone's duty to bring out the best in others.

In Phoenicia and Syria, Pythagoras learned the mysteries of Adonis, who was originally the Sun God to the Egyptians and who Phoenicians connected with the growth and maturing of flowers and fruits that depend upon the sun for life.

Pythagoras learned all he could from the Greek philosophers. He was initiated into the Babylonian and Chaldean mysteries. It is said that he studied with Zoroaster whose "Zoroastrianism" recognizes two creative powers: good and evil, and the triumph of the good over evil. It also teaches that there is life after death.

In the Euphrates, Pythagoras learned the secret lore of the Chaldeans. He studied for several years in Hindustan with Brahman priests who were the only ones allowed to interpret the sacred Hindustani texts, the Vedas. There he was known as Yavancharya, the Ionian teacher, a name he took because of his fascination and reverence for the letter "Y." It is the name that is still preserved in the records of the Brahmans.

Wisemen in those days were called sages or sophists because sage means "one who knows" and sophist means "wise." But when Pythagoras was no longer considered an Initiate, he felt there was still much more for him to learn. So instead of using sage or sophist, he invented the word "philosopher" for himself, the root "philo" meaning love and "sopho" meaning wisdom—philosopher: lover of wisdom.

The Pythagorean School

In 536 B.C., at age 56, he journeyed to Crotona, the Greek-speaking region of southern Italy, and established a school that combined religious ritual with scientific study. This was the first university in history.

Here, among esoteric lessons, the secrets of number vibration were revealed in personal discourse by Pythagoras to a select few; the discourse was so secret, it was never written. Later writers were very careful not to divulge the secrets openly, but followed a key statement with less important information that would divert the attention of all but the true seeker.

It is a little-known fact that 600 years later Jesus also established schools of mystery, five of them, one of which is in Palestine. The secrets were the same as those Pythagoras taught. This was uncovered by Max Heindel, the prolific writer of many books on the wisdoms, and a member of the Brothers of the Rosy Cross. The information that has come down to us about the school of Pythagoras is by word of mouth from his students and from a few manuscripts that were preserved.

We do know that his school followed very strict rules. His students never had personal contact with him until they passed several initiations and were in the higher grades. Even then he wore a robe, dressed so that he was hardly seen. They say he was awesome.

Children with a 7 Birth Path were readily taken into the school, since Pythagoras felt they were meant to learn the mysteries. But others who wished to study there had to pass certain tests first. They were taken to a secluded spot where they were left to concentrate on a given symbol, such as the triangle. They were to write down all ideas that came to them and to tie those ideas in with all life. The next morning they would report their concepts to all the others in the school.

Sometimes they would be ridiculed to see how they would handle themselves and criticism. If the candidate was too sensitive it was felt he could not withstand the rigor of the disciplines of the school.

After gaining entry, there was a requirement of five years of total silence. It was deemed necessary to learn to hold the tongue so it would not divulge all one's thoughts. It taught students to think well before speaking. Pythagoras said that quiet attention is the beginning of wisdom:

> It is better to be silent, or to say things of more value than silence. Sooner throw a pearl at hazard than an idle or useless word; and do not say a little in many words, but a great deal in a few (*The Secret Teachings of All Ages*).

In his lectures, Pythagoras stressed the value of wisdom above all else: you can continually give it away and still have more to spare. It is what makes the difference between a real man and a beast. There are so few men who possess it that he compared it to sports: in the Olympiad there would be seven outstanding men in racing, but in contrast, there were only seven men in all the world who would excel in wisdom. It was not wise to show a temper. About anger he said:

> Choose always the way that seems the best, however rough it may be; custom will soon render it easy and agreeable. Rest satisfied with doing well, and leave others to talk of you as they please.

Academically, the students were given what Pythagoras considered the triangular foundation of all arts and sciences: occult mathematics, music, and astronomy.

The word "mathematics," from the Greek word "mathesis," means "the learning." Its root, "ma," means the "mother wisdom," and the word was first used as their name for astrology. Astrology had originated in Babylon in the fifth century B.C. where it was first called "Babylonian Numbers." So mathematics developed from astrology *(The Knot of Time*, 16-20).

Since "number" was the underlying principle of all three sciences: math, music, and astrology, great importance was attached to it. The Science of Numbers was considered to be the origin of all things, and it was believed that greater knowledge of God could be gained by understanding numbers. So Pythagoras's Science of Numbers was built on kabbalistic principles.

Where we have been taught that a number depicts a quantity or an amount, Pythagoras taught it to be a living qualitative reality. Much of the Egyptian philosophy and religion that he studied for 22 years was built almost completely on the Science of Numbers. In fact, all of nature was explained entirely by this principle. For example, a rubber ball and the moon have identical mathematical properties, both being circular. Yet they are physically very different.

Nature was composed of groups of four such as the four geometrical elements—point, line, surface, and solid, and four material elements—Earth, Air, Fire, and Water.

Nature also supplied the clue to the law of contrasts: if there be light, then there is darkness; if cold, then heat; if height, then also depth; if solid, then fluid; hardness and softness; calm and tempest; prosperity and adversity; life and death. This proved the twofold activity of the one principle, the difference being only the degree of vibration—and vibration can be measured.

The Pythagoreans considered the triangle to be the originator of everything on Earth since it is the first rectilinear figure (bound by three straight lines), and it corresponds with the three attributes of the Deity, the Creative Trinity.

On studying the mystery of this sacred figure, Pythagoras established his famous theorem that has been of fundamental use ever since: "The square of the hypotenuse of a right-angled triangle is equal to the sum of the squares of the other two sides."

As influential mathematicians, the Pythagoreans made many outstanding contributions to both medicine and astronomy. Pythagoras taught that physical manifestation had to be preceded by mathematical conception—a builder cannot build unless he has a blueprint of measurements to go by. Nothing can exist without numbers.

The mathematical world makes everything so obvious that some members of the school were put to death for revealing math secrets, secrets which are now printed in schoolbooks.

Music underwent a change when Pythagoras began his study of it. Until that time, Greeks made music on a seven-string lyre. This seemed limited to Pythagoras, so he invented a monochord, a wooden resonator to which a single string was attached, with a movable fret that caused the tone of the string to vary according to the vibrations set up by the length of the string used. With this instrument he was able to construct a scale with accurate intervals and thereby invented the seven-tone scale, as we know it today.

He heard the eighth note was identical to the first, only an octave higher in pitch, so he added an eighth string to the Greek lyre. This gave musicians much more variety by enabling them to play various modes of eight notes.

Pythagoras found curative powers in music, color, and poetry. Certain melodies had a therapeutic effect on certain diseases. He discovered he could even control man's wildest passions with soothing music. He preferred the soft sounds of the lute or flute for they had the ability to keep a person in better mental balance.

The astronomy taught in Pythagoras's university included astrology, which relates man to the Universe. His knowledge on the subject came from the great Babylonian astrologers of 500 B.C., the Chaldeans, whose expertise was accepted by the surrounding countries *(The Knot of Time*, 22). Astrology and astronomy remained one science until the 16th century.

Pythagoras noted that the further from the Earth the other planets were, the faster they moved. He reasoned that since movement causes friction and friction causes sound, the planets must produce sounds in various tones: the faster they move, the higher the tone. He saw that their motion was related to the mathematical principles of the musical scale. He concluded that planets sing as they turn in their orbits, creating the music of the spheres, which he is said to have heard.

In the sixth and seventh centuries B.C., it was an age-old custom of the ancient Greeks to practice divination (foretelling of future events) by observing the entrails of sacrificed birds and animals. Pythagoras was upset by this practice and sought to put an end to it by perfecting a system using numbers. The system was based on secrets that originated from Orpheus, the patron of music, who represented the body of truth, the secret doctrine revealed through music.

Pythagoras also developed a wheel of letters with numbers and astrological signs on it that encircled a globe. By using the numbers of the inquirer's birth name or birth date, it was possible to foretell future events. However, divination was not the original intent for the use of numbers. Pythagoras was not the father of numerology as is so often stated, but it was Pythagoras who took numbers seriously enough to apply them to all teachings in his school.

Pythagoras married one of his followers, Theano, the daughter of Brontinus of Croton. They wed when he was 60 years old and together they had seven children. There are conflicting stories on the way he died, yet all agree that he was assassinated. They say he refused admittance to one man because of his bad manners. The man became so embittered that he returned with a gang of hoodlums and murderers who burned down the school and slew Pythagoras.

His widow and remaining disciples did their best to continue his work but were persecuted for it. Eventually the school was no more, but the students valued his teachings and his memory and preserved what manuscripts they could.

Later in history, Plato purchased some of these manuscripts *(The Secret Science of All Ages, LXVII)*. The basic tenets reappeared in the Middle Ages in a craft of stone masons called "Freemasonry," which was based on the Science of Numbers.

Masonry is identical to the ancient mysteries. The Freemasons had secret signs and passwords, and were interested in attaining spiritual knowledge that could only be learned from the arrangement of letters and combinations of numbers with their hidden meanings, which collectively are the key to understanding the mysteries *(Morals and Dogma, 625)*.

To their great credit, the Freemasons respect all religions, all peoples, and hold no prejudices. They understand that man is here to learn and grow at his own pace through his own experience.

> It was men with these beliefs who framed our Constitution and designed the Great Seal of the United States. The Eagle was the ancient symbol of spiritual vision and is meant to represent the people of The United States. The reverse seal with the eye in the triangle symbolizes the eye of God in His protective watch over our nation *(Our Great Seal, 41, 46)*.

The modern Masons' ninth commandment is "Hear much, speak little, act well"—very Pythagorean.

CHAPTER 9

The Roots of Numerology

We can see where the background of numerology is enmeshed in the moral philosophies and wisdoms of the ancient past. It was not just exalted thinking; its base was scientific. The very first alphabet was designed by the greatest spiritual and scientific minds of the day. Just as numbers were not only symbols of quantities, letters were not simply symbols of sounds. Both were designed to reveal deeper meanings to those initiated into the mysteries. Generally words were formed to embrace the attributes behind the words themselves.

Sixty percent of English words are based on their Greek and Latin origins, for example, "manus" in Latin is hand. Manual labor is work done by hand. Manuscripts are handwritten ("scribo" = to write), a manual is a small handbook, and so on.

The English and Indo-European alphabets are derived from the Roman (Latin), which we can trace back to the original Phoenician alphabet.

The 22 letters of the Hebrew alphabet were considered sacred, as they were believed to have been endowed with God's attributes. The actual formation of letters has been attributed to Hermes, the wisest of all the wise men, who was known to the Jews as Enoch, to the Greeks as Hermes, and to the Romans as Mercury (*The Secret Teachings of All Ages, XXXII*).

There were no vowels among the original 22 letters. Vowels were deemed too sacred to write, for they were the animating spirit of words, and the sound of them spoke the true and overwhelming name of God. Instead, vowels were assigned to the seven known planets. The consonants that made up the alphabet were all composed of the flame-like glyph called *Yod*. And it does represent a flame as it is meant to be a spark of the Divine Light that makes up the body of God used for all His creation. Each consonant contains some of God's attributes. Later on in history the meaning of the Yod degenerated from a flame of light direct from God to that of a phallic symbol representing mortal generation.

When the Greeks borrowed the alphabet, they added vowels for clarity, omitted sounds they did not use, and added ones they did use—as did all following Indo-European alphabets. Other than that, the letters are very close to the same sequence as that of the original (see Chart 1 on page 58).

Hebrew letters are read from right to left for a very special reason. God began creation by His own reflection. In a reflection right and left are reversed, as can be seen in a mirror. It was important to the Hebrews to show this reversal. By writing right to left they were going toward their source of life, toward God. It is important to note that Aramaic was the spoken language of the people, while Hebrew was reserved for sacred writings because of its magical qualities.

The letter name is the mystical name of a number, and every Hebrew word, when examined letter by letter, number by number, reveals a hidden meaning, for their letters and numbers are completely interchangeable. The entire Bible was composed of various combinations of those letter-numerals, giving important clues to the deeper meanings (see Chart 2 on page 59).

Hebrew is a very difficult language to translate because the vowels are omitted, the words are not separated for clarity, and there is no past, present, and future verb tenses. Add that to the fact that the original writers of the Bible felt it was not wise to give out certain information to the unholy, and therefore used every trick they knew to conceal the mysteries, and you can understand why translation of the Bible was such a major job.

An exact translation was made further impossible because the translators lived under an act that authorized them to translate but forbade them from upsetting or deviating from established beliefs.

In our translations only the names and numbers come to us untouched. But through the *Science of Numbers*, and methods known as *Gematria, Temurah,* and *Notariqon,* many secrets are unveiled. Gematria is the name given to a method of figuring hidden meanings from the geometric shapes of letters and from the numerical values of both words and phrases. Numerology gives meanings from the vibrational traits of numbers. Temurah is the art of finding words within words and from anagrams, and Notariqon derives words from abbreviations and the initial letters of words.

An example of Temurah is found in the Bible in the word SWORD. It is an anagram of WORDS, and it means "the utterance of a thought." "He has made my mouth as a sharp sword..." (Isaiah 49:2). Its meaning is defined in Ephesians 6:17: "And take the helmet of salvation and the sword of the spirit, which is the word of God."

Since the Hebrew letters were considered sacred and believed to have been formed by God and endowed with His attributes, the names people chose had spiritual significance to them. In many ancient civilizations people did not receive their own names until they developed their own personalities. Until that time they were given a childhood name that was known as a "milk name."

When they were older and initiated into the temple, they were given a name purely for spiritual unfoldment and for philosophical reasons. This name was used only in secret. The system of choosing that spiritual name was based on astrology. Vowels were assigned to each planet and consonants to the degrees of the zodiac. A mystical symbol would be created, probably by using the person's birth date, and from this symbol they were able to form the name and interpret the spiritual meanings behind it that revealed the true nature of the person to whom it belonged—just as we can through numerology today. In fact, all ancient names pointed out a person's true nature *(The Philosophy of Astrology,* 46).

Numbers in the Bible have an astrological meaning as well. When 12 is used as a number of nations, it represents all the people born under the 12 signs of the zodiac, and therefore, the whole human race *(The Sacred Word and Its Creative Overtones,* 138).

Saint John wrote the *Apocalypse* in such a way that only the Initiates would understand its meaning. It was meant to confound the masses by being written hieroglyphically with numbers and images, in which great mysteries are concealed. And he wrote, "Let them who have knowledge, understand! Let him who understands, calculate!" *(Morals and Dogma,* 321).

CHART 1
COMPARATIVE ALPHABETS (ENGLISH AND HEBREW)

Hebrew	Letter	Number	Final*	English Letter	Number
Aleph	A	1		A	1
Beth	B	2		B	2
Gimel	G	3		C	3
Daleth	D	4		D	4
Hé	H	5		E	5
Vau (Vav)	V	6		F	6
Zayin	Z	7		G	7
Cheth	Ch	8		H	8
Teth	T	9		I	9
Yod	I,J,Y	10		J	10 (1)
Kaph	K	20	500	K	11 (2)
Lamed	L	30		L	12 (3)
Mem	M	40	600	M	13 (4)
Nun	N	50	700	N	14 (5)
Samekh	S	60		O	15 (6)
Ayin	O	70		P	16 (7)
Pé	P	80	800	Q	17 (8)
Tzaddi	Tz	90	900	R	18 (9)
Qoph	Q	100		S	19 (10/1)
Resh	R	200		T	20 (2)
Schin	Sh	300		U	21 (3)
Tau	Th	400		V	22 (4)
				W	23 (5)
				X	24 (6)
				Y	25 (7)
				Z	26 (8)

* When the Hebrew K, M, N, P, or Tz occur more than once in a
word, the last occurrence is called the "Final."

CHART 2

HEBREW LETTER NUMBERS AND MEANINGS

1. **א** Aleph A *Oxhead:* (Taurus) Sign of physical generation.
   Air: (Element) Breath, spirit. Height and Depth and the path between.

2. **ב** Beth B *House:* Mouth cavity that holds sound.

3. **ג** Gimel G,C *Camel:* Product of A and B: The Word. Riches and communication.

4. **ד** Daleth D *Door:* The Cosmic Womb

5. **ה** Hé H,E *Window:* One's viewpoint. The sound of H is the breath of life.

6. **ו** Vav, Vau V,W *Peg,* or *Nail:* Joining link between the human and the Divine.

7. **ז** Zayin Z *Weapon:* Tongue
   Arrows, Sword: Words that cut.
   Scepter: Victory in the right use of words.

8. **ח** Cheth Ch(K) *Field:* Soil of consciousness; attainments.
   Fence: Self-imposed limitations.

9. **ט** Teth T *Serpent:* Wisdom.
   Roof: The protection that wisdom gives.

10. **י** Yod I,J,Y *Hand:* Our creative tool.
    Flame: Light of understanding within us.

20. **כ** Kaph K *Palm of hand:* Holds what we receive.
    final K, 500

30. **ל** Lamed L *Ox-goad:* A prod to express love and creativity.

40. **מ** Mem M *Water:* (Element) From which all life arises.
    final M, 600

50. **נ** Nun N *Fish:* Esoteric teachings and spiritual growth.
    final N, 700

60. **ס** Samekh S,X *Prop, Bow:* What we send out returns to us: Law of the circle.

70. **ע** Ayin O *Eye:* The Inner Spiritual Eye, beginning of expanded consciousness.

CHART 2
HEBREW LETTER NUMBERS AND MEANINGS (CONTINUED)

80. פ Pé or Phé   P,F   *Mouth:* Organ that speaks the Divine
final P, 800   Word.

90. צ Tzaddi   Ts,Tz   *Fishing Hook:* Catches fish (esoteric
final Tz, 900   teachings) that awaken the Christ
                         center in each of us. Tzaddic, in
                         Hebrew, is a righteous master.

100. ק Qoph   Q   *Back of Head:* Area of coordination and
                     balance.
                     Knot: Blending our consciousness with
                     that of God.
                     Mirth: Another great balancing power.

200. ר Resh   R   *Head:* (Pineal Gland) Organ of the
                     spiritual mind.

300. ש Schin   Sh   *Tooth, Fang:* Chewing assimilates food
                       for nourishment.
                       Fire: (Element) The purifying force that
                       completes creation. Divine Fire unites
                       perfect love.

400. ת Tau   Th   *Sign of the Cross:* The path that leads to
                     knowledge.

CHAPTER 10

Introduction to the Mysteries

The power of the word that formed the Universe, the Earth, and all that is upon it is what the ancient kabbalistic mysteries are all about.

The earliest Initiates believed that God taught these mysteries to the angels. After the fall of man the angels gave the secrets to Adam so that he would have an understanding of his error and gain back what he had lost.

These secrets are supposed to awaken in man when he studies the 10 numbers and 22 basic sounds formed from the letter combinations of God's own name. This, combined with the basic geometric figures of circle, triangle, and square, are the basis of the Kabbalah; the figures that were used in designing the alphabet.

The Kabbalah supplies the key to the spiritual truths of both the Old and New Testaments, a key which goes back long before Pythagoras to a dynasty of priest-kings originating on Atlantis, known as the Melchizedek.

The last of these priest-kings is said to have passed this knowledge on to Abraham, and then it went from one biblical patriarch to another—Isaac, Jacob, Moses, Joshua, David, and Solomon.

Abraham was supposed to have brought these wisdoms to Egypt where the Egyptians gained knowledge of them. Jesus was instructed in these mysteries about 600 years after Pythagoras studied there. Hebrew theology was separated into three definite parts: The Law, which was taught to all Hebrew children; The Soul of the Law (Mishna) that was made known only to the teachers and rabbins; and the Qabbala, or Soul of the Soul of the Law. This was so secret it was revealed only to the highest Initiates and never written. It is said that it is these secrets that God disclosed to Moses on Mount Sinai after the Ten Commandments were divinely inscribed and presented to him.

Briefly, all comes from naught: 0, the Cosmic Egg in which all numbers are contained. God was known as Alpha and Omega: 1 and 0, the first and the last. (0 is the last letter of the Greek alphabet.) Together

1 and 0 form 10, the perfect number, and since it is perfect, it is the sacred number of the Universe and is written as ① or ⊗ meaning "God in All."

In the 26th verse of the first chapter of Genesis, God said, "Let us make man in our image, after our likeness." The foundation of the Qabbala, or Kabbalah, are the Ten Sephiroth, or creative forces. They are also known as Sepharim and Elohim, and stand for the manifested Universe. All three words, Sephiroth, Sepharim, and Elohim, mean the same thing: numbers, letters, and sounds. Sephiroth comes from the root sephir which, when the vowels are removed, is S-ph-r meaning, "to cypher." Cypher is the figure 0, and it also means that there is a hidden message containing its own key.

These Sephiroth are depicted as 10 globes of light, each representing a number and each containing all numbers inside the 10 which is the cypher itself, thus:

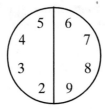

The large cypher divided in half is the 1 and the 0. In the Kabbalah these 10 globes of light are on a tree of the soul and are connected by 22 paths which are the 22 letters of the Hebrew alphabet, each with its own individual esoteric meaning. The light emanates from the dot point in the center of each globe, which is a reflection of the light of God, and when one understands the globes' deepest meanings, he receives the light of wisdom and knowledge.

Over the years, the kabbalistic approach has influenced both Christians and Jews. These are spiritual mysteries that are not easily grasped; the true answers are clear to those who "have eyes to see and ears to hear." Letters, numbers, and sounds are those keys and, like the wind, heat, and electricity, are powerful forces.

The word "mysteries" comes from the Greek word "muein," to shut the mouth, and "mustes," the word for an Initiate. The very word implies secrecy, not something for the masses, and not to be spoken of lightly.

There is a reason for this. It has been observed for thousands of years that as one begins to unfold the spiritual nature, the true nature comes to the forefront; and any repressed emotions, sensualism, or faults must be dealt with. This is so difficult that the majority will fail unless they are willing to fight every base tendency and win over it. If the inner person is wholesome and good, and not easily provoked to anger, the good is magnified. So those who would seek such enlightenment must have a high level of consciousness (*Strictly Private E.S.T. Instructions*, 5).

There were three views of creation perceived by the ancients: the Sepher Yetzirah, the Tree of the Sephiroth, and the Tetractys of Pythagoras.

Moses De Leon founded *The Sepher Yetzirah* (Book of Formation), in a jar in a Galilean cave. Rabbi Simeon, who was known to have taught and written in that very cavern, wrote the book. But the book was believed to have been originally written by Abraham.

Figure 1 on page 64 shows the double star of the Sepher Yetzirah with the letters in English rather than Hebrew, for clarification. Sepher means, "to cypher" or figure out.

In the double star, the center triangle contains the Holy Trinity, the Creative Principle.

The middle star contains the seven double letters that symbolize everything there is that life can be exposed to, good and bad. Those seven, with the first three, are the Ten Sephiroth, or attributes of God.

The outside star contains the 12 simple letters, which represent the signs of the zodiac.

The spirit of God dwells in the center triangle, the Holy Temple that sustains all. From this center He created all there is by the three Sepharim: numbers, letters, and sounds, which are one and the same.

The Voice, Spirit, and Word of the Holy Spirit formed these three. They were called the Mother Letters because everything came from these basic elements.

The Mother Letters are Aleph (A), Mem (M), and Schin (Sh). First the Holy Spirit created A and from A sprang Air, and in this was formed the sound of the remaining 21 letters. The sounds that came from A, or the Air of His breath, were designed to be uttered in five different areas of the human mouth:

1. Gutterals: Throat.
2. Palatals: Produced with the blade of the tongue near the hard palate, as the ch in child and the j in joy.
3. Linguals: Enunciated with the tongue, as in t, d, and l.
4. Dentals: Enunciated with the tongue against the teeth, as in t and d.
5. Labials: Articulated by the lips, as in p, b, m, and w, or by rounded vowels, o, oo.

From the formed letters He chose Mem (M) for the second Mother Letter and from it came Water, for Water is mute like M and it was extracted from the Air.

For the third Mother Letter he selected from His letters Schin (Sh) and from Sh came Fire (ether), for Sh is the sound of Fire and it was drawn from the Water. Air is the base of balance between Fire and Water.

FIGURE 1

THE DOUBLE STAR OF THE SEPHIR YETZIRAH

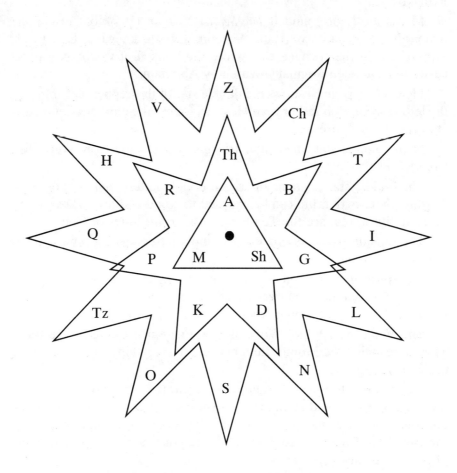

The Very Center
Invisible throne of the Supreme Definitionless Creator.
Center Triangle
Three Mother Letters: A = Air, M = Water, Sh = Fire.
The Holy Trinity. The Creative Principle.
Inner Star
Seven Double Letters: Wisdom.
Outer Star
Twelve Simple Letters - twelve signs of the Zodiac.

Those first three letters, or elements, are like a scale with virtues on one end and vices on the other, placed in balance by the tongue. He chose three consonants belonging to the first elements: I, H, and V, shaped them into a Great Name, and then fastened them with His spirit. This sealed the entire Universe in six directions: height, depth, east, west, south, and north.

The Inner Star holds the seven double letters: B, D, G, K, P, R, and Th that serve as a pattern for soft and hard, strong and weak. They symbolize all the good and bad that humans encounter in life. Each letter is like a balance board with its God quality on one side and its opposite extreme on the other:

1. B (B,V)   Wisdom   ⇔   Foolishness

2. G (ge, je) Riches   ⇔   Poverty

3. D   Fertility   ⇔   Sterility

4. K (K, Ch)   Life   ⇔   Death

5. P (P,Ph)   Power   ⇔   Servitude

6. R   Peace   ⇔   War

7. T (T, Th)   Beauty   ⇔   Deformity

Of these seven letters He formed the seven planets, the seven days of the week, and the seven openings for the senses in both male and female: two eyes, two ears, two nostrils, and one mouth. There are also seven each of heavens, earths, and sabbaths.

These seven and the first three, making up the Ten Sephiroth, are His qualities and attributes. They are the 10 emanations of number, which have 10 unlimited traits or infinitudes:

➤ Unlimited beginning and unlimited end.

➤ Unlimited height and unlimited depth.

➤ Unlimited east and unlimited west.

➤ Unlimited north and unlimited south.

Over all is the One who rules them and His Word is always in them.

In the Outer Star, the 12 simple letters, H, V, Z, Ch, T, I, L, N, S, O, Tz and Q, stand for the 12 basic traits of speaking, hearing, seeing, thinking, movement, work, sex, smell, sleep, taste (and swallowing), anger, and cheerfulness.

These 12 letters correspond to 12 directions: north in height and depth and northwest; south in height and depth and southeast; west in height and depth and southwest; and east in height and depth and northeast. By these God fashioned the 12 signs of the zodiac, the 12 months of the year, and the 12 major organs in the human body.

By designating the weights, amounts, and groupings of the 22 letters, God made all things that have existence.

First He formed the 22 letters with His voice, and with His breath He impressed them on the Air. He placed the letters around a spherical wall with 231 doorways, or gates and then turned that globe forward and backward. Forward was good and backward was evil, as all things must have a front and back. So there were altogether 231 methods to form ways for the powers of the letters to emerge. According to *The Sepher Yetzirah* (Book of Formation), everything that is made, from matter to language, proceeded from the utterance of words formed from the various combinations of letters of the awesome name of God that were spoken forth on His breath (*The Secret Teachings of All Ages, CXIII-CXV*). And, "by the word of the Lord were the heavens made; and all the host of them by the breath of His mouth" (Psalms 33:6).

Instead of a triangle within two stars, The Tree of the Sephiroth (Tree of Life) is a tree with 10 globes of light that is intended to symbolize the entire Universe, which is the body of God. It is sometimes depicted as three pillars with the globes (Figures 2 and 3).

The globes are the Sephiroth (numbers) and each represents distinct attributes of our Creator. Together they symbolize everything, which is contained in Heaven and Earth, and each contains a deep mystery (*The Pythagorean Triangle*, 19-21). The 10 globes are connected by 22 paths, which are the 22 letters of the Hebrew alphabet. Together they total 32 and are known as the 32 Paths of Wisdom. This is akin to the 32 degrees in Freemasonry.

Early Kabbalists envisioned the very beginning of all things as a vacuum of pure spirit not limited by conditions of time or space. This negative existence of pure spirit filled the circular void of space, or auric egg, and was called Ain (nothingness). It was also called "The Most Ancient of Ancients," and is the womb of the Universe.

This pure essence desired to express life and it moved toward the center of itself, producing a circle within the circle, which was without limit or boundary, and it was called Ain Sop or Ensoph.

It continued its movement to the center of its boundless, limitless circle where it became a dot that broke into light, Ain Soph Aur, meaning limitless light—three in one. This fills the whole circle of the Universe but makes its particular dwelling place in the very center where the point of light is at its brilliant Source, just as our own mind is our center encircled by our body.

That dot, the dwelling place or throne of God, contained within it all creation that is to be and is called Kether the Crown, the omnipresent Divine Will, first emanation of the Tree of the Sephiroth. Being All, It was androgynous.

This Monad, by its Will, gave birth out of itself to the other nine globes or spheres starting with the pair Chochma the Father (Wisdom), a male potency with the Divine Intellectual power to generate thought, and Binah, the Mother (Understanding and Intelligence), the female potency with the Divine Intellectual capacity to produce it, using for tools the 22 letters that make up the "too sacred to be spoken" name of God. Kether, Chochma, and Binah together are the Creative Trinity, which are the roots of the Tree.

FIGURE 2
TREE OF THE SEPHIROTH
(TREE OF LIFE)

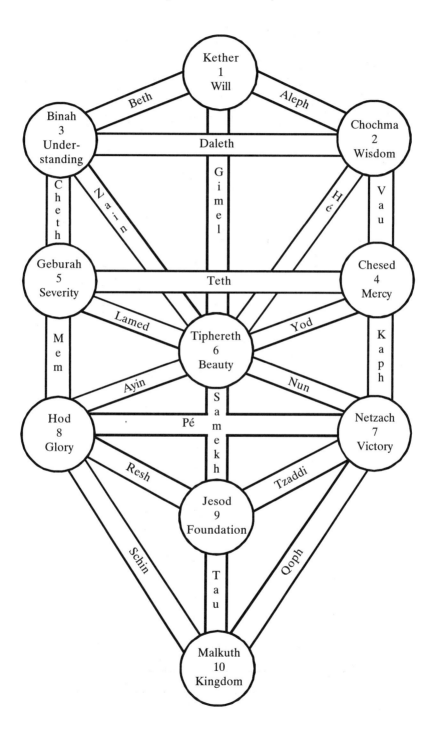

FIGURE 3

THE THREE PILLARS OF THE SEPHIROTIC TREE

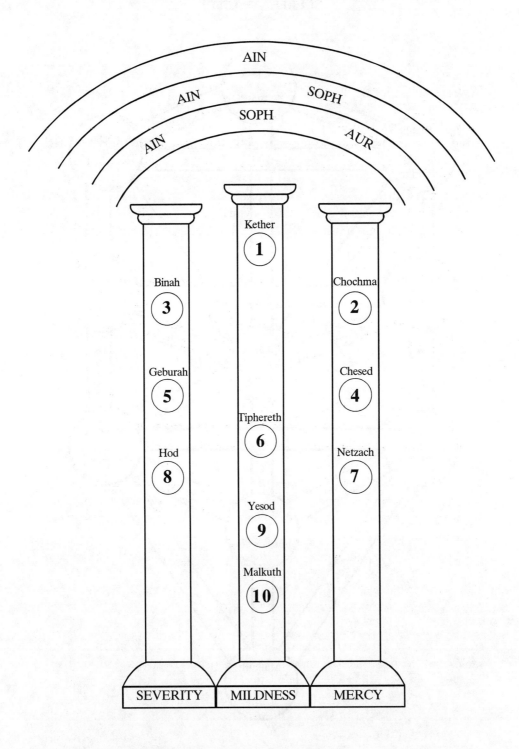

The first two letters of the sacred name Jehovah (IHVH) symbolize the creative activities of the Universe. There was no J in the Hebrew alphabet. They used I. Since they also used no written vowels, the first two letters became IH, the Father (Chochma) is the I, and the Mother (Binah) is the H.

The H is known as the childbearing letter because its numerical value is 5, the same as the Hebrew verb Awbab, or Abb, meaning, "to bear fruit." This coincides with the fifth house of the horoscope, which is the giver of children and creativity.

Before the remaining Sephiroth could be created, there had to be an active force to produce the idea put forth by Wisdom, Intelligence, and Will. This active force is the spoken word and it is called Daath. It is not a Sephira for it is not an attribute, but an invisible acting force. Yet some have called it the 11th Sephira. This is interesting because the force is the spoken word that sets the molecules awhirl into creation. "The Word" or "Logos" is the name given Jesus, "The Word of God without whom was not anything made that was made." And Jesus' name totals 11. So Chochma and Binah in Kether combine to produce Daath, which is the Word within the Deity.

These three: Kether the Crown (Will), Chochma (Wisdom), and Binah (Understanding and Intelligence), form the Creative Principle 1, 2, 3 or the Triad, or the Holy Trinity. And the Word (Daath) sets the creation into motion. This is why the scripture says that "without the Word was not anything made that was made." And, "For it is through faith we understand that the worlds were framed by the Word of God so that things which are seen came to be from those which are not seen" (Hebrews 11:3).

Initially, the idea of something being formed from a word sounds ridiculous. But on further study it begins to make scientific sense.

When a word is spoken it sets up a vibratory condition that allows it to be heard. Without vibration, all that is would cease to exist. This is because everything is composed of a basic universal substance that appears different only because of that substance's groupings of atoms and their rate of movement.

From the Creative Trinity the remaining seven Sephiroth were formed by action of the Word (Daath) and spewed forth in receptacles (Yods). These were filled with Light from Ain Soph Aur centered in Kether the Crown, which contains All.

Each receptacle contains a Sephira (number) and its attributes. From these seven were named the seven planets, the seven notes of the musical scale, and the seven colors separated by a prism. Each of the seven planets was assigned a metal, a Greek vowel, a color, and a musical note.

And so each of the 10 globes on the Tree has its own particular name which shows the qualities and attributes of the Creator. The number is the vibrational rate of those qualities. These are the ingredients for all creation.

The laws of the Universe were established by various groupings of the 22 Hebrew letters which are the pathways of the Tree. Creation, in order to take place, has been pictured as going through four Sephirotic Trees, each representing a world, or plane of existence. All emanates from the dot, the light in the center of Ain Soph Aur. The names of the worlds are taken from the Hebrew verbs that mean, "will take of the spirit" (Atziluth), "have created" (Briah), "have formed" (Yetzirah), and "have made" (Assiah).

1. **Atziluth:** This is the sphere of perfection, of pure spirit where God manifests Himself first as archetypes—ideas born to become models for every part of creation that is to be. To become manifest they must be reflected to the sphere below.

    The first reflection is seen between the Creative Trinity: Kether, Chochma, and Binah as: and the next three: Chesed, Geburah, and Tiphereth as: . This all comes about from the union of God with His feminine counterpart known as the Shekinah. The next three worlds are the result of this union.

2. **Briah:** This is the creative world of pure intellect and unconscious mind. This tree is slightly dimmer than the first since it is a reflection. In this world reside the 10 great spirits (archangels) who aid in bringing about divine order and intelligence in the cosmos.

3. **Yetzirah:** This is the creative world of formation; conscious mind; personality. This tree of 10 globes is reflected from Briah. It is called the formative world, for here are seen the vibrational patterns behind matter, the fourth dimension.

4. **Assiah:** This is where matter forms and the vibrational energy patterns behind it are no longer seen. This is the three-dimensional Universe we see that includes the planets, the Earth, and our body. In death only the physical body disappears and the true ray of light continues on its journey back through the upper worlds to reunite with Ain Soph.

The tree is a concept of eternal truths put into a form that we can relate to, and so much can be and is related to it. It represents the states of consciousness man experiences as he journeys in life through the Sephiroth and learns the lessons of each from the physical to the spiritual.

We are told that for any creation to take place, it must go through these four planes:

Atziluth	Briah	Yetzirah	Assiah
Spirit	Mind	Soul	Body
Idea	Plant seed	Incubation	Birth

This is why later Kabbalists perceived four Sephirotic Trees as lightning energy that starts at the very top of the first and zigzags through its 10 Sephira. Its idea is planted in Briah as it zigzags through those 10 Sephira, and the zigzag continues on down through Yetzirah where the vibration attracts the molecules to its own keynote. Lastly it zigzags through Assiah where it has its birth in form *(The Qabalistic Tarot*, 39).

FIGURE 4

THE FOUR WORLDS

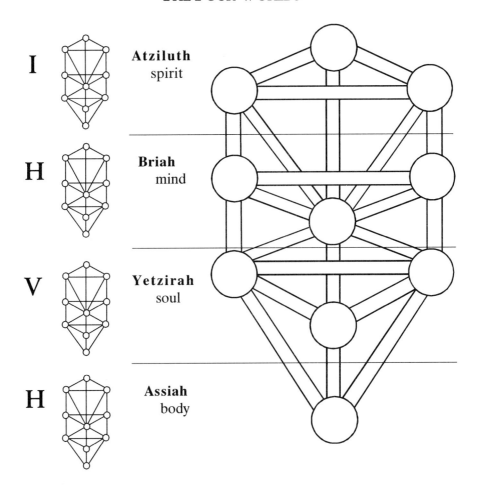

Four trees and 40 Sephiroth later is the birth. Anywhere we see 40 in the Bible—it means completion.

In Genesis two trees are mentioned: the Tree of Life and the Tree of Knowledge of Good and Evil. One interpretation is that they are one and the same; the Tree of Life being the original while the Tree of Knowledge of Good and Evil is its reflection on the waters *(The Bible and the Tarot*, 21-22).

They have also been described as being contained in the one Sephirotic Tree: evil being the left side called Severity, good being the right side of Mercy, and the Tree of Life being the central pillar of Beauty. This is more clearly seen as The Three Pillars (Figure 3). The central column is the trunk while the right and left sides are its branches.

The Sephirotic Tree is sometimes depicted as a giant cosmic man making up the entire Universe (macrocosm). His image is of man on Earth (microcosm). Viewed this way we can more readily perceive what is meant by "For in Him we live, move and have our being...." (Acts 17:28).

In this concept the lights, or globes of each of the Sephira, are related to the organs of the human body:

Kether:	Head. The pineal gland.
Chochma and Binah:	Right and left hemispheres of the great brain.
Chesed and Geburah:	Right and left arms.
Netzach and Hod:	Right and left legs, supports of the world.
Tiphereth:	Solar plexus.
Jesod:	The generative system, or foundation of form.
Malkuth:	Two feet, or the base of being.

As the body of man, the central pillar of Beauty, or trunk of the tree, is the spinal column with Tiphereth centered in the solar plexus area. One must obtain a sense of balance from that area in order to balance out the opposing forces in man. This microcosm is the image of the macrocosm, the original meaning of "being made in the image of God."

Mystically it was Adam Kadmon who became the Tree of Knowledge of Good and Evil from which Eve was tempted to take the fruit, which was supposedly the knowledge of human procreation in a material sense—bestial desire rather than spiritual love. This refers not to natural union but to the abusive use of the creative power and wasting precious life essence on self-gratification.

According to ancient cosmogyny, Adam and Eve were not individuals, but representative of root races. As Adam Kadmon is a collective name for the entire Universe, likewise Adam is a collective name for mankind (*The Secret Doctrine,* Vol. 2: 4, 128*)*.

Now we can see the pattern of Creator to that which is created; from macrocosm to microcosm, all a reflection of the Creator's thoughts at the time of conception. By analogy, the words we speak are our own creations. The Bible points out another Tree of Life, the tongue: "A wholesome tongue is the Tree of Life, and he who eats of its fruit shall be filled with it" (Proverbs 15:4).

The **Pythagorean Tetractys** was the symbol of greatest importance to Pythagoras and his disciples. By understanding it, the mysteries of the Universe were revealed to them.

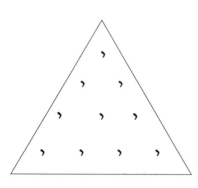

The Pythagorean Tetractys

It is called "The Tetractys of Pythagoras," although it was not his invention, having been part of the mysteries long before his birth. It was, in fact, invented by the ancient priests long before man developed any true method of writing.

Tetractys comes from the Greek word "tettares," which means four. There are four dots (Yods) across the bottom, along each side, and one in the center, 10 in all.

When you add the first four numbers: 1 + 2 + 3 + 4, the total is 10. To them this was proof that all 10 powers of creation (Sephira) exist in the number 4. So 10 was the ideal number and represented the Universe.

Pythagoras learned of this when he studied in Egypt in his youth. It became an important part of his teachings, and all his students are said to have been bound by an oath:

> I swear in the name of the Tetractys, which has been
> bestowed on our soul. The source and roots of the
> overflowing nature are contained in it.
> *(Mathematics and the Search for Knowledge,* 41)

The dots in the triangle are called "Yods," and according to the very first ancient written doctrines of kabbalistic knowledge, *The Zohar* (Book of Splendour) and *The Sepher Yetzirah* (Book of Formation), the Yod is a point of light called Auir, ether, or space. It sprang forth from a source of infinite light.

That ray of light is shot directly from the Deity in the form of numbers and letters, and a point of light remains in each one. These are the cause of all that exists.

Yod is the name of the 10th letter of the Hebrew alphabet, and there it means "the origin of all things." It is translated as "hand," meaning the creative hand that fashions and makes things *(The Key to the Universe,* 356).

The first three Yods represent the threefold white light which is the Godhead, containing potentially all sound and color, the unconscious universal mind—the Creative Principle of Will, Wisdom, and Activity.

All things come from that light and all must return to it, Ain Soph Aur, where all things have their genesis. That light is the first form of intelligence *(The Secret Doctrine,* Vol. 2, 128).

The last seven Yods, or receptacles of light, held much meaning—seven visible planets, the seven notes of the musical scale, and the seven primary colors, all of which are the creative forces which emanate from the Primordial Cause that established the Universe.

Pythagoras said that every letter of the alphabet has its own rate of vibration and color. Everything from a grain of sand to a human being is vibrating at its own rate and around its own center, producing its own particular sound or keynote. This means that everything, without exception, is in a vibratory condition. The higher the rate of vibration, the more spirit force an object contains.

He noted that planets moved in their orbits, proceeded to calculate their distance from each other, and thereby figured the keynote of the planet. Each one sounded a separate note on the musical scale.

The Greeks assigned their seven vowel sounds, one to each planet, for they believed that the musical notes the planets each sang in their orbits were the mystical vowel sounds forever singing the name of God:

First Planet	Moon	A (Alpha)
Second Planet	Mercury	E (Epsilon)
Third Planet	Venus	H (Eta) Long E
Fourth Planet	Sun	I (Iota)
Fifth Planet	Mars	O (Omicron) Short O
Sixth Planet	Jupiter	Y (Upsilon)
Seventh Planet	Saturn	O (Omega) Long O

They believed that by intoning the "aum" they could become one with the highest vibration of the Godhead. "God," said Pythagoras, "is the Supreme Music, the nature of which is harmony."

When vowel sounds are aspirated, they set up a vibration that draws a like vibration to itself. This can be shown by a tuning fork. When plucked, its vibration touches anything in the room of a sympathetic nature, and it too will begin to vibrate.

So, to the initiated, the placement and number of Yods held a great deal of information, and by concentrating on all the attributes therein, they gained an inner awakening: "Concentration is the secret of intellectual power; without will-power exercised in effort we can acquire nothing" *(The Power Within*, 122).

Occultists believe that the Tetractys is the missing capstone of the Great Pyramid of Giza.

PART THREE

Mystical
Letters

CHAPTER 11

Prelude
to Letters

A photograph can stir up so many memories. A picture can tell a whole story without words. A logo design can hold so much meaning that many have become well-known symbols. That is what letters were originally meant to do.

Letters were created as more than the tools to form written words. The shape of each one was carefully considered in order to convey the meaning behind the letter. You see, the shape of each one, based on the geometric figures of point, line, circle, triangle, and square, creates an energy field with its lines of force. These influence their characteristics. Just meditate on each shape and you will sense the individual properties of these forms, i.e., the circle, having no edges, suggests unending energies, while the square with its edges has an entirely different energy reaction.

In order to create the world, God had to use the only substance in existence: Himself. So these building blocks are His attributes. Now here is the secret: the sound of each letter sets up a vibration that conforms to those attributes; the shape of each letter is designed to call them to mind; and their numbered place in the alphabet is their actual rate of vibration when thought or spoken. This gives them a scientific cohesiveness.

Hebrew Kabbalists planned their letters and corresponding numbers to be interchangeable: A means one, B-two, G-three, and D-four, etc. While each is a picture that gives something of face value, by understanding the symbolism an even deeper meaning is revealed.

That alphabet was the model for hundreds of others, and though the letter sounds have come to us untouched, the symbols have changed to suit our needs. Yet amazingly, the attributes still apply, as we shall see when we analyze words.

Seen as a whole, letters tell of every possible life experience. Mystics know that by meditating on a symbol it will reveal itself, and the meditator's awareness will expand. In the letters are the answers to all of life's problems, for each one is a path on the Tree of Life.

A letter is considered from every aspect. The upper half is the mind, thought, spiritual plane; the lower half, the material, physical, Earth plane. A letter that is the same inverted—H, N, O, S, X—is active on both planes. This may bring out the double strength of the letter.

A letter that becomes a different letter when inverted is considered to be dual. For example, M has feet firmly planted on the ground, so M is well-organized and stable. But inverted, it is W, reaching up for spiritual help in times of emotional upheaval (*A Guide to Cosmic Numbers*, 125-6)

The events of your lifetime are recorded in the letters of your name. Each one tells the nature of the experiences, and the root number of the letter tells its duration:

A, J, S-one year	**D, M, V**-four years	**G, P, Y**-seven years
B, K, T-two years	**E, N, W**-five years	**H, Q, Z**-eight years
C, L, U-three years	**F, O, X**-six years	**I, R**-nine years

This lifetime of events, called "Table of Events," is discussed in numerology books such as *The Romance In Your Name* by Dr. Juno Jordan (Chapter 16), and *Your Days Are Numbered* by Florence Campbell (Chapter 14).

Each name works separately, and the full name works as a unit. Each experience is drawn from the positive or negative aspects of the letters and their corresponding numbers. They are influences in our lives and we are the ones who ultimately choose our destinies by the way we handle each experience.

This was thoroughly tested by the California Institute of Numerical Research, Inc., which was founded for extensive analysis of the science of number vibration. Numerologists from all over agreed with the findings of this Institute. Satisfied with their conclusions, the Institute closed after 25 years of research.

Regarding the spelling of names, two may sound the same though they are spelled differently, for example, Sean and Shawn. The letters are as important as the sound, for each time we speak a name we subconsciously see the letters, and their numbers make a mathematical statement of vibration.

The first letter of your name tells your nature, your initial reaction to things, and the way you approach situations. Likewise, the first letter of words tells us the nature of the word, sometimes even by the shape alone:

Mountain: The M has peaks and crevices.

Valley: The hills on both sides of the V form the valley.

Hills: The H is a ladder. Hills are easier to climb than mountains with their steep sides.

Bumpy: The B is made of two bumps.

Sudden: The S makes an abrupt change in direction.

Tree: The T has a central trunk and outstretched branches.

When we study the meanings of each letter, we see where this holds true for all words. But most important of all is your name. Those particular letters are the divine gifts bestowed on you at birth, and you can choose to live up to their full positive potential.

It has been observed that numerology works as well with the Chaldean alphabet as with the English. It works in any of the Indo-European alphabets where the letter and number are interchangeable. Though the letters in these alphabets are different, they are set to their own rate of vibration. Numbers are a universal language.

FIGURE 5

ENGLISH LETTERS IN RELATION TO THE
TREE OF THE SEPHIROTH (TREE OF LIFE)

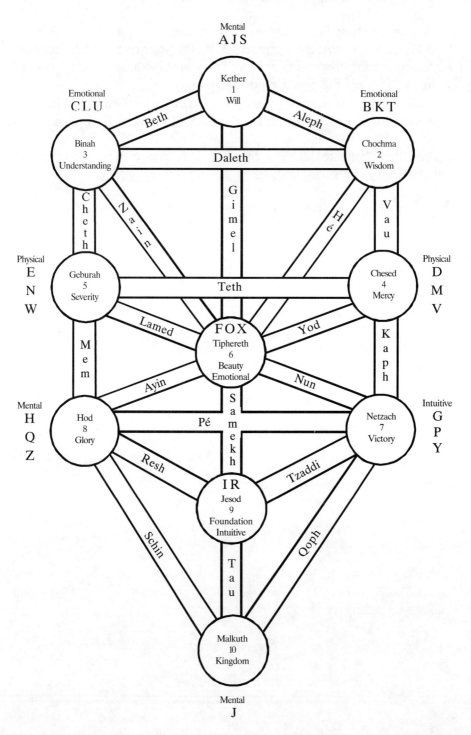

CHAPTER 12

The 1 Letters:
A, J, S

A

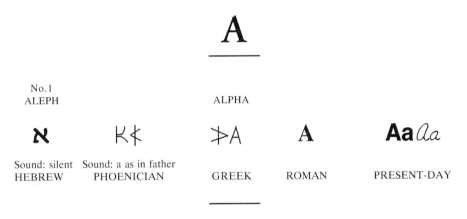

No.1
ALEPH   ALPHA

Sound: silent Sound: a as in father
HEBREW   PHOENICIAN   GREEK   ROMAN   PRESENT-DAY

A – 1

According to the mysteries, Aleph (pronounced aw-lef) was the first letter designed by God. Its sound was necessary to breathe out the other letters, for it is the breath of God. It is the Element of Air and is called a Mother Letter because it is one of the basic elements of creation.

Aleph means "oxhead" and its astrological symbol is Taurus, the sign of physical reproduction. The constellation becomes visible at the spring of each year, the time when the Earth grows warm in temperate climates and flowers spring up to herald the start of a new season of growth. The oxhead itself is the shape of the uterus, the horns being the fallopian tubes—all signifying physical reproduction.

Aleph is the breath of life in every man. Adam did not become a living soul until God breathed into his nostrils the breath of life (Genesis 2:7). Here we learn when life as a human really begins—not at conception, for that is when the physical body has just begun to be formed.

Until the moment of birth the soul hovers near the mother, attached to the fetus by the silver cord. It is at the very first breath that the soul enters the new body, and like Adam, becomes a living being *(The Wisdom of the Mystic Masters*, 28). This is why the time of birth, rather than the time of conception, is of key importance to astrologers.

Aleph is the vital principle of all, the breath of life, and it flows even through inanimate objects. Nothing can exist without Air—so we find Aleph in height and depth and also the path between the two. We can see that pictorially in the shape of the English letter A as well as in the Hebrew letter symbol א.

Aleph is not a vowel sound, but like that of soft breathing from the back of the throat, Air that is necessary for the creative words to float out upon, giving them sound and life. There was no sound in Greek to compare with the glottal consonant of the Hebrew Aleph, so they used this first letter for their A vowel and named it Alpha, meaning "first."

The Romans borrowed it from the Greeks and called it simply, "A." All of the Indo-European languages have this A as their first letter, and they all kept the same shape which, ironically, is like that of a diaphragm which helps to push forth air. And A, like the glyph for Aleph, has three lines which represent the Creative Principle: the trio of Will, Wisdom, and Activity.

The lesson of A is that of self-control. The balance line in the middle separates the upper spiritual world from the lower material world, giving the "A" a balance of forces, or energies to help with this lesson.

The A is a picture of a man standing well balanced on two feet. This shows initiative and leadership ability. A also stands for ambition. In a name it adds strength of character. During the year the A is in force, there is a feeling of being in charge, wanting to take the initiative and not be subservient; a person may even feel a little too self-important. The A wants to be in charge. A stands for Aggressive.

When things go wrong, A becomes disturbed and is better off making decisions quickly. The A can become uptight because it usually has its feet firmly on the ground, so when it's upset (upside down) it must try to keep its balance on a point. Unless it decides quickly, it can lose its sense of balance. A is an article that stands for one, i.e., A house, A person.

The negative A is very self-centered, opinionated, and selfish, for it is 1 and thinks of itself as number one.

Since Aleph is "soft breathing" and represents the Element of Air, A is susceptible to colds and respiratory problems. Anyone whose name has A for the first letter or vowel should never smoke. And during the year any A in the name has an increased danger in smoking. It is important for A to learn how to breathe properly, letting lungs expand with each breath. Fresh air is most beneficial.

Aleph is both life and breath. Breath and life are all one. This oneness of life and breath is called ruach in Hebrew, and in Sanskrit it is prana, in Greek it is pneuma, and in Latin, spiritus. Breath, life, and spirit are one. And one is Aleph and Aleph is one.

Aleph stands for the hidden seed of the Godhead and is representative of the secret God Power that manifests in man. This makes it clear why the First Commandment is "Thou shalt have no other Gods before me."

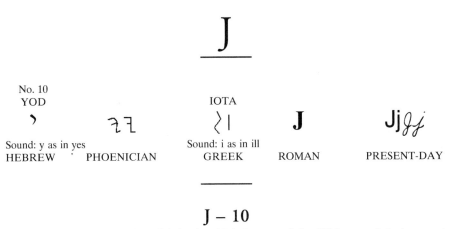

No. 10
YOD   IOTA

Sound: y as in yes   Sound: i as in ill

HEBREW   PHOENICIAN   GREEK   ROMAN   PRESENT-DAY

J – 10

Yod (pronounced yode) is the 10th letter of the Hebrew alphabet and corresponds to the letters J, I, and Y, of which J is the 10th letter of the English alphabet.

Yod is the sixth of the 12 simple letters and its main influence is in *work*. Yod means "hand," and the symbol itself has been described as "a finger pointing heavenward."

With his hands, man is able to work and to fashion things. Yod refers to the hands of God originating all there is (*The Key to the Universe*, 356).

God, the 0, creates man and his world. Man comes from the center of the 0, and stands beside it in 10 as a creator in his own right, using the tools God has provided. With his hands, man fashions his own lesser creations through diligence in work.

All the Hebrew letters were made up of these Yods, for every letter was considered as a creative force. And just as the number 1 is in all numbers, Yod is a portion of the Creative Light Force of God that exists within all of God's creation.

When the Greeks borrowed the Yod, they changed the name to Iota and used it for the vowel I. In Hebrew, of course, there were no letters for vowels, so the Yod corresponds to the consonant forms of J and Y in English.

At one time the I, J, and Y were interchangeable, J being pronounced as a Y, as in Jesu (Yesu). Sometimes the word Yod was spelled "Jod." In the 19th century the use of these letters was finally made distinct and Y became the diphthong ee-ah, except when it took the place of a vowel. I then became the ninth letter, J the 10th, and Y the 25th. Since J is the 10th letter of the English alphabet, it is the first letter on a new level of consciousness; 10 higher than 1. The number 10 means it has been here before and now has new paths to explore.

J's are usually religious, for J carries a cross that is also a crown. The number 10 is self (1) and God Power (0), so J's seek an ennobled or advanced position in life.

The shape of the letter is like a fishhook with the hook facing the left. Since we write from left to right, the left indicates the past and the right, the future. So the hook facing left tells us that the J has a good memory, and it acts as a cup to retain that memory and knowledge.

J's do not like to be told what to do for they are not natural followers; they are leaders. They have much ambition and creative ways to accomplish their goals.

J's seldom ask for advice, for the 10 insists that they have total self-reliance, drawing upon God Power within. This demonstrates why so many religious leaders had names that started with J: Jesus; John the Baptist; John the Apostle; Jacob, who became the father of the Jewish nation; James the apostle; Jeremiah, a major prophet of the Old Testament; and Joshua, Son of Nun, who took Moses' place.

Also, J starts such words as judgement, justice, and judges. If J is the only number 1 letter in the name, the person can lose confidence. This is because the J is on a rocker, not firmly in position. At times J's procrastinate. J's must be careful of accidents because the 1 is so daring and the rocker is a precarious balance.

The truly negative J is dishonest. But as a rule the J is witty and humorous, cautious and clever. It can be outstanding in its work.

Yod corresponds to the Tenth Commandment: "Thou shalt not covet …" because Yod is the hand that works to create, it is representative of honest labor. We are all entitled to all we earn. To desire what someone else has worked for is a form of self-condemnation. The good we do is a positive force that returns our good to us, while evil, being the opposing or negative side, continually destroys itself.

S

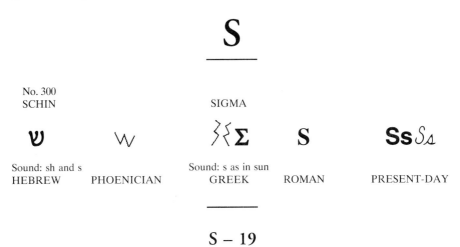

No. 300
SCHIN   SIGMA

Sound: sh and s   Sound: s as in sun
HEBREW   PHOENICIAN   GREEK   ROMAN   PRESENT-DAY

S – 19

The 19th letter of the English alphabet, S, relates to the Hebrew letter Schin, **ש**. Schin is the third Mother Letter of creation and represents the Element of Fire, for Sh is the sound of Fire, and Schin has two sounds: S and Sh. As the 21st letter of the Hebrew alphabet, it reflects the creative trinity (2 + 1 = 3) of which it is a part. The Elements of the Creative Trinity are Aleph (A) = Air, Mem (M) = Water, and Schin (S, Sh) = Fire.

Kabbalistically, Schin means tooth. This relates to Fire in that by chewing we make food ready for assimilation, just as Fire produces life-giving heat that is necessary to creation *(The Key of Destiny*, 297).

Schin represents the Christ principle: "I Am (My teachings are) the Way, the Truth, and the Life," which is the basis of the Christian mysteries *(The Bible and the Tarot*, 103).

The shape of Schin suggests a choice of paths: to choose to attain Christ-consciousness or to continue in the realm of the senses. By choosing the higher path, our love becomes the Fire of divine love, which expands our awareness. It is the Way, the Truth, and the Life; thus the Christ principle.

The Phoenician sign for Schin was almost identical to the original glyph, **ש**, looking more like our modern W. When the Greeks borrowed the sign, they stood it on end and eventually settled on their classic form, Σ. They called it Sigma and used it for their S consonant. This form was passed on to the Romans who rounded out the shape to the modern S.

As the 19th letter, 1 and 9, alpha and omega, S barely finishes one project when it's ready to start another, so S is a self-starter and achiever. S is very creative and sets its sights high, for it is 1 and 9 striving for the perfection of 10. This often makes S a symbol of success.

The 1 also makes S's enjoy working alone; they do their best without interference. They dislike taking orders for they know intuitively what must be done and are capable of doing it. They enjoy expressing their individuality and don't worry what others may think.

The 9 makes S very dramatic and emotional. People with these two qualities make good actors, for they can draw from their sensitivities to portray a character.

This letter consists of two C's: one open to the spiritual/mental plane and the other to the material/physical plane, so it not only "sees" both realms and is psychic, but can control both worlds as well. Its serpentine shape symbolically reveals the fact that it has the wisdom of the serpent.

Each C is like an open moon shining its light in its area. The upper half faces the future and is open to spiritual insight as well as talents, intuition, and ideas from the creative level. Being so receptive on the spiritual plane, it enjoys dwelling there in daydreams. Once it discovers the world in the mind it is intrigued by all it can learn.

The bottom half faces the past from the level of the material world, so it remembers back to a younger age than most. Actors whose names begin with S or have S's in their names find that their good memory helps them draw on past experiences.

S may change direction mid-stream in search for the right way to approach a problem. The reverse curve in the letter means sudden changes: changes of mind, of place, of direction. Because of this it is often difficult for an S to plan ahead.

S will, at some time, have to choose between the lower C of sensuality and the upper C of spirituality.

Negative S's think too much of themselves. They assert their independence sometimes to their own detriment. Some turn from the light to the baser path. Otherwise, S seeks wisdom as the serpent form represents.

CHAPTER 13

The 2 Letters: B, K, T

B

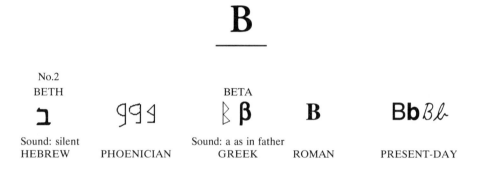

No.2
BETH

ב   999   β   B   Bb Bℓ

Sound: silent
HEBREW   PHOENICIAN   Sound: a as in father
GREEK   ROMAN   PRESENT-DAY

B – 2

The second letter designed by God was called Beth (bayth). Its three basic meanings are *house, mouth,* and *womb.* Beth literally means house and its sacred context is "birth place." The Earth is our house and according to ancient Hebrew tradition, it was the letter B that created the Earth. Anytime we see "Beth" in the Bible, it means house, as in Bethlehem—house of bread, Balbeth—house of the sun, and Bethel—house of God. Bethel refers to the body as the holy temple, for El means God and refers to the true ray of light which is part of the existing God within us all, that is receptive to wisdom and good.

Beth is the womb because that is the dwelling place of the fetus while it is being made ready for birth.

Beth is the mouth, the dwelling place of words about to be born. B is an explosive sound from the lips suggesting the primal explosion, which spewed out the planets. Beth is the first of the seven "double letters" of the Hebrew alphabet. Each one of the seven form the seven opposites of qualities, Beth being Life/Death.

Originally, Beth was drawn as a square to represent a house, then the left wall was omitted leaving a roof, one side, and the floor. When the

Greeks took the letter, they doubled the square. The Romans kept the straight side and rounded out the "rooms."

Those enclosed rooms are able to house collections. B likes to collect things from ideas to books. B also likes to be close to home.

Pictorially B is the nurturing breast, the mother's bosom. The first letter of any word tells the nature of the word. Baby has two B's, and needs nourishment from the mother's breast for it is in the process of building its body. Body begins with B for it is the house of the soul.

B is the builder. The number of the builder is 4, and 4 is made up of 2 plus 2.

B, being 2, is the feminine principle. It leans toward A just as 2 leans toward 1. B is shy and needs affection. B can be all "boxed up." It is very sensitive because it holds so much inside. It has a definite dividing line between the top and bottom rooms, the top being the spiritual world and the bottom, the physical.

As an enclosed letter, B shows secrecy. When negative, B's can be secretive or sneaky.

B's remember. B holds fast to memories in its enclosed double house.

B has a solid base line, which indicates fixed opinions. We saw how A expresses a quantity of one and can be used that way, for example, "A" car or "A" bird.

B is not used as an alternate for two the same way A expresses one, but instead as "bi"; as in biannually meaning twice a year; biped meaning two feet; and so on.

B is pronounced as "be" meaning "having existence." And as 2, B is a straight line down from spirit becoming manifest in the physical, so that it is, or literally, "it be."

Beth is the individualized use of the one pure essence and corresponds to the Second Commandment "Thou shalt not make for thyself any graven image."

K

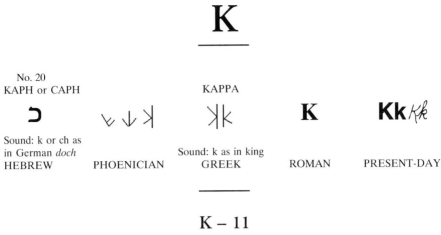

No. 20
KAPH or CAPH

KAPPA

Sound: k or ch as
in German *doch*
HEBREW   PHOENICIAN

Sound: k as in king
GREEK   ROMAN   PRESENT-DAY

K – 11

The 11th letter of the Hebrew alphabet, Kaph (caf), was one of the seven double letters having two sounds, K or Ch, and representing opposites in nature: divine love and human love. Venus, the planet of love, rules it.

Kaph was given the number 20 for there was no number 11 in Hebrew. It is a higher expression of Beth (2) as K (11) is to B (2). This gives Kaph the qualities of Beth on the next octave, which indicates mastery of the lower self—human love on a higher level.

Kaph means the hollow or the palm of the hand and symbolizes the act of holding. It means taking hold of opportunities that present themselves or retaining what we receive. To the seekers of wisdom this is a sign of the Initiate who welcomes the opportunity to delve further into spiritual truths; the one who has passed through the lessons of all the numbers 1 through 9, reaching perfection in 10, and then radiating an outpouring of love in 11.

When reaching 10, these people should be well-acquainted with and follow the divine law established in the Ten Commandments, and then in 11 be ready to bring their light to the people, to put their palms out to bless them.

11 is the number of light, and of Jesus who brought light to the world. Positive 11's do bring light (29/11) and laughter (38/11) for they are in that vibrational harmony.

Every letter and number has its negative polarity as well. The destructive side can double the errant vibration of the base number 2. This means "overly sensitive." Nervous tension. Dishonesty. Hidden motives. Unsympathetic. Narrow. Intolerant. Moody. Kleptomania. Thievery. Sneakiness. Glibness. Liar. That is why it is important to overcome the lower nature and, like the upper part of the K, reach upward for light and be receptive to a higher awareness and intuition, spiritual help, and creative ideas. K is intuitive and can follow hunches.

The lower part of the K is a V upside down with its feet firmly planted on the ground, suggesting material influence. The side of the K is a wide

V like a crescent moon giving its light to all and, like C, scatters its energies. Its success depends on how it uses its talents. K is as spiritual (upper V) as it is material (lower V), hence, divine love or human love.

K needs music (20) to calm itself and give inspiration. When it allows its light to shine, it is a great inspiration to other people.

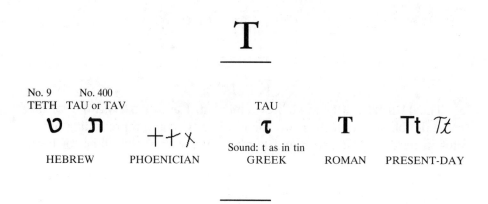

No. 9	No. 400		TAU			
TETH	TAU or TAV					
ט	ת	✝✝𐤗	τ	T	Tt	*Tt*
			Sound: t as in tin			
HEBREW	PHOENICIAN		GREEK	ROMAN	PRESENT-DAY	

T – 20

There are two letters in Hebrew that correspond to the English letter T: Teth (tayth) (t) and Tau, or Tav (tawv) (t, th).

Teth, the ninth letter, means *serpent* or *roof.* At first thought there is little connection between the two, but we shall see where there is a definite spiritual relationship.

The 9 completes its exams and garners wisdom from all that has been learned. The serpent represents that wisdom.

The Bible tells us that "wisdom strengthens the wise" (Ecclesiastes 7:19) and that it is "far better than weapons; yea it is better for those who see the light of truth. For the protection of wisdom is like the protection of money, and the advantage of knowledge is that wisdom gives life to him who possesses it" (Ecclesiastes 7:11-12).

The wisdom we gain is a protection to us as a roof protects us from the elements. The T has a horizontal bar that is the roof of the letter representing that protection. Teth is the fifth of the simple letters and represents hearing. When we listen with our inner ear and understand what we hear, we gain wisdom.

As the giver of wisdom, Teth is the serpent on the Tree of Life. It is the coiled fiery power also known as the Kundalini force and often pictured as a coiled serpent.

The ancient form of this letter was a circle surrounding a cross. The circle is the serpent encircling the Tree of Life, which is Tav. The circle also represents the 22 letters in which all knowledge is contained. Every circle is numbered as 22.

The cross in the center is a plus sign, or tally. It is the force that continually "adds" to its creation. So it has been called Jehovah (IHVH). It refers to IHVH because the total of the circle, 22, added to the cross of four sides, 4 equals 26, the number of IHVH in Hebrew:

$$
\begin{aligned}
I &- 10 \\
H &- 5 \\
V &- 6 \\
H &- \underline{5} \\
& 26 \text{ or } \oplus
\end{aligned}
$$

This is meaningful to us in English as well, for the word for Jehovah, God, also totals 26 by its full number:

$$
\begin{aligned}
G &- 7 \\
O &- 15 \\
D &- \underline{4} \\
& 26
\end{aligned}
$$

The horizontal line is matter and the vertical is spirit descending into matter. When they cross (t), they make a plus: creation. "In the sign of the tally is concealed the building of the whole creation" (*Book of Tokens*, 91). And, "By this letter I show all is brought forth through number" (92).

The Hebrew alphabet is constructed so that there are three groups of seven letters. The number 7 denotes the end of a cycle, and is a number of rest and reflection on things learned and completed. The end of each group of seven is an initiation to higher study.

To know all is symbolized by the cube. Unfolded, the cube becomes the cross, and the 22nd and last letter of the Hebrew alphabet is Tav, meaning the sign of the cross. As the final letter it represents the end of a cycle, just as the cross means rising above all physical limitation and soaring free in spirit (*The Bible and the Tarot*, 4-5).

Tav is the seventh double letter (Th), assigned to grace and the beauty of holiness (wholeness), and its opposite, deformity of sin and imperfection (*The Key of Destiny*: 319).

There is no letter in Hebrew that is actually shaped like a cross, but when the Phoenicians borrowed from them, they took the meaning "sign of the cross" literally and made their glyph a cross shape.

When the Greeks borrowed from the Phoenicians, they raised the horizontal bar to the top and called it Tau. The Tau cross also represents ten because its sacred meaning was perfection, Heaven, the Tetractys and all it stood for, plus the ineffable name of God. It was inscribed on the forehead of every person admitted into the mysteries of Mithras, the ancient Persian God of Light and Truth who was often identified with the sun, and also known as Abraxas. It was "mystery" *(The Secret Doctrine*, Vol. 1, 384).

Tau later became the Roman T. In a name it means "you can make your mark in the world."

In English, T is the 20th letter. This gives it a distinct relationship to Teth (9) and Tav (22) because: 9 must learn to give selfless service to others; 2 desires partnership in business and marriage and must learn to give and take. The 0 following the 2 increases the power of the 2's qualities; and 22 is double the lesson of the 2, but with the mastership attained to give so much more of itself; hence "the sign of the cross."

The T reflects that self-sacrifice by the crossbar load on its shoulders over a precarious one-line base.

All 2's have a difficult time making decisions because of their ability to see both sides of a question. T, by its shape, shows why this is so. The T can go three ways. It makes an equal triangle on either side. Which path should it take?

Carrying the cross also signifies an interest in religion. T can be spiritual because it is 20, and the God Power of the 0 is always there. T needs spiritual unfoldment or it feels burdened. T can be easily hurt and often feels used, as 2 is a very emotional numerical vibration and feels things deeply. The cross means self-sacrifice, martyr, or self-pity and "poor me."

The negative T has a temper it must learn to control. It is stubborn and must learn to have patience and to be tolerant. Where positive 2's are cooperative and outgoing, the negative side is unfriendly.

Otherwise, the positive traits of the 2 are magnified in the 20: cooperative pays attention to details, neat, diplomatic, a peacemaker; all are intensified by the cypher beside it. That top bar is a protective wing. T loves its family and is protective of it.

The top bar also means "high strung." T's are often tense and, when carried away by negative emotion, will use sarcasm and cruel words. Remember, 2 has a way with words, good or bad. Those negative emotions, if not controlled, can stir up difficulties in partnerships and in marriage. T has more of these qualities than the other "2 letters," B and K, which do not carry a load on their shoulders.

Two T's in a name can mean getting all bottled up over situations. Even the word bottled has two T's. It can "double-cross" itself, and be in "tied-up" conditions.

The 2 is the peacemaker, so peace is important to the 20th letter. It will carry a grudge rather than argue because of that, and it will often agree with others just to have peace. As the 20th letter, T takes on the qualities of the 20 in its collective nature. T is easily turned into a plus sign and plus means to add more, just as 20 adds more. So the letter and its number agree, as do all letters and numbers; the agreement is more easily seen in certain cases such as this one. T, particularly as the first letter in a name, needs a partner. To be a good partner, T must be honest and true to itself and in its relationships. In Hebrew it is the ninth letter, Teth, that corresponds to the Ninth Commandment "Thou shalt not bear false witness against thy neighbor."

We are all sons of God in that we have a spark of that divinity within, and that is the good we see and respect in each person. To bear false witness against anyone is to ignore the divinity in others and belittle that which is in ourselves. We bear witness to truth when we quietly salute the divinity in others in our deeds as well as in our words.

CHAPTER 14

The 3 Letters: C, L, U

C

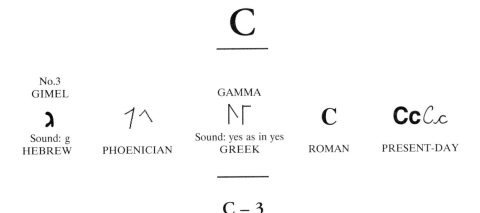

No.3 GIMEL		GAMMA		
ג			C	Cc Cc
Sound: g		Sound: yes as in yes		
HEBREW	PHOENICIAN	GREEK	ROMAN	PRESENT-DAY

C – 3

The third letter of the Hebrew alphabet is Gimel (ghee-mel), meaning *camel*, and it corresponds to the letter G. There is no C in Hebrew. The governing influence of Gimel is riches, and camels were often laden with many rich possessions. Likewise, C's love to adorn themselves with beautiful clothing and jewelry.

Whether C or G, this letter is good with words because it is a 3. The camel's hump holds a lot of water so that it can go for days in the desert without thirst. When the throat is dry it is difficult to speak. To have a sufficient amount of water means to have a lubricated throat, and the throat is the resonator of sound. All 3's have fluidity of speech, so "camel" is a perfect name for the 3 letter.

The Greeks took the glyph and called it Gamma. They also used it for the G consonant. But when the Romans borrowed the symbol, they used it first for both the sound G and the sound K. They would write "Gaius" for "Caius." Later they developed a second symbol, C, for the K sound, to distinguish the two. C became the third letter of the Roman alphabet. The letter still means "camel" and camel begins with a C, while in Hebrew the word is Gimel (Geemel) and starts with a G.

Ironically it is the Third Commandment that tells us not to take the name of the Lord God in vain. There is power in our speech. It can be healing or hurtful and every word we utter returns to us, whether blessing or curse, each one being a seed sent forth only to return to us in full maturity. Harmful words create inharmonious vibrations which, according to the law of the circle (cycle), return to the giver or speaker.

C is pronounced "see" and it does indeed see for it is psychic, though not always aware of it.

The shape of C is the half-moon giving light to the Earth. 3's do enjoy letting their light shine and are happiest when they can bring a smile or entertain others.

C is also like an open mouth; it loves to talk. Negative C's tend to gossip—use words unwisely.

C is open to receive talents. They have many kinds of creative self-expression. It is just as easy for them to scatter their energies. Some are real show-offs. They want to enjoy life, have fun, and not take things so seriously. They love to inspire people with their words, oral or written. And they do, for they have a marvelous creative imagination.

It is difficult for C to save money. Money is energy and it is tempting to scatter it, causing money worries. Anyone with a 30 birth date who has a C in their name is apt to leave covers off things like toothpaste tubes, camera lenses, anything that has accessory parts. Rather than keep a set of like equipment together in one box, the parts disappear one by one. That is a scattering of energy too.

C's are artistic and prefer professional work. They hate mundane jobs and manual labor unless it is creative. They want to enjoy everything they do, even in their work. They need someone to manage their business needs so they can devote their time to creativity. They see the abstract and can capture it in words, paintings, and ideas.

C is shaped like a U sideways. Where U holds things like a cup does, C lets it all flow out, so the emotions cannot be held in.

The negative C's may have loose morals, or be too serious or critical of others. They are intolerant. They gossip.

Words that describe C are: Careless, Character, Communicative, Confident, and Creative.

C likes to travel. Here again Gimel (camel) has its influence, since the camel was used for transportation, to travel to distant places.

L

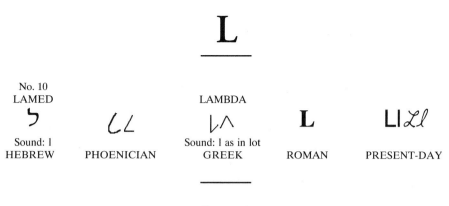

No. 10
LAMED
HEBREW · Sound: l

PHOENICIAN

LAMBDA
GREEK · Sound: l as in lot

ROMAN

PRESENT-DAY

L – 12

In Hebrew, the 12th letter is Lamed (law-med): the outstretched arm of God in the act of accomplishing. "I am the Lord and I will save you with an outstretched arm" (Exodus 6:6).

Lamed means *ox-goad*, which is a pointed stick that urges oxen to move on. L's have the ability to encourage others to make the most of themselves. They can inspire people to make a move in the right direction, like the outstretched arm of the Lord in Exodus.

Lamed is sexual desire, the force behind all evolution, the power of the life force to produce manifestation *(The Key of Destiny*, 72). This force of desire must be balanced between the physical and spiritual so that it is used wisely: "Be ye fruitful and multiply and replenish the earth and subdue it" (Genesis 1:28).

When the Greeks borrowed the letter from the Phoenicians, they called it Lambda. It later became the Roman L and is the same number in the English alphabet as in the Hebrew: 12. Only there was no 12 in Hebrew. After 10 they numbered by tens: 10, 20, 30, etc., the 30th being Lamed. The root of either 12 or 30 is 3.

L is for "loving." Its nature is romantic and devoted to family. In order to "subdue" the passions, it must find the balance between the higher and lower natures. L has no visible balance line as in A, for example.

L's can be warm, expressive, and loving, but when upset by circumstance, become cold, aloof, and sarcastic: two ends of the same balance board. L's need self-control. Sometimes they feel they don't need this self-control because they feel attractive and expect others will admire them just the same. They think they can get away with being critical and still remain attractive. (So they think.) Yet they are very sensitive.

L is highly creative since it is the 12th letter and 12/3 is the number of the creative trinity. L has a firm base line so it is balanced on the Earth plane. It doesn't rock or scatter so it is not apt to be as impulsive as C. It gathers where C scatters; it is open to receive its good and tends to hold it better than the C, so it is wiser in its approach.

L is not as spontaneous as C, for its base is straight and will not move as quickly, so it considers things before acting.

Expressive L's find popularity and success through creative self-expression and are usually happy and outgoing. They do need to channel their talents toward study and self-improvement.

Along with artistic abilities, the L has a good legal mind because it knows the basics of law. L is 12/3, A, B, C, basics. Both law and legal begin with L, the picture of the outstretched arm of the Lord (Law).

L has a good legal mind because its intuition gives it insight into people's motives. It understands why they act as they do and its first impressions are often right. L's are very intuitive because they are completely open to the mental and spiritual plane, as their shape shows, and upside down L is 7, an intuitive number vibration.

This gives L psychic awareness. It often desires occult and religious training. The 7 gives L the ability to think things through, for 7 is very analytical and has good reasoning abilities.

It is not strange that L's are good speakers, singers, teachers, and preachers, or that they are equally vocal when negative by use of hurtful words, sarcasm, and criticism. Together the vocal numbers—2, 3, 6—are what compose an L: 12/3 = 6.

The L loves to sing and has a good voice, especially if born on the 12th or 30th. Lamed's value is 30. The negative L has absolutely no patience and finds fault with everything. They can see both sides of a question and tend to be indecisive. Some feel held down by their environment and that can be a source of frustration. They must feel free to express themselves.

Also, since L's are upside down 7's, they bring in the negative polarity of the 7 when things don't go right for them: fear, sorrow, frustration, and coldness.

People with more than one L in their name are prone to accidents and carelessness because they have so much on their minds that they do things too quickly.

Otherwise they have a happy disposition and are friendly and sociable.

L: Law. Learned. Legal. Life. Light. Likeable. Loquacious. Loving. Lust. Lyrical.

U

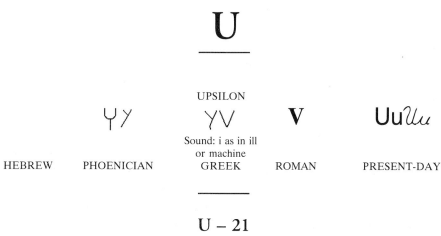

UPSILON

Sound: i as in ill
or machine

| HEBREW | PHOENICIAN | GREEK | ROMAN | PRESENT-DAY |

U – 21

Of the 3's, C scatters, L gathers, and U is most receptive. U is open to receive talents and good fortune (horseshoe shape), but it can rock and spill out contents like a rolling cup if U's fill their cup through selfishness and greed. This cup called U is endowed with creative imagination, inspiration, and charm along with nervous tension in maintaining its balance. The base rocks from past to future, left to right, an indication of uncertainty and indecision.

U can hold a lot inside but when it becomes too nervous or emotional it will rock over too far and spill its contents. So U should not gamble, especially if it is with a Q; that signifies losses.

Inverted, U makes an umbrella. This shows that it needs protection and will set up its own defenses. U must prepare for the future. It tries to fill its cup and may hold onto too much for too long. U is an enthusiastic collector.

Though it is a 3 vibration, U has strong characteristics of the 7 because 21 consists of three 7's. The 7's are either warm and spiritual or cold and materialistic. U is so entirely open, with no balance line between the spiritual and material areas, that it can be all one or the other. It is so wide open to the spiritual realm that, with the 7 influence, it can become overzealous and fanatically religious.

All 3's are good with words. Like 7's, U either speaks well or remains silent and uncommunicative.

U has high ideals and, like 7's, is usually quite conservative. The other 3 letters, C and L, are more faddish and liberal since they are not influenced by strong 7's. C is 3 and L is 12 (which is 2 × 6).

This conservative aspect is noticeable by the high sides on the U. It makes its own boundaries. The straight lines on both sides mean there are two emotional outlets as well. Sometimes two distinct personalities are seen: a dual nature. U's have musical ability and good voices. The 6 (21/3 = 6) represents the voice; 2's are good speakers and 3's know how to project. Because the 2 comes first, the U leans toward the opposite sex. It is not the initiator that the L is, whose 1 comes first (12/3). All of the 3's are emotional, but U holds so much inside that it can be overly sensitive and can't always express those feelings.

Negative U's are jealous, temperamental, quarrelsome, and sarcastic. They use words to win or war (negative 7 characteristics). They must be careful to maintain their balance with self-control or they easily lose all they gain.

There is no comparative letter in Hebrew. U is a descendant of the letter V. When the Greeks borrowed the alphabet from the Phoenicians, they developed two signs from their "waw" which they used as the semi-consonant W, as in the word "know." The first sign actually became F and this one became the vowel U and was called upsilon, or bare-u.

The Romans used it as both the consonant V and the vowel U. English dictionaries did not separate them until approximately 1800 and later.

U: Urbane. Unconventional. Useful. Uncanny.

CHAPTER 15

The 4 Letters:
D, M, V

D

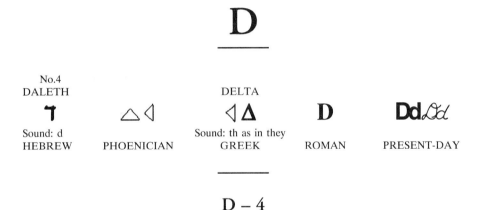

No.4
DALETH
Sound: d
HEBREW

PHOENICIAN

DELTA
Sound: th as in they
GREEK

ROMAN

PRESENT-DAY

D – 4

The fourth letter of the Hebrew alphabet, Daleth (daw-leth), is one of the seven double letters of creation that has qualities of opposites; Daleth being knowledge versus ignorance.

Daleth means *womb* or *door*. In a way, the womb is a door; the door of birth. The graphic sign for Daleth is **ח**. It is clearly open, for door to the Hebrews means a way to go freely in and out.

When the Greeks borrowed the sign, they called it Delta, also meaning door, but they enclosed it into a triangle: **Δ**. To them a door is something you can shut to keep things in or out. Pythagoras felt a great mystery was revealed by the fact that 4 equals 10 $(1 + 2 + 3 + 4 = 10)$. 10 means a new beginning; when one door closes, another will open. The only other number that totals 10 this way is 7: $1 + 2 + 3 + 4 + 5 + 6 + 7 = 28/10$.

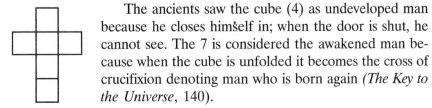

The ancients saw the cube (4) as undeveloped man because he closes himself in; when the door is shut, he cannot see. The 7 is considered the awakened man because when the cube is unfolded it becomes the cross of crucifixion denoting man who is born again (*The Key to the Universe*, 140).

D corresponds with the Fourth Commandment, "Remember the Sabbath, to keep it holy."

When the Romans took the letter from the Greeks, they put the straight line to the left and rounded out the opposite side into a half-moon. It is similar to a cube, or square with four sides.

D is closed in, so anyone who has a name that begins with this letter will often feel enclosed by limitations, especially if there are several D's in the name. They find they must often rise above unfavorable circumstances.

D sits firmly on the line, so it is a letter of balance; it understands the material side, and it can be opinionated. It can also be ultra-conservative, held in by self-made boundaries.

D is not open like C, so it does not "see" as a C does. It believes more in things seen, and has to see to believe. D should avoid business with a 3, for 3 is an artist, while 4 is a worker, and the two seldom agree. Nor do they get along too well with 1, 5, or 7. But 3 needs 4 to manage its career.

D's can be workaholics and very dull, but they love their families, are patriotic, trustworthy, and dependable. D will work hard to achieve. Just don't expect a D to be overly demonstrative.

Since D is almost a square, it believes in "a square deal," it is "fair and square," honest, and expects the same in return. A strong foundation of security is important to them.

Negative D's are gloomy, too straight-laced, opinionated, argumentative, and stubborn.

M

No.40 MEM		MU		
Sound: m		Sound: m as in mother		
HEBREW	PHOENICIAN	GREEK	ROMAN	PRESENT-DAY

M – 13

Mem (mame) is the 13th letter of the Hebrew alphabet, and as 13, it is numbered 40. It is the second of the Mother Letters and represents the Element of Water, which is necessary for all of creation.

The letter itself is a glyph that suggests movement, a wave showing the motion of Water. In most languages words that represent the Mother or Water aspect begin with M: Mother (English), Mere (French), Mor

(Swedish), Madre (Spanish), Mutter (German). And the word water in Latin is mare, and in French, mer. Then there are such aquatic words as marine and marsh. Mother and Water are synonymous with this letter because prenatal life begins in the amniotic sac of Water within the womb of the mother. M is the 13th letter of all Indo-European alphabets, the center, just as the womb is located in the center of woman. And, interestingly enough, M is the center of the word "woman."

In the Bible we read how the Pharaoh's daughter found a baby afloat in a small ark: "And she called his name Moses; for she said, I drew him out of the water" (Exodus 2:10).

The Bible does not explain what the name had to do with Water because in those days it was well known that Mem (M) represented Water. Over the years the deeper meanings have been lost to the world in general.

All letters and numbers had mystical meanings in all languages, but M was considered the most sacred of all since Water is necessary for all life. It is both feminine and masculine, or androgynous.

There is a connection with W, the first letter of the word Water; for M is a W upside down, and the womb, which starts with W, is in the Mother, which starts with M.

The first Phoenician hieroglyph for Mem was a W with a tail down the right side: \/\/) . When the Greeks borrowed the sign they eliminated the tail, turned the letter around, and called it Mu. The Romans adopted it for their M.

The Romans thought the M looked like a face. They added a dot on each side for eyes, and when they made the dots larger they became circles, thus creating "omo." This became homo, the Latin word for man.

M shows strength of character, and stands well balanced on its own two feet. The V is prominent in the upper middle of the M. This shows that it is open to ideas from a higher plane and gives M management abilities. It is good in positions of authority as it has an orderly mind and excellent memory.

The 4 is a number of business, and M's root is 4. The V inside it is the 22nd letter and its root is also 4. Adding 4 plus 4 equals 8, the number of the executive. This means the managerial abilities are strong in the M. Women whose names begin with this letter are exceptional homemakers, and men with this initial like to manage the home.

M is the only letter that is pronounced with the mouth closed. This signifies the quiet of the great sea whose deepest waters are mute, yet from it springs all life.

This mute letter ties in with the 13th card of the Tarot, Death. But this symbol represents change, not the end. A prominent sun on the horizon in the background is to remind us that while the sun sets every day, it also rises again the next morning. Every symbol on the card points out a continuation of the life force.

As with the mute M, there is great strength in silence. For it is in rest that we renew our energies. Noise is disturbing; silence relaxes. The body is renewed in the silence of sleep, and so is the mind. The continual change from rest to activity and rest again is vital to a healthy life.

Because M is pronounced with the mouth closed, it is the most inexpressive of all the letters. The negative M appears dull, cold, hard, and unfeeling. M's feel hemmed in, as do all 4's. They are hard workers and conservative to the point where they forget to take time to relax and enjoy what they have earned.

There are ups and downs in the glyph that suggest upsetting qualities; M's can be careless. It is important for them to keep their thoughts above the earthly things. That middle V with its arms upstretched suggests a calling for spiritual help, and it does receive help through intuition.

Another aspect of M is greatness in height or visual impact, as in such words as Mountain, Majestic, Millionaire, Magical, Momentous—all words that start with a glyph of height. Or the opposite: Minimal. Then there is greatness in quality of being, such as in Master.

V

No.6

VAU or VAV	WAW	UPSILON & DIGAMMA		
٦	Ψ Υ	Υ V Ϝ	V	Vv Ṽʋ
Sound: v or w	Sound: w as in know			
HEBREW	PHOENICIAN	GREEK	ROMAN	PRESENT-DAY

V – 22

Vau or Vav (vawv) is the sixth letter of the Hebrew alphabet and the second of the 12 simple letters. Its governing influence is *thought* (*The Secret Teachings of All Ages*, CXVI).

Vau means *peg* or *nail*, and also *eye*. In its astrological connection it is the eye of Taurus. In the Taurus constellation, there is a brilliant star called Aldebaran. Now, what does a nail or peg have in common with thought and a star that is the eye of Taurus?

Pegs or nails are connecting links that hold things together. Taurus has good physical coordination and likes to put things together. Words are the connecting links, which form a sentence to express a thought. Taurus rules the neck and this is the location of the voice. If we are to express a clear thought we must first *see* it clearly with our inner vision.

"The eye is the lamp of the body; if therefore your eye be bright, your whole body is also lighted" (Matthew 6:22). That beautiful red star, Aldebaran, which is the eye of Taurus, has long been used as a guiding point in navigation confirming sailors' sights. It is a material representation of the spiritual insight that guides us when we desire enlightenment.

When we become one with the Divine thought, love, and light of the Christ-consciousness, we then have that inner vision and light of knowledge that gives us the joy of constructing treasures of lasting value, and we ultimately contribute to the upliftment of mankind and our own soul's growth.

Esotericists know that the eye referred to in the scripture is the pineal gland that fills with spiritual light when it is activated, the gland also called "the third eye." When one becomes evolved spiritually to the point where the pineal gland fills the body with light, the Christ-consciousness is developed and we feel a love for our fellow man that we have never felt before *(The Bible and the Tarot,* 65-6). When this is developed in man he knows the difference between the sensual physical love, which is nothing more than sense gratification, and the pure love of the God-light that is present in every living being.

Light and love compose the link between the human and the Divine. These are the attributes of our Creator and are expressed in the third letter of the Tetragrammaton IHVH: His Name. When the Phoenicians borrowed Vau, they gave it the name Waw and used it for the semi-consonant W, as in "know."

When the Greeks borrowed from the Phoenicians, they developed two signs from Waw: Upsilon (U) and Digamma, which they used for their semi-consonant W. This disappeared in later Greek. The Romans took the Digamma from the Etruscans and used it as the consonant F, and they used the Upsilon in the form of V to stand for three sounds: U, V, and W.

We still see the letter V in ancient Roman script in place of U on government buildings today. The two letters were not separated in written form until the 18th century.

The letter V, being completely open above, is very intellectual, and has a good business head. It is the 22nd letter and those 2's show that the V will work very well with others. 22 is the number of the Master Builder, so V, especially if it is the first letter of the name, has what it takes to be a good leader, or to be evil if the person works on the negative side of the vibration.

V's need to study metaphysics because they have no line to separate the spiritual from the material plane. Therefore they can easily be all one or the other. Those who are filled with materialism are unscrupulous business people. Those completely lacking in spiritual light become hardened criminals. They need good moral precepts if they are to be fulfilled and able to contribute something of worth as they are meant to do.

Inverted, V is a mountain peak, and V's have so much nervous energy that they often feel they must climb mountains to achieve all they desire.

Otherwise, V stands on a precarious point that touches the Earth line. They will spend all their money on their desires and then feel the need for financial security. But the point of the V is insecure and the desires are many, so it is important for V's to have an understanding of finance.

V's need spiritual enlightenment to balance out their nervous energies and bring peace within themselves. The letter V is a picture of arms lifted upwards asking for spiritual help. It is entirely open to receive ideas to build upon. It has Vision. It also has strength and the will to work hard, as it is 22/4, the number of the tireless worker.

V's are able to make their ideas work for them better than anyone else since they have a natural gift for channeling their energies into their projects. V is definitely for Victory, and they are able to set new goals and achieve them again and again.

V's love their families and are definitely the marrying type. They will work hard to provide for their family. Life in Latin is Vita, beginning with the letter V (Vau) which is the sixth letter in Hebrew, and six is synonymous with sex. Vau is the connecting link between man and woman, not only physically, but in the sacred spiritual love-force that unites us all with the divine.

Yod Hé Vau Hé is the name of that part of God that gives life to His creation. Yod is the male principle, Hé is the female, and Vau is the "nail" or connecting link that joins the two for the outflowing of birth and all creation from the womb of the final Hé. All life is a sacred gift, and V corresponds to the Sixth Commandment, "Thou shalt not kill."

CHAPTER 16

The 5 Letters: E, N, W

E

NO.5 HÉ or HÉH		EPSILON		
ה	ヨ≩	∃ᖴE	E	Ee*Ee*
Sound: he as in head		Sound: e as in red		
HEBREW	PHOENICIAN	GREEK	ROMAN	PRESENT-DAY

E – 5

There was no graphic sign in Hebrew for E since their alphabet contained no vowels. The Phoenicians took the consonant Hé (hay), which is equivalent to the English consonant H, and changed the symbol ה to ⅄ for their own consonant. After 900 B.C. the Greeks borrowed the sign, reversed it ⅄ to E, called it Epsilon, and used it for their short E vowel, in order to differentiate it from their long E vowel, Eta.

Like 5, E is open. It is open to talk, sing, and speak, so it is a letter of communication, of words. When negative it can be vocally critical of others.

E-5 is open all around so it needs its freedom. It tends to have a nervous temperament and a temper. It is the 5 of the five senses so it is "open" to try, test, and taste everything. It may overdo things because it is so open.

The 5 is on a rocker so it is changeable, and will frequently change its mind. It has a tendency to lie. Negative 5's can get into trouble with the law.

The E is so energetic and restless, it needs something worthwhile to keep it occupied. E can be openly affectionate and loving or the opposite, cold as ice. It is generally extroverted.

When the E is doubled it gives a wider expanse of expressions in either space or the senses. We see this in the words that suggest space: Freedom, Deep, Meet, Keep, Seep, Fleet, and Seek.

We see it in the sense words: See, Feel, Sleep, Speech, and Teeth.

The E is progressive. The letter is open to the future (the right). It doesn't look back, but looks forward to new experiences. It is important for E to have a good education.

There is a good balance line between the spiritual and physical, for the middle line is centered. This makes E interested in the occult as well as the material.

Since it is the fifth letter, the five senses predominate, and sensuality makes the E more worldly than spiritual. But those who do seek the higher level become idealistic and very intuitive.

E: Energetic. Effective.

N

NO.50 or 700 (Final N) NUN		NU		
Sound: n HEBREW	PHOENICIAN	Sound: n as in now GREEK	ROMAN	PRESENT-DAY

N – 14

Nun (noon) is the 14th letter of the Hebrew alphabet and the eighth of the 12 simple letters. Its governing influence is the sense of smell. Nun means *fish* and is the symbol of the Initiate. Nun also means *growth*, meaning spiritual growth.

Fish became representative of the deeper teachings for several reasons. Christianity was born in the Piscean Age, and the first letter of Jesus' title in Greek, translated "Jesus Christ, Son of God, Savior" (ΙΧΘΥΣ), spells out fish. And Jesus was able to live without sin while surrounded by it, just as fish live deep in cleansing waters.

In other faiths, fish were drawn in pictures of gods and goddesses to represent divinity.

The 5 is the mysterious middle of numbers that refers to man and his five senses. 14 is 5 on a higher level and is the number of the Sage (14/5) who has conquered the lower nature of the five senses and seeks the spiritual path by mastering his thoughts and actions.

Thoughts are like fish in the great sea of the mind, and it is important what fish we feed on or what thoughts we choose to make part of our being. The Initiate chooses to attain the Christ-consciousness and remain on that level.

Joshua, the son of Nun, was an Initiate of the Old Testament whom God appointed to take Moses' place in leading the people. He promised He would be with him as He was with Moses. Later, those who chose to become disciples of Jesus were known as fishermen. There are always only a handful of individuals who seek the true wisdom, and out of the multitudes only 12 became disciples. In the Bible, bread and fish were related to spiritual teachings. The number 7, referring to the loaves, tells us that the teachings were of a spiritual nature. This bread, or teachings, filled the multitudes, while the few fishes were all that were needed to fill the 12 disciples, who sought something deeper. Jesus explained this point to them himself. He had told them to beware of the leavening of the Pharisees. The disciples thought it was because they had not brought bread with them, but Jesus was referring to the teachings of the Pharisees as leaven. Leaven is the yeast that changes the characteristics of the dough and causes the bread to rise. Teachings are like leaven in that they can change a person's attitudes and beliefs.

> How is it that you did not understand that I was not talking to you about the bread, but to beware of the leaven of the Pharisees and of the Sadducees?
> Then they understood, that he did not say that they should beware of the leaven of the bread, but of the teaching of the Pharisees and of the Sadducees (Matthew 16: 11, 12).

The bread that Jesus gave was the bread of Heaven.

> This is the bread which came down from Heaven; it is not like the manna which your forefathers ate and died; he who eats of this bread shall live forever. (John 6:58)

It is Jesus' teachings that are the "bread of Heaven." Whenever he says, "I am" or "I give you," the correct translation is: "My teachings are," because the direct translation has no "am" (See Max Freedom Long's book, *What Jesus Taught in Secret*, pages 7-8.) The correct text of John 6:51 is:

> My teachings are the living bread [not "I am the living bread"] because I came down from Heaven; if any man eats of this bread [meaning, "takes in knowledge of"] he shall live forever; and the bread which I will give is my body [the outer teachings for all but his disciples] which I am giving for the sake of the life of the world.

Max Freedom Long tells us that the code meaning for "No man cometh to the Father but by me" is really, "No man cometh to the Father but through what I teach." And from this misinterpretation the Christian religions have used as dogmas, "only through me" and "in my name" (*What Jesus Taught in Secret*, 8).

Those who do seek higher consciousness have much revealed to them in meditation. Seldom is there a teacher of flesh and blood who appears out of nowhere to reveal the mysteries. True enlightenment is a very personal thing. The great spiritual teachers who have progressed beyond their earth's incarnations are ever ready to reach out to the true seeker—who is made known to them by the light of the seeker's aura. So it is true that when the student is ready, the teacher appears.

In order for the student to know he is in the presence of his spiritual teacher, he must have his senses under control, free and clear of any physical stimuli. Through the ages, students have noted that when a spiritual Master is near, there will be a lovely scent to signify his or her presence. This can never be detected in a room filled with heavy perfume, smoke, or even incense, nor is a Master attracted by them. These substances cannot overpower the physical sense of smell. This is why Nun refers to the sense of smell (*The Key of Destiny*, 162).

As the eighth of the simple letters, Nun is astrologically associated with the sign of Scorpio, which represents the reproductive area of man—the sacred center of generation and regeneration.

The low Scorpio seeks sensual gratification and stimulation. The high Scorpio is the eagle that soars above all the mundane, sensual desires and seeks the flight of the soul to the upper regions of wisdom and unfoldment (*The Bible and the Tarot*, 87). The difference is great—being merely mortal or being master of one's circumstances.

When the Greeks borrowed the glyph Nun from the Phoenicians, they changed the name to Nu, reversed the symbol, and then later made it symmetrical, as the present N in English. From there the Etruscans and then the Romans adopted it. When it came to us it kept its 14th place in the alphabet.

N is well balanced on the Earth plane and is the very same when reversed. It can be very sensual or spiritual since there is no line separating the two worlds as there is in A, B, or H (*A Guide to Cosmic Numbers*, 128).

Its inverted V on the left is open to the material world. Those who never develop their higher natures remain attached to the material, sensual world and never venture ahead to the V on the right that is open to something higher than themselves.

The right V is looking up to something greater: to ideas, spiritual understanding, and it is receptive to spiritual unfoldment. Hence Nun is either Scorpio or the Eagle.

Because N is open above and below, it is versatile and encounters many changes in life. It is associated with marriage and with travel.

On its side, N is a Z. This gives it psychic awareness that is subtle and often not used, but it is evident by the two intuitive 7's that make up the Z.

These subtle 7's also account for the great imaginations N's have. In fact, the ancients used this symbol to signify a scribe, as writers must be endowed with a good imagination *(Numerology and the Divine Triangle*, 73).

N is able to pick up ideas out of the air just as an antenna captures radio and television waves. N even looks like an antenna. The word is pronounced "N-tenna," and of the seven letters in that word, four of them are 5's: N, E, N, N, so the predominating trait of the word reflects the qualities of the 5.

W

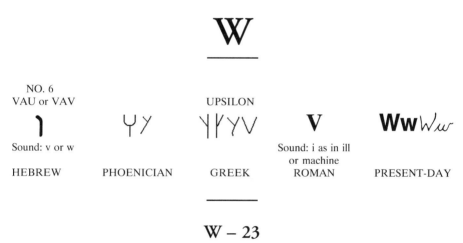

NO. 6 VAU or VAV		UPSILON		
Sound: v or w			Sound: i as in ill or machine	
HEBREW	PHOENICIAN	GREEK	ROMAN	PRESENT-DAY

W – 23

The W is a descendant of the letter V. The Phoenicians' glyph was more like a Y, but they used it for the semi-consonant W (oo). They called it Vau or Waw and it signified the eye of man that sees light and the ear that hears the sound of Air and the wind.

In later Roman times, the W sound was written as a V. But the sounds U, V, and W were all shared by the same letter, and this caused confusion. So they formed a new graphic sign, W, by putting two V's together for the light "oo" sound, while the U retained its vowel form and V was used purely as a consonant. When used as a consonant, W was a picture of Water and represented the taste and the appetite. The symbol W was regarded as the likeness of deepest mystery because of the two deep valleys the letter stands on; the mystery is the point which sets apart being and non-being.

W is the 23rd letter of the English alphabet. This gives it a deep, sensitive nature, for both 2 and 3 are emotional number vibrations. They add up to 5, which represents the five physical senses and a need for freedom in order to cope with the changing aspects of the 5. Overindulgence in sensual pleasures, or expressing any of the other negative traits of the 5, is living in the valleys or pits of the W.

The peaks of the W are very high, and 5 is the middle of numbers, known by the ancients to be "the limited master." The wise men of old called themselves sages for they had mastered themselves by overcoming the temptations of their five senses and touched on the spiritual.

Persons with a W in their names have a change of consciousness at some time in their lives. They have experienced the consonant form of indulgence, some in a lesser degree than others. Those who dissipate themselves are in the deep valleys, a pit that is difficult to ascend. Only through a change of consciousness can they pull out and scale the peaks, which are like arms upraised seeking the light.

This accomplished, it is indeed like the eye of man that sees the light and the ear that hears the Air and wind, for only the ear that is attuned to these subtle sounds hears the inner voice. That is experiencing the peaks of the W. (For more on W see Double-You, page 233.)

CHAPTER 17

The 6 Letters:
F, O, X

F

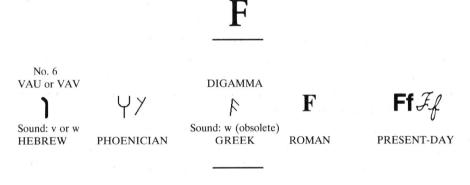

No. 6 VAU or VAV		DIGAMMA		
Sound: v or w HEBREW	PHOENICIAN	Sound: w (obsolete) GREEK	ROMAN	PRESENT-DAY

F – 6

F is a descendant from the Hebrew letter Vau (V). All 6 letters, F, O, and X, are good teachers, for 6's are concerned with their communities and want to be of value. They understand the law and desire to uphold it. They care about their environment and the people with whom they associate. Some are drawn to politics, some to counseling, and many to teaching itself. The 6 also represents the voice that must be heard, and is important to 6's in their careers. They will take on responsibilities as their duty.

This propensity toward responsibility can be seen in the shape of the letter. F carries a double cross. Everyone comes to them with their problems, and they will "carry the load" for them and take an active role in helping all they can, or just worry about it.

F is not as well balanced as E. It needs to be calm and to avoid confusion. Being 6, it wants to finish things and do so in a peaceful atmosphere.

The two horizontal lines of the F are like arms outstretched to help those near them, and 6 is a numerical vibration of service. They are most fulfilled when they accomplish something that is of benefit to other people, whether their own family, friends, or community.

F is the sixth letter, and 6 desires artistic surroundings. This number is prevalent in the arts. The 6 may enter a field of music, decorating, acting, or performing, which is, in a sense, serving others. A good performance brings joy to many people.

F has an open mind and a sixth sense. It is similar to the letter P, the only difference being that the F is open to new ideas. P is opinionated and has a closed mind. (See the closed-in circle at the top of P?) It is the 16th letter, which is 7, and 7 turns its back on the other numbers and chooses its own counsel.

F's are idealistic and as a rule they wish to express beauty. Their calm exteriors give them a kind, parental look.

The negative F carries the responsibility trait to an extreme. This is the meddlesome know-it-all who thinks no one else is right, that he/she alone has all the answers, and is smugly self-righteous.

This is the voice that must be heard, which, when negative, will display a stubborn streak, using the voice as a silent weapon and not speaking for days.

Those who live mainly on the negative polarity of this vibration are people who want to control their families and friends. They can be tyrants and not even realize it because they are so sure that they are absolutely right. By their stubbornness, they make many people unhappy and uncomfortable in their presence.

Otherwise F is a happy family vibration. It stands for Family, Fatherliness, and Fidelity. F can be very passionate. It expresses the full 6 vibration, which is the number of Venus, the planet of love. It will mother or smother.

O

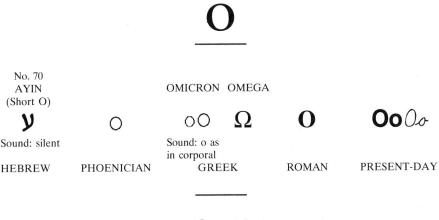

No. 70 AYIN (Short O)		OMICRON OMEGA			
Sound: silent		Sound: o as in corporal			
HEBREW	PHOENICIAN	GREEK	ROMAN	PRESENT-DAY	

O – 15

The letter O corresponds to the 16th letter of the Hebrew alphabet called Ayin (ah-yin), which is the 10th of the 12 simple letters, and whose main influence is anger.

Ayin means *eye*, and refers to the inner spiritual eye that comprehends and interprets what we see. There are two ways we see: with the physical eye, and through the mind by understanding. This second way is when the light dawns on us and we say, "Oh, I see." This is the spiritual eye, Ayin: the window of the soul.

Physical sight is the letter Vau (V). Vau means peg or nail: that which attaches one thing to another. In the case of Ayin, the physical eye is linked with the mind, for only when that which we see physically is interpreted by the mind, do we understand what we see. *(The Key of Destiny*, 219).

The shape of Ayin, O, is like that of an eye and was used by the early church to represent the all-seeing eye of God. The word "church" is from the Anglican root Circ or Cyrc, meaning circular. The first churches were circular designs to represent the eye of God *(The Key to the Universe*, 35-6).

Anger is an emotion of the lower animal self of man. It is a force that can be used to build or to destroy. When a man learns to control his temper he "tames" the animal and his greater power unfolds. Then he is able to build his good rather than destroy his chances. "The man who ruleth his temper is greater than he who taketh a city" (Proverbs 16:32).

Ayin was used by the Phoenicians and Semites for an emphatic laryngeal consonant, C, which is not found in English or in any other Indo-European language. Since the Greeks had no use for that Semitic sound, they used the glyph to represent the vowel O. They called it Omicron, meaning "short O" to distinguish it from Omega, "long O," which they originated and placed at the end of their alphabet *(American Heritage Dictionary*, 903).

The Romans used the sign for both the short and the long O. With O it is all or nothing. It stands for the Cosmos and all within it, as well as the empty zero. No matter how you turn it, it retains its shape. This means that it has fixed opinions, especially if it is the first letter of a name. O is moody, but can cover its feelings well. O is possessive; it wants to hold its own within its enclosed circumference.

O represents home, family, and finances. It attracts money but should never take chances. It is highly protective and responsible, and has a conservative nature.

O is a picture of an eye and starts the words Ophthalmologist and Occultist. Two O's in a word look like a pair of eyes and often refer to "seeing." Through those eyes we look. And we can see with the inner eye when we read a book.

O is an open mouth: Ora and Orthodontist. As the ear it is Otic. As a container full of luxury it is Opulent; full of knowledge it is Omniscient; full of power it is Omnipotent. Empty it is Oppressed, and full of self it is Ornery.

Negative O's are nervous, smug in their self-righteousness, worrisome and meddlesome. On the destructive side they can be jealous, suspicious, cynical, or tyrannical.

O is saint or sinner, either honest or dishonest. It is all or nothing as the circle suggests, and since very ancient times it has been a letter of magic and mystery.

X

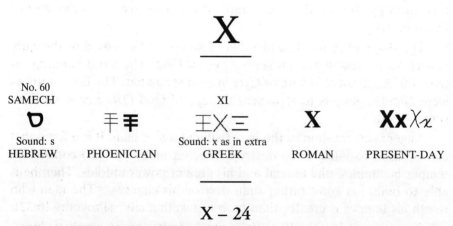

No. 60
SAMECH   XI

Sound: s   Sound: x as in extra
HEBREW   PHOENICIAN   GREEK   ROMAN   PRESENT-DAY

X – 24

The Hebrew letter that corresponds with our letter X is Samekh (saw-mek) (S and X), a picture of a serpent swallowing its own tail.

The Greek name Sigma (S) was confused with the name Samekh (X) which is related to the cross, or Christ principle, so S and X were mixed up. And where Schin represents Fire as the force, which purifies and completes creation, Samekh is the fire that burns in the world of the senses. There still are Kabbalists who relate X to Samekh by writing it as Xmach *(The Bible and the Tarot*, 90).

Samekh, the 15th letter of the Hebrew alphabet, is the ninth of the 12 simple letters. It means *prop* or *bow*, and refers to the bow used to shoot an arrow.

Its sound is like that of the hissing of the serpent, or of the sound made by the string of the bow when the arrow is released from the prop. The arrows that shoot from the bow are, esoterically, the words we speak that either hiss and wound or kiss and heal.

Samekh's governing influence is sleep. If we are seekers of truth and make study and meditation a part of our growth, our spiritual teachers meet and guide us while our bodies are at rest. Often we awake with an answer to a problem or have a new enlightenment. Those who are spiritually unaware often have confusing dreams and nightmares, for they wander unguided in the strange astral realms—realms they do not understand.

The serpent always represents wisdom, and the picture of a serpent swallowing its tail makes a circle, which is akin to a full cycle. A cycle means completion, and like the snake who sheds his old skin to start life anew, this sign represents the shedding of old conditions and completing old projects so that it can begin a new cycle.

This is dealing with the "law of the circle." "What ye give out shall return to you. As ye sow, so shall ye reap." It tells us we must ultimately face what we have created; what we sow becomes our destiny. If we sow good, X is our cross of resurrection; if evil, it becomes the cross we must bear.

When the Greeks borrowed Samekh from the Phoenicians, they changed the glyph and renamed it Xi. It became the Roman X. As the 15th Hebrew letter it is Saint or Sinner. It meant that the animal nature had to be conquered, or "ex-ed" out and the emotions brought under complete control before one could become saint-like.

As the 24th letter of the English alphabet it shows a magnetic personality. Magnetic attraction is X in the + position, a definite love and family vibration. The 6 is the number of love and family, so it is interesting that both the Hebrew 15th letter (ס) and the English 24th letter (X) total 6. (1 + 5 = 6, and 2 + 4 = 6.)

On the negative side, it exes itself out. If it feels another has crossed it, it becomes bitter and seeks revenge.

The glyph itself, X, is a symbol of self-denial. It is open on all sides so it is vulnerable. Through hasty action it can X itself out as former President Richard M. Nixon, who had to resign from the presidency or face impeachment, and actor John Eric Hexum who played Russian roulette with a revolver at his own head and lost.

The X stands strong on the Earth plane and thus open to materialism. But arms are upstretched asking for spiritual help. It can be all spiritual or all material, high-minded or abased.

X has a V on all sides, and V, being 22, has much nervous energy: 4 V's (4 × 22) = 88. The 8 has a fine sense of balance and rhythm, and like the X it can be all spiritual or all material. 88 (8 + 8) = 16, a malefic number. In the Tarot it is the Lightning-struck Tower and can depict losses, accidents, and setbacks. X's have falls and accidents *unless* the person finds his/her spirituality in 7 (1 + 6 = 7).

Because X is so open it is receptive to psychic powers, but it rarely uses them. X feels things so deeply, its sorrows can be intense. Its desire to improve conditions for mankind or to help family and friends can be so great, it will sacrifice to do so.

X is often used in commercial products and names with much success because it is providing a service to people—a strong vibration of the 6: love and service.

X is used as a symbol for a kiss. Some sources say that it became so because Judas gave Jesus the kiss that pointed him out to the enemy. So it is used to mark a person or place: X marks the spot. It is related to the cross, or Christ-principle.

CHAPTER 18

The 7 Letters: G, P, Y

G

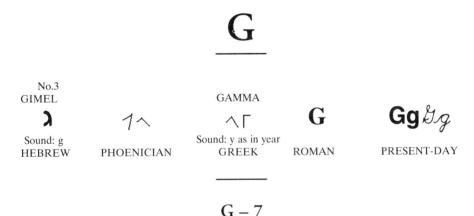

No.3 GIMEL		GAMMA	**G**	**Gg** *Gg*
Sound: g HEBREW	PHOENICIAN	Sound: y as in year GREEK	ROMAN	PRESENT-DAY

G – 7

Gimel, which corresponds to letters C and G, is the third letter of the Hebrew alphabet and the second of its double letters. It is double in its hard and soft sound, and in its strength in health and its opposite, disease. The astrological association is Mars and its governing influence is riches. This stems from the fact that camels were laden with costly merchandise.

Gimel means *camel* (See C, page 95) and the shape of G resembles the outline of a camel's head and neck. The Phoenicians and other Semites used Gimel for their G consonant.

Mars, being the red planet, rules the blood as the life force in man's body. Blood and Water are necessary for life. The camel is known for its ability to store water just as an artery is the vessel for blood.

The Talmud says that Gimel is equated with the loving kindness that is shown to the poor. Science has learned that loving deeds promote good health, and that bad feelings and deeds create "bad blood."

C (3) and G (7) are related health-wise, since Gimel is related to health and disease. As the third letter of Hebrew, it is our foundation because it is through the Trinity of Father, Mother, and Son that we are created.

That Trinity is synonymous with the three Mother Letters, Alef (Air), Mem (Water), and Schin (Fire), that are necessary to our physical makeup and good health. When we maintain perfect harmony of that Trinity, it is reflected in the sevenfold aspect of our bodies, bringing perfect health.

Notice, the original Holy Trinity was Father, Mother, and Son. Early church fathers, influenced by Paul, changed the Trinity to Father, Son, and Holy Ghost in order to reflect more perfectly their belief in the Mother aspect as being below the Father rather than equal with it.

When the Greeks borrowed the letter they changed the name to Gamma, but continued to use it as their G consonant. It was the Romans who used the C for both the C and G sounds until the third century B.C. In order to end confusion, they added the horizontal bar line for the G and left C as it was for the K sound. G is inclined toward religion because it is the seventh letter of our alphabet and 7 is inclined toward spirituality. It turns in on itself to show that it is apt to be more self-searching, more analytical, and more deep thinking than C.

It is a good vibration for any of the arts since it will practice until perfect. It is also a good vibration for writing, science, and religion because of its analytical abilities and desire for perfection. This makes G conservative, and to prefer quality to quantity.

G can speak beautifully but is not as talkative as the C. C is an open mouth while G reflects on its words, speaks little, and says much. This is purely a reflection of the 7 vibration which is spiritual, scientific, or silent.

G is not quite as outgoing as the C, for it is a C turning toward itself. This also manifests the following qualities for G:

➤ It prefers to be alone more than the C.
➤ It keeps its own counsel and can be secretive.
➤ It works best alone and should not go into partnership.
➤ It is more concerned with self than others.
➤ It is reserved, opinionated, and strong-willed.
➤ It wants to solve hidden meanings.
➤ It wants to understand people's motives.

Peace is necessary to a G; time alone to think, to rest, and to balance out its energies. When negative, the balance is upset and G will appear to be cold and unaffectionate. As a result it is often misunderstood and may really be lonely.

The negative G can be very critical, sarcastic, aloof, even morbid, and use hurtful words. It can be nervous or crafty. But it can also be easily hurt. Spiritually mature G's are looked up to for their willpower and wisdom.

As the camel is a means of communication between tribes, G reflects on the deeper values and in its own way will uplift and inspire mankind with its few choice words of wisdom.

P

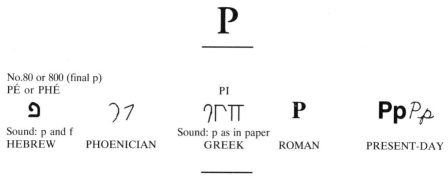

No.80 or 800 (final p)
PÉ or PHÉ
PI
Sound: p and f
HEBREW   PHOENICIAN
Sound: p as in paper
GREEK   ROMAN
PRESENT-DAY

P – 16

Pé or Phé, the 17th letter of the Hebrew alphabet, and the 16th of the English alphabet, is the fifth of the double letters having both a hard and a soft sound: Pé as in pen and Phé as in phenomena. Its double traits are power and servitude, and its letter name, Pé, means *mouth*.

The "power" is the power of expression in either writing or speaking, or both. The mouth is the organ of speech that can be used to express thoughts in a negative or positive way, for evil or for good. Our words can be beautifully constructive and equally destructive.

The thoughts we entertain are food for the mind, just as the food we eat with the mouth is that which sustains the body. We have the power to choose our thoughts as well as the food we eat, and when we choose wisely we gain in health and wisdom.

If we eat something we don't like, we can spit it out since our mouth can accept or reject. It is the same with our thoughts. We have the power to control our thinking, to choose constructive thoughts.

Physiologically, Pé is the pituitary gland, which endows us with intuition, thought transference, and an "inner knowing" when it is awakened in us. So if we direct our thoughts toward achieving a goal we can meet with success, which is an aspect of power. Misuse of energies will surely lead us to the opposite trait: servitude.

Pé was adopted by the Greeks, who renamed it Pi and reversed the glyph. The Romans enclosed the top circle and called the letter P, and it became the 16th letter of the English alphabet.

Geometrically, P is a circle on a line, the head on the self, so it is an intellectual vibration, has mental curiosity, and is good at concentration. But it also indicates a bent toward being opinionated and stubborn. P can be either very spiritual or agnostic or atheistic with a closed mind.

A great deal of power is felt and expressed by persons with many P's in their name, so it is important for P-predominant people to balance their interests with studies in philosophy, to use their power for good rather than for selfish gains. This is also true for those whose first letter is P, because the first initial is the cornerstone of the name, and that cornerstone tells our natural approach and reaction to life's experiences.

When unbalanced, P can be very domineering, have a "big head," and therefore not be a good business or marriage partner. Such people become more possessive than loving. Being so top-heavy, the foundation of P is not secure, and without spiritual awareness it can be very moody and ill-natured. And, being 7, sufficient rest is important both physically and mentally.

P can accomplish anything when it Perceives what it must do, does it Promptly, and Perseveres until it is done to Perfection *(The Key of Destiny,* 240-41).

All words that start with P denote Power, both physical and mental. People who Plot and Plan use mental Power. There are Pilots and Politicians, Pathfinders and Physicians.

Those who use P physically are Physical: they Produce, Pluck, Pack, Pace, Paddle, Paint, Party, etc.

As a 7, the letter P is drawn to the scientific and/or spiritual. There are Popes, many of whom were Pauls and Peters. There are Pastors and Philosophers, Parishioners and Peacemakers, Pharmacists and Physicists, and on and on. All P's have a Purpose.

Y

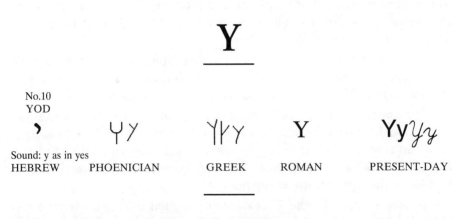

No.10
YOD

Sound: y as in yes

| HEBREW | PHOENICIAN | GREEK | ROMAN | PRESENT-DAY |

Y – 25

From Yod, the 10th letter of the Hebrew alphabet, come the letters I, J, and Y. (See I and J for more on Yod.) The Y shape was derived from the Phoenician Vau, or Waw. Waw was Y-shaped and eventually developed into four letters: U, W, Y, and F.

When the Romans first borrowed the letters from the Greek in the first century B.C., they used Y as a vowel. Later on it was used interchangeably with I as both vowel and consonant. Since it was used phonetically as an I, it is considered an offspring of Yod.

Whereas the W has its valleys and peaks denoting change, the Y is a crossroads of decision. Pythagoras said the stem of the Y is youth. When that person reaches adulthood, there is a crossroads where a decision has to be made about which path to take. It is either the broad left path of materiality (often the Y is printed with a wider left side) where there is trial and error, or the right-hand path of godliness and virtue known as "the narrow way."

In the mysteries, Y was symbolic of "the forking of the ways." Pythagoras drew it this way: ⌐ . The branch to the right was called Divine Wisdom and the left, Earthly Wisdom. So the left broad path signified the lower nature of man, and the right was the path to wisdom *(The Secret Teachings of All Ages*, LXV).

People with this letter in their names have a leaning toward the mystical, a desire to learn the mysteries of life. Y is shaped like the divining rod that is used to find water far beneath the Earth. Likewise, the Y in the name works as a divining rod drawing the person to a deeper study of the spiritual. There may be psychic experiences and/or a true search for wisdom. Whichever it is, there is bound to be spiritual unfoldment because of the drawing power of the 7 vibration to a deeper inward reflection.

Y is a deep thinker. Idle talk can be most discomforting. The V is up on the mind level, and it is a deep cup open to ideas and deep thoughts. There is a feeling of desiring quiet, more rest, and peaceful surroundings.

The materialist with the Y will have urgings to study something deeper but may ignore these feelings and take instead the broad material path. If extremely negative, they become loners during this cycle and are prone to excess in sensual temptations.

Because of the abrupt branching out of the two roads, there will be decisions that will have to be made quickly and there may be difficulty in making them. If the bearer has learned to listen to the still, small voice within and be guided by it, decisions will be much easier to make.

Y points out the path to God. It is the initial letter in God's true name, Yod Hé Vau Hé , and the Yod is the light of God that is within all of us. (See I on page 133.)

CHAPTER 19

The 8 Letters:
H, Q, Z

H

No .8 CHETH or HETH,	No. 5 HÉ or HÉH		ETA		
ח	ה	⊟	⊟H	**H**	**Hh** /th/
Sound: ch as in German *doch* (Pronounced Kayth or Hayth) HEBREW	Sound: heh as in head	PHOENICIAN	Sound: i as in ill or machine GREEK	ROMAN	PRESENT-DAY

H – 8

Cheth, or Heth, is the eighth letter of the Hebrew alphabet representing the number 8. It corresponds to the English letters "Ch," the sound being guttural as in the name of the German composer Bach.

Cheth is the fourth of the single letters whose governing influence is sight, and whose meaning is a *cultivated field*. The sight alluded to is that of intuition and the field is the person's own consciousness.

Just as a field must be made ready for crops by proper plowing, irrigation, fertilization, and seeding, a person's own consciousness must prepare itself for spiritual illumination, much of which comes through intuition.

When one has advanced along the first 7 paths, learning the lessons of the vibrations of each letter and its corresponding number, one reaches in 8 the chance to test all he has learned in his own field of endeavor. (Consciousness.) It takes effort, for the field must be tilled and seeded in order to bring forth crops. (Accomplishments.)

125

The number 8 is a pictorial representation of the celestial orbits and of cycles in life; never ending and constantly moving. Seed that is planted goes through a cycle of growth and returns to the sower as mature fruit.

On its side, 8 (∞) is the nourishing breast that gives forth needed nutrients for growth. It is also the scale of justice where our words and deeds are all carefully weighed out. The cycle always returns to us in just measure. This is reflected in the Eighth Commandment, "Thou shalt not steal" (Exodus 20:15). Whatever we take that is not rightfully ours will impose a karmic debt on us that will impede our progress. We must pay it back in either this life or one to come.

In the seventh letter, Zain (Z), we were given a weapon to master. In Cheth we have made the weapon into a plowshare to till our creative field of consciousness with honesty and integrity so that our labor rewards us with a fulfilling harvest. Cheth can be summed up in, "As ye sow, So shall ye reap."

Hé (pronounced hay or heh, as in head), the fifth letter of the Hebrew alphabet, is the first of the twelve simple letters and its governing influence is speech.

The very act of verbalizing the letter, Hé, or H, causes the breath to come forth. Hé is the second and last part of God's name, Yod Hé Vau Hé. Yod is the masculine and Hé the feminine potency. Their union brings life, and Vau is the androgynous link that connects the two.

Because of this life-giving force, Hé is sometimes called the child-bearing letter. This is dramatically related in the story of Abram and Sarai in the Old Testament. When God chose Abram to be the "Father of Many Nations," he first changed his name to Abraham and his wife's to Sarah. A year later she gave birth to Isaac, and from his lineage grew many nations (Genesis: 17).

The life-giving force of the letter Hé is kabbalistically related to the Hebrew verb that means "to bear fruit" or "to blossom," Awbab, or ABB, for its numerical value is 5, the same as Hé (The Book of Tokens, 60).

Hé, being the fifth letter, corresponds to the Fifth Commandment, "Honor thy Father and thy Mother." The mystical meaning refers to our Father-Mother God, the two forces of our Creator that join to give us our being, our Cosmic Parents. We are all children of God.

Hé means window and refers to the eyes as the windows of the soul. The Hebrew glyph for Hé even looks like an open window since it was changed to ⊟.

Now, a window lets in both light and air. It also offers a view and that view can be happy or depressing. This equates with our own viewpoint, which can be positive or negative. When we see beauty our eyes fill with light and our facial expression is soft. Likewise, a negative viewpoint will cause the eyes to look steely and seem hard and unkind. We can see out and others can look in, just as through a window, and the viewpoint in either direction depends on how we choose to see and be.

When the Greeks borrowed the sign, they eliminated the top and bottom bars, changed the name to Eta and used it for their H consonant. Later they used the sign for long E to distinguish it from their short E, Epsilon. This form was passed via the Etruscans to the Romans who again used the sign for their H consonant.

H resembles a ladder, and a ladder has two directions, up and down. We can descend into the negative or ascend into the positive by our thoughts as well as our deeds.

H is the eighth letter of our alphabet, and 8 is a symbol of "As Above, So Below," the principle of cause and effect. One who sets a good cause into motion is, in a sense, climbing a ladder to reap the reward of a good effect. Likewise, a negative cause will send one in the opposite direction to reap a negative effect.

H has both feet solidly on the ground. Being a window, it sees well what must be done and how to do it, so it is important for H to keep that window clear, and that means a positive frame of mind and a good viewpoint.

H will either be very successful or will face some hardships. There is much power with this letter and many opportunities that present themselves. As the breath of life must continue incessantly, the H must continually put forth effort for its success and it earns every penny.

It must be careful of spending; for being open-ended it is easy for H to turn over and empty out all it has gathered. One H in a name gives such people a drive to accomplish and a good sense of self-control. Theirs is a desire to excel, and perhaps become an authority in a certain field.

As a boss the H is either a loving leader or a terrible tyrant. The negative H is too demanding, draws conclusions quickly, and is selfish and miserly, whereas the positive H uses good judgment and enjoys being a humanitarian. H must decide whether to remain material-minded or to advance mentally. H both starts and ends Health. Good health is of extreme importance for physical coordination. H, the breath, must be strong and constant. It is interesting that many athletes have an 8 for their total name number. Balance is important for this eighth letter: balanced mind, body, and checkbook.

When there is no 8 (H, Q, or Z) at all, the person must learn to control the temper. Remember, the governing influence of Hé (H) is speech. In a fit of temper there is an abuse of words. The breath for speech is being contaminated from within and spewed out in an unsavory energy that poisons the air. And it does so physically, for the chemistry of the breath changes into poison. This was proven in an experiment by capturing the breath of an angry person in a test tube. When analyzed it was found to contain enough venom to kill a small animal very quickly (*The Finding of the Third Eye*, 141). So the term, "a poison tongue" can be taken literally. Loving words are chemically as life-giving as hatred is poisonous.

H is more than the breath necessary for speech. It is the breath that gives and renews life. The spoken word can be the lower part of H—all material and mortal, or it can be the upper part—the loving, creative breath of God that revitalizes and renews; a healing energy. So well-chosen words develop a sense of balance and harmony in all of our activities. "The speech of a wise man is like a honeycomb, sweet to his soul and health to his bones" (Proverbs 16:24).

Q

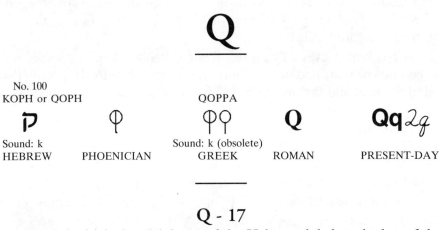

No. 100
KOPH or QOPH

ק

Sound: k
HEBREW

PHOENICIAN

QOPPA

Sound: k (obsolete)
GREEK

Q

ROMAN

Qq

PRESENT-DAY

Q - 17

Qoph (cofe) is the 19th letter of the Hebrew alphabet, the last of the 12 simple letters. Its governing influence is mirth.

Qoph means *the back of the head*, and the glyph, ק, a half circle on the right with a sharp vertical Yod down the left, resembles a profile of face and neck pointing out this area. It is here, at the base of the brain, that is the center of balance and coordination for the entire physical body.

We must learn to balance the feminine and masculine forces within us: the masculine as the active physical force, and the feminine as spiritual inspiration. The balancing and blending of these two forces is what the ancients called "the mystical marriage." This is not a sensual, physical union. It is the blending of our consciousness with the consciousness of God, which awakens the soul to an indescribable elation of knowing. All around us are positive and negative forces that we must learn to keep in their proper perspective. A balance must be maintained on the physical level by having a solid, constant, and unchanging moral structure and discriminating thought.

The 19 is the number of initiation, and that means there will be trials and tests. The secret solution is balance. Then 1 + 9 becomes 10, the number of perfection, the grade for passing the tests of the initiation.

Throughout time, 19 has been identified with the sun in mythology and in folklore. The sun is the vitalizing force that brings life and light to perfection just as 1 + 9 = 10, the number of perfection.

There is a bit of that sun's revitalizing force in all of us, and it is centered in the spleen, which is regarded as the seat of the emotions. A large network of the sympathetic nervous system in this area behind the stomach is called the solar plexus. It is in the center of our body just as the sun is the center of our solar system, and the active force of the sun is related to the power of the solar plexus in man. This is the point where we balance our positive and negative forces.

We can feel when this center is out of balance: shocking news, angry words, fear, and all negativisms hit us in that area likes a physical blow. Likewise, great joy and feelings of deep love give us a feeling of lightness there. In the mystical marriage the strong, unchanging moral fiber keeps these energies in their proper perspective and no man can split them asunder.

Our most useful tool for keeping the forces balanced is that of mirth. Mirth is defined as rejoicing or enjoyment. It is a cheerful attitude, a positive reaction. It is the release valve on the pressure gauge. Seeing the funny side of a negative circumstance releases the pressure of the moment. Humor is a great healer both physically and psychologically.

Qoph was used by the ancient Hebrews as a voiceless velar (a sound formed with the back of the tongue touching the soft palate). When the Greeks borrowed the sign they changed the name to Qoppa, or Koppa, and put the straight line down the middle through a full circle: ϙ . But they had no use for this sound in their language as they already had the K sound in Kappa, so they eventually omitted it altogether.

The Etruscans passed it on to the Romans who used it as the K sound before U. They kept the circle and put the line outside of it thus: ϙ. Then they began curving the line to the right: ϙ , and eventually **Q** as in the English capital **Q**.

The circle represents the spiritual sun. The line is the rod of balance. In depicting mirth it has been alluded to as the head with the tongue protruding.

We spoke of Qoph balancing the physical and mental forces. Ironically, Q's are active on both planes. The O stands for all or nothing, and Q's are willing to give of themselves 100 percent. They are loyal, sympathetic, and understanding.

They seem to have a knack for making money, and they truly want to be the very best they can be. If well balanced, they are likely to enjoy outstanding success. There is a feeling of uniqueness or peculiarity with Q since it is found in so few names. It is an original.

The circle of all or nothing really demands the balancing rod because Q can easily go overboard in either direction: it can be too spiritual or too material. Too negative, even dangerous, or overly positive. The forces need to be balanced as in 8: dividing itself equally in both worlds.

The O is a mirror that reflects from the spiritual realm to the physical, so Q's are often quite psychic. Man's connecting link to the astral world is the solar plexus, so the Q must have an understanding of his psychic energies and know how to maintain their balance in the light of spiritual knowledge. Without that light and understanding, the psychic force will draw from the lower astral world, causing fearful experiences, even insanity. The same psychic force used positively gives the Q a most vivid imagination to draw from to be an inspired writer. Being the 17th letter, Q has the individuality of 1 and the regal bearing of the 7; 1 + 7 = 8, the number of balance which the Q must maintain.

Often the Q needs help. This is why it is usually followed by a U. But U is a cup with a rocking base, so it is not entirely secure itself. Another vowel almost always follows the U. In spite of this help, which equates with the rod of balance protruding from it, the Q does like to be alone. This is due to the 7. The world of thought, dreams, and imagination is very real and the Q can easily lose itself in this land of "let's pretend." But once it finds that state of equilibrium, it is able to take an idea from the mental/spiritual world (bottom of the 8). When that happens, success is assured.

Z

No. 7 ZAIN		ZETA		
ז	Iiz	Iz	Z	Zz
Sound: Z		Sound: z as in zero		
HEBREW	PHOENICIAN	GREEK	ROMAN	PRESENT-DAY

Z – 26

Zain, or Zayin (zah-yin), is the seventh letter of the Hebrew alphabet and is used for the consonant Z. It is the third of the single letters whose governing influence is movement, and whose meaning is *weapon, sword,* or *arrow,* and also *scepter.*

This suggests some type of conquest where the arrow or sword will, by exact aim, hit its mark by movement in the right direction, resulting in victory.

The first seven letters are born of Aleph (Air), and in Zain perfection should be reached in right use of Air; mastery of the spoken word. The main weapon that Zain refers to is the tongue, and its arrows are words, which can cut like a sharp sword or dispense love that can heal any situation. The conquest of Zain is mastery of the tongue, and the scepter is the symbol of the victory gained in its spiritual illumination. "There are those whose speech is like the piercing of a sword; but the tongue of the wise heals" (Proverbs 12:18).

When the Greeks borrowed the glyph, they too used it as the Z consonant. They renamed it Zeta, meaning life, for to them 7 symbolized life. They changed the glyph to its present shape which is actually two 7's, one being upside down. They used Z for the first letter of their verb Zaw, which means, "I live," and in the name of the Father of All Living, Zeus (Jupiter).

The Romans borrowed the glyph for their Z consonant and it became the 26th letter of the English alphabet.

As two 7's, a Z has a vibration conducive to detective or secret service work. The 7 is analytical and investigates things. It has the ability to discover hidden purposes. It is for this reason that Z is interested in, and can get to the bottom of mysteries.

The shape of Z resembles lightning, which is created from atmospheric electricity, so there is much vital energy with this letter. Electricity can be used for good or evil, to make things run smoothly or to destroy. And so it is with Z in the name.

There is a feeling of much power. There is no limit to fine achievements, but if used for evil purposes, the "weapon" becomes a boomerang that will ultimately destroy the sender.

Z cannot abuse its powers without negative results. Anything it gains can be quickly lost: monetarily, politically, or any other way. The Z demands integrity if it is to remain in charge. Greed will destroy it.

The middle vertical line goes straight from the physical to the spiritual, a direct line of current supplying energy, ideas, and inspiration. Z has deeper insight than H or Q and it is more spiritual, so it makes an able leader who can inspire others.

The Z analyzes everything. Mental strain will drain its energy and it can suffer a mental breakdown. But with proper rest it can maintain its balance. Being a double 7 (its shape), it needs more rest than normal. It needs its ZZZZ's. Negative Z's are deceptive and sly. They tend to exaggerate and even believe their exaggerations. Unless Z finds its spiritual side, it does not make a good marriage partner. It will want to control the other and it is not comfortable with sharing.

But the Z who has learned the sixth lesson of responsibility and has learned to control the five senses, will take aim with good intent and its arrow will hit the right mark, resulting in victory. In the process it will gain its own perfection. The full number of God is 26. There are 26 letters in the English alphabet, and Z is the 26th, so Z corresponds to God. In the Hebrew alphabet Zayin is the seventh letter and corresponds with the Seventh Commandment, "Thou shalt not commit adultery." The 7 is the spirit within the body of six sides, and adultery is a sin against the holy Spirit within, which is the pure spirit of man in the likeness of God (*The Bible and the Tarot*, 210).

CHAPTER 20

The 9 Letters: I, R

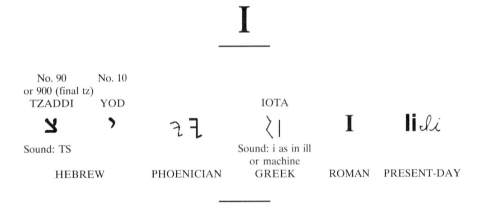

No. 90 or 900 (final tz) TZADDI	No. 10 YOD		IOTA		
Sound: TS			Sound: i as in ill or machine		
HEBREW		PHOENICIAN	GREEK	ROMAN	PRESENT-DAY

I – 9

Tzaddi (tsaw-day), the 18th letter of the Hebrew alphabet, corresponds to the English double letters Ts or Tz. It is the 11th of the single letters. Its governing influence is in taste, or swallowing, and its hieroglyph means, a *fishing hook*.

Fish, we have learned, refer to the esoteric teachings, or spiritual food of the Initiate. The fishing hook is that force in man that draws and connects him to esoteric study. Jesus was such a drawing power and taught his disciples to be fishers among men. The fishing hook can be words from an inspired teacher or minister, or it can be from an awakening within us. The governing influence of taste and swallowing refers to the taking in of spiritual food. If we like the taste we, in a sense, swallow and it becomes a part of our belief pattern just as surely as the nutrition in physical food supplies our bodies with good health.

The general meaning of Tzaddi is that of a goal or purpose. When Ts or Tz begins a word it means working toward a goal, and at the end of the word it signifies that the goal has been reached.

In a way, 18 is a picture of goal setting. It is the self (1) standing next to the evolutionary path (8) of accomplishment. Or it is the one (1) setting the goal in motion (8). The 1 and the 8 total 9, the number of completion and of initiation. In 9 the goal has been reached and the person is ready for a new experience. There will be trials and tests for the 9 to pass, tests that will result in wisdom.

We must take care to choose and taste of the wholesome fruits, choosing good over evil, for that which we taste is swallowed and becomes a part of us. Each taste should advance us toward our goal: spiritual understanding, brotherly love, and becoming the "hook" that draws other seekers to the path of wisdom.

The letter I, like the J and Y, is from the Hebrew letter Yod. (See J, letter number 10 of the number 1 letters.) The Yod is a candle within the circle of our being, from the light God called upon in the beginning: "And God said, Let there be light; and there was light. And God saw that the light was good..." (Genesis 1: 3,4).

Yod represents reproduction and is the female symbol of the Orient called Yoni, which is egg-shaped. The egg and sperm unite, forming the Yod of creation, ờ.

The time of year when all of nature reproduces is during the sign of Cancer, which has always been 69. When combined they form the Yod, which is currently drawn like a flame (ʾ). The flame more correctly corresponds with the globes of light on the Sephirotic Tree which, when understood, is the light of understanding, and the bearer of light.

Yod is the first part of God's name, Yod Hé Vau Hé. Yod is male, Hé is female, and Vau is both. Yod is the point in the very center of light. It is the only symbol in the alphabet that stands for both God and man, and it is the smallest letter. It stands for God's name, the I of IHVH, yet as a suffix it means "my," and refers to man.

The vertical line depicts spirit descending into matter so that man becomes a living soul. That portion of God remains as a light within each person, and at the same time reflects outwardly in personality.

In Latin the word for "I" is Io, and it is pronounced like Yod without the d: eee-oh. The ancient mystics regarded I as the Higher Self, the God within each of us, whereas "me" refers to the personal self, or ego.

There is more stature to the I than to the me. It is that something within all of us that gives inner strength, that still, small voice; the Yod; the Light of God within us all.

When the Greeks borrowed this consonant, they changed the name to Iota and used it for their vowel I. It became the Roman I and also the Roman numeral for 1.

There were times that two I's came together in a word and were confused with U, so in the 11th century the tittle (dot) was added over the small letter i.

The I became our ninth letter, and 9 is the numerical vibration of emotions and sensitivity which is felt by the personal I. Opinions are strong and emotions run deep. It needs to master the self and have total reliance on the big I within that gently directs the little i, which is the ego, or me.

The 9 is also the number of humanity, so "I" must be thoughtful of others, and learn compassion and understanding.

Negative I's are too steeped in self and are too critical and arrogant.

Like the Yod, the I has all the creative abilities. Here is the artist, actor, performer, musician, and a doer. The I always strives to achieve perfection because 9 becomes 10 when it completes its work, and the tail of the 9 detaches from the circle and stands alongside it making 10.

The I is like 1 (one) in that it is the initiator and can start things. Being the ninth letter, it is able to finish things as well. I is the shape of a pen or needle. Those who have an I in the name can be good at writing, sewing, and designing. I is also the shape of a knife, so the bearer must be careful in handling knives, to avoid cutting the self.

The I does not have a strong balance line on the Earth. It is an emotional vibration; it can be either up or down. It refers to the "I am," so it is sensitive to its needs. Through that it understands the needs and sensitivities of others, and is helpful and will serve the "I am" in others. It is the "I am" consciousness.

The greatest truth revealed by the mysteries is the fact that God dwells in man. That in the soul of each and every one of us there is that abiding light which is a ray from the Divine Being, just as Yod appears in every letter of the Hebrew alphabet with its light of knowledge. All of our God-like qualities—love, compassion, understanding—emanate from this light.

R

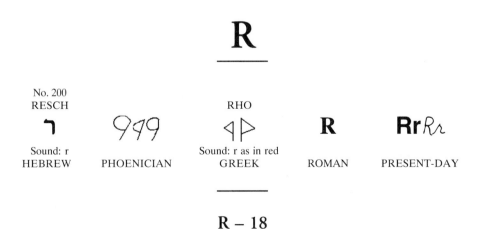

No. 200
RESCH

RHO

Sound: r
HEBREW

PHOENICIAN

Sound: r as in red
GREEK

ROMAN

PRESENT-DAY

R – 18

Resh (raysh) is the 20th letter of the Hebrew alphabet and is used for the consonant R. It is the sixth of the seven double letters and its opposites are peace and strife (or war). Its meaning is *head*.

This letter is concerned with man's spiritual unfoldment. The man who lives only for material things does not waken his spiritual centers and true peace is unknown to him. It is in ignorance that man expects accomplishment through war.

The man who seeks spiritual unfoldment finds in his meditations the peace which passes all understanding (Philippians 4:7). The spiritual center for this is found in the head: a small gland in the forehead area that is known by mystics to be the dwelling place of man's spirit and his point of contact with the higher planes. It is called the pineal gland because of its resemblance to a pinecone. Some call it "the third eye," for when it is opened, spiritual illumination takes place and all knowledge is available to us. It is the organ of the spiritual mind (*The Key to the Universe*, 265).

The interesting thing is that R is a picture of the pineal gland: a small rounded body with two cords attached that connect it to the brain.

As the 20th letter, Resh signifies death and resurrection. When the spiritual centers are awakened, there is a tingling sensation that raises the vibratory rhythm so high that an exaltation of consciousness is experienced. To one who has reached this level of awareness, death has no sting. "Oh death, where is your sting? Oh grave, where is your victory? The sting of death is sin ..." (1 Corinthians 15:55-6).

Death totals 20 (4 + 5 + 1 + 2 + 8 = 20). The 20 is not a finishing number so death is not the end. It has been noted, though, that persons who have a prominent 20 in their chart are inclined to fear death unless that fear has been replaced with a faith.

When the letters of death are added according to their exact numbered place in the alphabet, T would be 20 instead of 2 and the total vibration of the word death would be 38/11 instead of 20. The 11 is the number of light, so death is not darkness but light to the man who is spiritually aware. It is the man meeting the Master 1 to 1, a resurrection—a new birth.

When the Greeks borrowed the sign for Resh, they changed its name to Rho but kept it as their R consonant. They changed the glyph by reversing it and the Romans added the leg at the right.

R begins with a vertical line on the left, which represents upright man. The loop at the top is the head and it stands for the ability to think, to draw in knowledge, to have creative thought. At this point it resembles the letter P, which is a symbol of the creative force in a paternal way.

The added leg at the right, R, is a picture of a man with one foot forward showing that he is moving ahead. This depicts activity in the person's life. Since the leg is attached directly to the head it means to move ahead with one's thinking. Esoterically it means to raise one's thinking above the purely material and to seek spiritual understanding.

R's are intellectual. Here we find teachers, writers, and leaders. That enclosed circle tells us they retain knowledge and that they think deeply about things.

The R is the most understanding of all letters, since it is necessary for R to develop the spirit of brotherhood. R is the eighteenth letter of the English alphabet and $1 + 8 = 9$, the numerical vibration of humanity and brotherly love.

Because 9 finishes the cycle, it is an initiation: the completion of the old, passing tests, and making ready for the new. Being the 9 letter makes R quite emotional. Unless honest and unselfish, there can be failures for the R. To pass the initiation requires integrity, tolerance, compassion, and a sincere search for truth.

There is so much power with R that can be used for either constructive or destructive purposes that man must use his head to discriminate in its use.

The R has been comically referred to as the "dog letter" or the "snarling letter" because of the sound of "rrrr" is like that of a dog snarling. In man, the very negative types grumble a lot. They let their uncontrolled emotions take over. They must learn to control their basic human responses: temper, jealousy, and physical desires. They need patience, which is removing that active right leg on R to make it stand still like the P, initiating patience.

There are many criminals with an R prominent in their name. R starts the words Robber, Ruffian, Rebellious, Rude, and Rough. Until the bearer of the R outgrows his self-seeking interests, gains emotional maturity, and seeks higher levels of expression, life will manifest one difficulty after another. Law totals 9, and an R (18/9) who allows himself to continue breaking the law will find he no longer has freedom, for to work against the law is to lose one's freedom.

When positive, this is the most beautiful letter, for it can inspire confidence in people like no other. It gives without thought of return, for the sheer joy of it. That is when R is rewarded. Such an R is Radiant, Refined, Reliable, Remarkable, and Respected.

Tests passed, initiation completed, and the final initiation known as death means not the end, but the Resurrection into the light.

"Death is swallowed up in victory"
(1 Corinthians 15:54).

PART FOUR

Number Groups
and Numbers

Number Groups

The name for each number group is derived from the Greek word for that number: Monad, Duad, Triad, Tetrad, Pentad, Hexad, Heptad, Ogdoad, Ennead, and Decad. Each group held the underlying deeper meanings of the number to the Kabbalists.

\\ Monad //

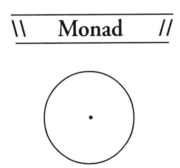

There is a difference between 1 (one) and the Monad. The 1 is applied to each of the essential parts in any group, so the 1 is simpler than the Monad, which is the part considered as a unit.

Pythagoras did not even see 1 as a number. To him it was the Monad, the Father, and the symbol of wisdom; the principle underlying all numbers and from which all numbers come forth.

This is easier to understand if we see it as he did—a circle with a dot in the center. It was *one* in the midst of *all*. Ain Soph Aur. Infinite. So the Monad was considered as a unit just as a man, like the Universe, is a unit composed of many individual parts. According to Cato:

> God makes himself known to all the world; He fills up the
> whole circle of the universe, but makes His particular abode
> in the center, which is the soul of the just (*The Pythagorean
> Triangle*, 51).

The beginning of all things lies motionless in Ain Soph Aur, the Monad, in the form of ideas that have yet to become real. Since the Monad is this original mind, it is the origin of all thoughts and contains all wisdom, for all numbers proceed from and are hidden in the Monad.

Pythagoras's description of God was that He is everywhere present in the Universe as Supreme Mind, Who is the original cause of all things that exist and have being; the source of every Divine good; that His motion is circular, His nature is truth, and His body is light.

In the Pythagorean triangle, the Tetractys, the Monad is the top and first point.

In the Tree of the Sephiroth the Monad is Kether, the Crown whose attribute is Will and whose essence is Divine Love. It contains within itself all the other Sephira. All ideas that are, were, or ever will be are contained within that point of light.

In the Grand Man of the Universe, the Adam Kadmon, the Monad is the crown above the head that is the genesis of all creation. The vibration of the Monad corresponds with the C below middle C: 128 vibrations per second. This is the seventh octave above the fundamental tones of the Cosmos (*The Sacred Word and its Creative Overtones*, 7).

Kether is a symbol of unity as it is indivisible. Divide 1 into 1 and you still have 1. Multiply 1 by itself and the 1 remains, so it represents the unity of all life. Every number is made up of 1's. The 1 is the self that performs, learns, and grows in each lesson.

\\ Duad //

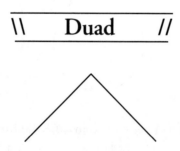

The Monad was depicted as a point in a circle. In order for it to reach out and take form it had to cast its own reflection. By so doing, it created a positive and negative pole: unity separating itself. The original Monad is the positive male principle, electricity, and the opposing end is the negative principle, magnetic attraction. Both are necessary for creation since it is spirit's descent into matter.

Thus the Duad is the dividing line between spirit and matter. It represents all duality, all opposites, all diversity. The hieratic secret of the Duad is the Tree of Knowledge of Good and Evil, the fruits of which can be beneficial or deadly (*The Mysteries of Magic*, 66).

These fruits are the five senses, which can be used or abused. For example, the sense of taste is a blessing, which helps us enjoy wholesome food for our nourishment. But it becomes perverted through overindulgence and gluttony.

The serpent on the tree has several meanings. Some say it is the serpent of wisdom. Others say it is the devil who entices. The least-known aspect is that it symbolizes electricity, the male positive force in nature. Because electricity moves in a serpentine motion when it passes between the poles of a spark gap, it was called "The Great Snake," symbolized by the serpent. Since electricity is a universal force that can be used for either constructive or destructive purposes, the serpent was an emblem of both good and evil. The apple represents the knowledge of the procreative process *(The Secret Teachings of All Ages*, LXXXVIII). An apple cut in half crosswise reveals a perfect five-pointed star, one point for each of the five physical senses and the star itself representing man and his extremities.

It is through misuse of the wholesome fruits of the Tree of Knowledge of Good and Evil that all ills befall the world. God does not cause illness, disease, and destruction. We do that ourselves when we partake of the evil side of the fruit.

So the Duad represents the beginning of the knowledge of good and evil, error and truth, and all contrasts of nature: night and day, cold and heat, wet and dry, as well as male and female. Pythagoras taught that every man was placed between vice and virtue and would eventually have to choose between the two.

The number 2 consists of the straight base line which is good, and the twisted line which is evil. If man follows the twisted path and is burdened by his evil doings, at death he must face the misery he created in one of two mansions of the lower realms: Tartarus, where he suffers for eternity, or Elysium, where amends can be made for an eventual return to Heaven *(The Pythagorean Triangle*, 71).

In the Pythagorean Tetractys, the Duad is the first of the second two points near the top.

In the Tree of the Sephiroth it is Chochma, the Father whose attribute is Wisdom. Chochma could come from the original Monad, Kether, only by reflection. It is the Divine Intellectual power to generate thought. Wisdom contains the entire zodiac, each sign being dual.

Chochma is above and to the left of Adam Kadmon's left shoulder. Whereas the original Monad is androgynous, Chochma is the potency of positive, vital, outpouring energy.

\\   Triad   //

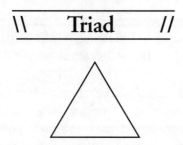

The Triad was highly revered by the ancients. One or two lines could not represent a figure, but three lines form the triangle, the first figure. And since it is first and is perfect, it represents God.

It is the first three Sephiroth, the Godhead: the Creative Principle. It is the supreme expression of love; two who seek each other only to become three. But also two who seek each other that they may become one *(The Mysteries of Magic*, 67, 343). To Pythagoras, the union of the Monad and Duad produced the Triad. To him, the right-angled triangle represented this world.

The tripod is the first structure that can give support to a physical thing. 1 lacks base, 2 lacks steadiness, 3 gives support (and 4 gives solidarity).

According to the Kabbalah, 3 is associated with triangles, tripods, bodies with three divisions, and bodies that can expand and contract because the triangle is the primal or first shape. Salt in a solution will form triangular shapes as the molecules begin to cluster *(The Secret Doctrine*, Vol. 2: 594).

The triangle is the shape of the pyramid, and the pyramid is said to hold the secret to Fire. So words referring to Fire begin with "pyro." Particles of fire are pyramidal in form.

Pythagoras taught that everything in nature is divisible into three parts, and that all things consist of three, including our problems. The problem itself is one side. When we see the other point of view, that establishes the second side. Then it is easier to supply the base, which is the answer *(The Key of Destiny*, 120). "Establish the triangle and a problem is two-thirds solved" (Pythagoras).

The third Sephira on the Tree of the Sephiroth is Binah, or Understanding and Intelligence. Binah is the female energy from which all life becomes manifest. As the female potency it is the negative, passive energy, not sexuality.

In Adam Kadmon, Binah is above and to the right of the Grand Man's shoulder, directly across from Chochma (Wisdom), the male energy. Here we see male and female absolutely equal. It was not until the church came into power that woman was put below man. According to the Kabbalah, they are equal before God.

When Understanding joins Will and Wisdom in the form of Divine Love, it completes the creative triad, forming a triangle of power: the Holy Trinity. Only through Understanding are we able to manifest the power of Wisdom and Divine Love in our lives.

\\ Tetrad //

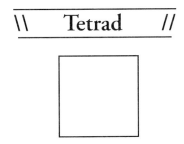

The four-sided figure was considered sacred because it represented the beginning of form. The sacred Trinity spoke the Word which set up a vibration that sent the molecules whirling into visibility clothed in form *(The Secret Doctrine,* Vol. 1:351).

Everything that exists has to start with 1 and go through three successive stages to reach form in 4:

1 — Idea.

2 — Seed planted.

3 — Growth.

4 — Mature product; matter brought into being by the Holy Trinity.

So 4 represents the generative power from which all combinations are derived, the root of everything that can be named. The Pythagoreans concluded from this that there is a connection between God and numbers *(Morals and Dogma,* 633).

In his law of opposites, Pythagoras called the 4 "Right and Left" for when you are standing, the Earth spreads out from your left and from your right. It is the physical plane, the Four Corners of the Earth, the four directions: North, South, East, and West; the four Elements: Fire, Water, Air, and Earth; and the four geometrical forms: point, line, plane, and solid. This is why the ancient Greeks considered the Tetrad to be the root of all things.

They also noted that there are four liberal arts: geometry, astronomy, music and arithmetic, all of which are important in understanding the other sciences.

4 doubled is 8, or the cube, which was the symbol of truth, because no matter how you look at it, it is always the same. It also had significant reference to justice because the cube could be divided equally *(The Pythagorean Triangle,* 103-106)

Many ancient peoples gave God a name containing four letters: Amun (Egyptian); Sura (Persian); Deus (Latin); Odin (Scandinavian); יהוה (Hebrew); Gott (German); Dieu (French); etc. *(Morals and Dogma,* 633).

The Hebrews and "Tetractys" called the four-letter name "Tetragrammaton" by the Gentiles *(The Pythagorean Triangle,* 103-106).

Pythagoras claimed that man's soul has four powers: mind, science, opinion, and sense, making it a Tetrad. Since the Tetrad is the first solid figure, it represents immorality. The universal symbol for immortality is the pyramid because of its four-cornered base *(Morals and Dogma*, 633).

Geometrically, 4 is related to horizontal lines, squares, crosses, and rectangles.

The fourth Sephirah is called Chesed, or Mercy. This is the first Sephira following the trinity of Kether (0), Chochma (Wisdom), and Binah (Understanding): the Holy Trinity that makes up the Creator, also known as Macroprosopus. Chesed is the next Sephira, the first of the six Sephiroth below which illustrate the law "As Above, So Below." Its place as the Grand Man of the Universe is the left shoulder, and is directly opposite the fifth Sephira, Geburah (Strength), which is the right shoulder. So our bodies are related in this Tree of Life. Chesed is the beginning of manifestation, just as the number 4 shows the beginning of solid form. Particles of earth are cubical in shape. Chesed establishes the basic structure on which matter is built *(The Qabalistic Tarot*, 79).

Paul Case tells us in his *Book of Tokens* that the riches of the kingdom are hidden in Chesed. "Kingdom" is the 10th Sephirah. If you add the numbers 1 through 4, which is Chesed, $1 + 2 + 3 + 4 = 10$. And, since Chesed is the fourth Sephira, it suggests that 1, 2, and 3 already have existence. So you can see how the riches are hidden in Chesed: the richest of all 10 Sephiroth.

\\ Pentad //

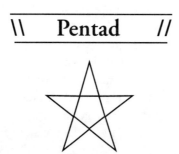

The 5 represented equilibrium. In numbers 1 through 10, 5 is the exact middle. The Decad (10) is Divinity, and the five (5) is the Demi-Goddess because it is half of 10. It is the number of the Sage (14/5): one who has limited knowledge of that which is higher than itself.

The ancients said the row of numbers 1-9 in sequence, formed a beam of balance, and man is perfectly balanced in the center. 1, 2, 3, and 4 add up to 10 and are the animal forces below; 6, 7, 8, and 9 add up to 30 and are the spiritual forces above. The Pentad was often called "Justice" and sometimes "Nemesis" for it was the instrument keeping the balance between the celestial and the bestial. Pentad refers to the number 5. The pentagram is an emblem, the five-pointed star representing the Pentad. It became the symbol of safety, that middle ground of balance that is necessary because of the dual influence of the 5.

It is also the number of man because man has five senses and five distinct extremities: two arms, two legs, and a head that directs the other four.

The pentagram is actually a figure of the microcosm, man, and represents the soul (1) rising above the animal nature.

Sometimes the body of man is drawn on the five-pointed star, the head at the single point at the top, the arms outstretched on the two points at the upper middle, and the legs on the two lower points. Drawn this way it locates the five mysterious centers of force, which have great meaning to the mystics, the study of which leads to remarkable understanding. Man is the pentacle.

But inverted, the pentagram represents a perverted power, for it takes man off balance by standing him on his head. Black magicians distort it by breaking a line somewhere or by using it upside down so that the two star points are at the top resembling a goat's horns. The ancients considered the Pentad as a symbol for marriage because it contains the first female number, 2, and the first male number, 3. (The 1 was not considered the first male number because it is found in every number and its addition makes odd numbers even.) Five candles are lighted at the wedding ceremony. The minister performing the rites holds one hand, five fingers spread, above the bride and groom while declaring them to be husband and wife (*The Pythagorean Triangle*, 136-7).

The Pythagoreans noticed that the five points resembled five capital A's interlocked, so they called this symbol "Pentalpha." Alpha represents the Element of Air and is everywhere present—in, through, and around—all creation.

The 5 is the number of nature because above the four Elements of Earth, Fire, Air, and Water is the fifth and celestial Element of Ether. Pythagoreans called it "quintessence," which means "the purest and most essential part of anything." The number 5, by its shape, symbolizes this quintessence because it has a serpentine form showing pictorially the animating spirit or vital essence that flows through all of nature (*Morals and Dogma*, 634).

Most flowering plants have petals or leaves in clusters of four or five. Like nature, 5 reproduces itself by its own seed, because when it is multiplied by itself it returns to itself by producing its own number, showing up as part of the total, for example, $5 \times 5 = 25$, $5 \times 15 = 75$, $5 \times 25 = 125$, etc.

The 5 is related in form to sharp shapes, forms that lack order or coherence, and to jointed and disjointed bodies. The fifth Sephira is called Geburah, or Severity. It means strength. It is opposite of Chesed (Mercy) on the Tree, and where Chesed is the builder, Geburah is the destroyer, both necessary to ongoing creation.

Being the destroyer means eliminating that which is no longer useful. It also demands payment where it is due, and fulfills karma. "Chesed giveth, Geburah taketh away." So it is called "The Sphere of Fear," but it means to be in awe of God, for that is the beginning of wisdom.

In the Grand Man of the Universe, Geburah is the right shoulder, being Chesed's perfect balance.

In the law of opposites, the 5 is masculine and feminine, and for us to be well-balanced, we must all have a small amount of the opposite force. Man must have some receptivity to soften his nature, and woman must have some positive force to give her strength.

\\ Hexad //

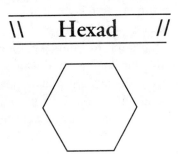

The Hexad was considered a sacred number because the world was created in six days, and on the sixth day man was created. Pythagoras called the Hexad the "form of forms, the articulation of the universe and the maker of the soul." His followers called it "the perfection of parts" and "Venus, herself." The Hexad was the source of harmony, and Venus is the "Mother of Harmony" (*The Theoretic Arithmetic of the Pythagoreans*, 194).

The Hexad was the perfection of parts because it is the only number from one to 10 that is completely equal in its divisions, and it produces a hexagon when six lines are circularly drawn and adjoined, like individual pockets in a honeycomb.

Its consistence of form in the honeycomb, or in a double triangle, also signifies good health, for health is perfect form. It was also noted that nature is partial to six-cornered formation of crystals (*The Pythagorean Triangle*, 151-2). The relation of the 6 to body and form is also seen in the fact that the world consists of six sides: north, south, east, west, height, and depth. There is no existing body that does not have six sides (*Morals and Dogma*, 635).

The very vowels of World (O = 6) and Earth (E = 5, A = 1, and 5 + 1 = 6), add up to a 6 soul urge, the urge to propagate the species and to nurture.

The 6 was an ancient symbol of marriage because the male (3) times the female (2) equals 6, the two becoming one body. And because it is a number equal to its parts, it produces children resembling their parents (*The Pythagorean Triangle*, 158).

So 6 is associated with symmetrical and well-formed bodies, graceful curves and rounded figures where symmetry and balance are evident.

In the law of opposites it was "rest and motion," the necessary ingredients for bodies to remain in health.

The sixth Sephira is called Tiphereth, which is Beauty and Mildness. It is in the exact center of the Tree. In the Grand Man, the Adam Kadmon, it is the solar plexus or sun center in man, the exact center of man, and is like a sun shining from within.

It is from this center that we first feel great joy or great sorrow. If something goes against our higher nature, we feel as if our breath has been whacked out of us from that area. Elation brings a feeling of lightness there. So this is a very important spiritual center that we can learn to trust.

It is the power of nature and of the Christ Force within working toward perfect expression, so that God's attributes can be reflected in man's life.

The 6 is a symbol of creation and no creation would have taken place without the Word of God which is the Christ Force. The Hexad is a double trinity: the first being God and the second, His reflection. God's brow and eyes form a triangle in the heavens, say the Kabbalists, and its reflection in the waters formed a second triangle, which was the beginning of creation. A double triangle has six sides. Six equates with sex to bring about creation that can continually renew itself through its 6-Force *(The Secret Teachings of All Ages,* CXX).

The Sixth Commandment is "Thou shalt not kill." That takes away the Christ Force from another. This in turn brings destruction back to the slayer. We cannot set into motion any word, act, or deed that does not return to us, for we are dealing with the law of the circle. Everything from the paths of the planets to the circulatory system, to people lost in the woods, to words and deeds, ad finitum, all are subject to this law.

\\   Heptad   //

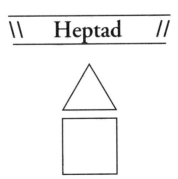

Throughout the ages in every religion the 7 was a symbol of the ensouled, living man. The Pythagoreans called this number "the vehicle of life" since it contained body and soul: 6 applies to the physical dimensions of height and depth, front and back, right and left sides, and is animated by the seventh dimension, the living, vital essence within which is the immortal spirit.

Spiritual man is known to have seven senses, the five physical, including sight, touch, smell, taste, and hearing, plus the sixth of mental perception and the seventh of spiritual understanding.

The 7 was sacred because it contained 3 and 4: 4 being matter and 3 being the spirit that activates it. The Kabbalah shows the cube representing matter when it is unfolded and becomes the cross of four squares down and three across. This is the Tau form that symbolizes the Element of life (*The Secret Doctrine*, Vol. 2: 600).

Sometimes it is shown as a triangle above the square. The triangle is the threefold spiritual body of spirit, mind, and soul descending into the physical form (the square) on Earth. After death they disconnect, the lower quarternary turning to dust and the spiritual body continuing. "Then the dust shall return to the earth as it was; and the spirit shall return to God who gave it" (Ecclesiastes 12:7).

The 7 was sacred to life because babies who are born in the seventh month generally live, while those born in the eighth month perish. Pythagoras said this was because 7 is composed of 3 and 4, masculine and feminine forces. But 8 is composed of 4 and 4 which is a purely feminine number or force and unable to supply the strength needed to survive.

The Heptad was called "Minerva," the unmarried virgin goddess who was said to have sprung from the forehead of Zeus, or Jove. This was the same as if she had come directly from the Father of All, the Monad.

The figure 7 is like the Monad (1) but with a line extending from the head, thus: 7, to depict the event. It also portrays the helmet that Minerva wore. So 7 is representative of helmet shapes, horned shapes, crescent forms, and shapes with curves on the right side. In the law of opposites, 7 is "crooked and straight."

There are seven creative double letters in The Sepher Yetzirah and there are seven Elohim who make up the manifested aspects of the Godhead. These are the same seven. In Christian scripture they are referred to as "the sons of God" and are the ones who say, "Let us make man in our image, after our likeness...." (Genesis 2:26).

Every culture has reference to these seven primordial powers, which are the Elohim, nature powers, or planetary gods, the creative hierarchies. Their tools are the seven primary colors and the seven tones of music that supply the keynote of vibration to every living thing.

Pythagoras calculated the tones of the planets according to their distance from each other, reasoning that their movement creates a vibration, which in turn creates a musical sound.

He was led to this enlightenment by observing that the effect of a sound emanating from a vibrating string was controlled by mathematical proportions or by the length of the string when plucked.

There were seven tones in all and each tone emitted was a step of the musical scale of seven tones. The whole Cosmos is in a state of vibration, the overtones emanating from the fundamental tone of the original Monad, or Creative Deity. These tones compose the "Music of the Spheres" and the "Voices of Nature" (*The Sacred Word and its Creative Overtones,* 3).

There were also seven vowels in the Greek alphabet, seven basic colors, and seven metals, and Pythagoras assigned one of each to the seven known planets:

Planets:	Moon	Mercury	Venus	Sun	Mars	Jupiter	Saturn
Vowels:	A	E	ee	I	O	U	oo
Notes:	Si	Mi	La	Re	Do	Sol	Fa
Colors:	Violet	Yellow	Indigo	Orange	Red	Blue	Green

Each planet corresponds to one of seven basic wavelengths. Like music, they have their octaves depending upon their rate of vibration: the slowest is the color red, the musical note C, the planet Mars, the vowel O, and the metal iron. The lower the rate is more physical, and the higher the rate is more spiritual.

Pythagoras was known to have taken children with a 7 Birth Path into his schools of mystery without first testing them, for the 7 meant they were born to pursue this course.

The seventh Sephira is called Netzach, "Firmness and Victory," for this is where perfection is reached. Through the first six Sephiroth a man can evolve intellectually, but until he responds to his center of spirituality, which is the light of illumination within, he cannot achieve Victory.

The body has six sides. Netzach, 7, is the spiritual center that represents the spark of the Deity within every man. It is also the first Sephira that makes up the personality. It has to do with expressing the arts, music, poetry, and all that takes creative imagination. In creating things of beauty through the use of imagination, the person develops his ability as a creator and that is his likeness of God.

Netzach is the right leg of the Adam Kadmon and stands for the instincts and emotions; while its opposite and balance called Hod (8) is the left leg and stands for the intellect. A proper balance is needed between the two because intellect alone is cold and calculating.

Here is the difference between material and spiritual man. Material man is able to gain much through intellect, but until there is that inner illumination of the spiritual self, he cannot grow into his full perfection.

\\ Ogdoad //

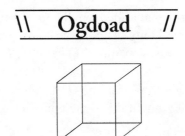

Any group or set of 8 is called an Ogdoad. The Gnostics of old portrayed this by eight stars for it was sacred to them. To philosophers, the Ogdoad is the first cube of energy having eight angles. The number 8 was considered the only "evenly even" number between 1 and 10, meaning it could be divided by any other lower number and not leave a remainder.

This was also true of 4 except that 4, unlike 8, could not make a three-dimensional figure. And so 8 proved to them that idea produces form: God "geometrizes"(*The Pythagorean Triangle*, 191).

The Ogdoad is like a double mirror that sees (understands) both worlds, so it represents good judgment. It stood for justice because it could be divided into equal parts. 8 on its side represented the scales: ∞, a symbol that has always stood for man being equal under the law. "False scales are an abomination to the Lord but just weights are his delight" (Proverbs: 11:1).

The ∞ was also a pictorial symbol of the orbital movement of planets and their regular and constant serpentine paths in the Universe. Because they were always perfect, it came to mean perfection *(Morals and Dogma*, 635).

The 8 also referred to time because it depicts the hourglass, which the ancients used to measure time.

Because the 8, like the O, can be written over and over without lifting the pen from the page, it symbolizes divine power and material power; the higher "As Above" flowing serpentine into the lower "So Below." So 8 is the symbol of all coiled, intertwining serpentine and scroll forms *(Numerology and the Divine Triangle,* 146).

There is a discovery known as "The Law of Octaves" in modern chemistry. John A. Newlands was making a list of the elements according to their atomic weights and found that every eighth element had a definite repetition of characteristics. *(The Secret Teachings of All Ages,* LXXXII).

This is also true of colors and of sound; when one octave of music other begins, there are twice as many vibrations as there were and three times as many in the third. There are seven eighth making the octave that vibrates at twice the unity of pitch on a higher level.

Likewise, as C is the bottom of the musical scale, consisting of the coarsest waves of air, red is at the bottom of the color spectrum, consisting of the coarsest waves of luminous ether. Together they traverse the scale: sound and color, side by side through the octaves of vibration, each octave showing a repetition on a finer scale.

Sights and sounds that are out of our range of seeing and hearing continue on in another realm invisible to us, but existent nevertheless in the fourth dimension.

8 symbolized friendship and love because they were considered to be in perfect harmony, love being an octave above friendship in vibration (*The Pythagorean Triangle*, 192).

The eighth Sephira is called Hod and represents Glory, or Splendor. Where 7 (Netzach), its opposite and balance represents the arts, feelings, and instincts; Hod stands for the sciences, literature, and all that is part of the intellect, or the concrete mind.

In the body of the Grand Man of the Universe, Adam Kadmon, Hod is the left leg. Instincts and intellect: two legs that give balance to the mind of man. Here ideas take form and can be put into words so there is a deeper understanding.

\\ Ennead //

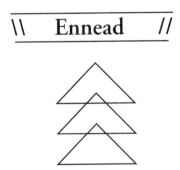

The Pythagoreans called 9 "the Ocean and the Horizon" because it had all numbers within it and none beyond it, as the ocean contained all the Water and all that is within the Water and continued to the horizon as far as man could see. For after 9 is 10. And all numbers following, when added together to the last digit, cannot produce a number higher than 9 as its root. So it returns to itself as water to the ocean.

The 9 is called the number of Initiation for the same reason. No matter how much we learn, we must return to our source in 10, forming the never ending circle of existence which, at each graduation, begins at the same point on a higher level, ever spiraling upward, 1 through 9 on higher levels. Each 9 we come to is an initiation to a new cycle.

Often we experience an initiation in a dream, which is in fact a true experience in the higher realms of the astral world. It may be forgotten, but its equivalent will come about in our physical world. The way we handle the situation constitutes our understanding of the lessons we should have learned first inwardly. Those who pass the test start anew at 10 on the next level and work toward the next initiation. The reason we experience our tests first on the higher inner level is because it is in accordance with the law of all material manifestation: all that manifests is first an idea. Then comes the Will to create, followed by the Wisdom or Intellectual power to plan, the activity to produce, and finally comes the production, or manifestation. This is the same procedure as that of the creation of the world, and it is the power that we, as minor creators, follow.

Sometimes a person fails to follow his inner promptings, and delays the graduation even to another incarnation. But those who do pass realize a new strength surging through them and a feeling of a "job well done" (*The Key to the Universe*, 315).

Matter was represented by the number 9, or 3 × 3. It was noted that all material was composed of three Elements: Water, Earth, and Fire, and that those three elements each contained a little of each other. Therefore, 3 x 3 became a symbol of all body formations of matter (*Morals and Dogma*, 636).

The 9 has come to be known as "The Great Lover." This stems from the story told about the brother-in-law of Alexander named Caleron, who was able to become invisible by carrying a piece of silver with the number 9 engraved upon it. He would make love to his brother's concubines and never be caught.

The 9 was the finishing number, a bringing to an end, because it takes nine months for a baby to be formed, and when it is completed there is birth. Hence 9 is perfecting and finishing for the new birth which is in 10.

Still, there were many ancients who feared 9 because it signified the end of something and unknown changes to take place.

The number 9 looks like a spermatozoon, so it is associated with germinal life. And because there are nine months of embryonic life, the 9 came to be known as the number of humanity.

The Kabbalists saw the 9 as the generative egg, the stem being the spirit of life flowing into it. The circular part also represented the planet that is animated by the spirit of life (*Morals and Dogma*, 636).

In the Law of Opposites, 9 is "Good and Evil:" good because 9's are known to be filled with brotherly love and seldom focus on the evil in things, and evil because it is an inverted 6. By inverting numbers, the destructive aspects become prominent.

The 9 is associated with shapes that are sharp and pointed, especially if made of steel or iron: spears, knives, swords, and scalpels.

The ninth Sephira is called Jesod, or Foundation. It is the stability and foundation because it causes continuity of life, and is situated in the generative (sexual) area of the Adam Kadmon. And 9 is the sperm-shaped glyph that is the visual representation of that germ of life (*Morals and Dogma*, 767).

It is in this area, at the base of the spine, that the Kundalini force (the Serpent of Wisdom encountered in the Garden of Eden) lies coiled. It can be awakened to the strictly physical sex force and orgasm or, in the spiritually awakened man, will undulate upward through the 33 segments of the spine, opening each chakra on its way. When this occurs, a tingling sensation is felt all over the body. When this force reaches the pineal gland (the Eye of Horus) the spiritual eye is opened and the Initiate is ready for wisdoms to be revealed. From then on the still small voice becomes very clear, for these seven centers (chakras) are the seven seals spoken of in the Bible that cannot be opened until the individual evolves spiritually. They are the means through which man comes into conscious communion with the higher realms *(The Rosicrucian Cosmo-Conception,* 478).

It is very hard for material man to understand the spiritual man. Material man always has been and always will be blind to spiritual truths. "For the material man rejects spiritual things; they are foolishness to him; neither can he know them, because they are spiritually discerned" (1 Corinthians 3:1).

\\ Decad //

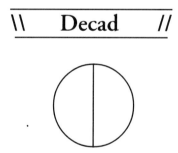

Decad comes from the root word dechomai, meaning, "to receive." It represents Heaven, the origin of number, the container of all things, the attributes of all Ten Sephiroth.

To the Pythagoreans, 10 was "the great number" symbolizing perfection: 1 being the spirit, embodied in nature which is 0. The 10 Yods in their sacred Tetractys explained the nature of God and the Universe and all its elements, and even included the unspeakable name of God.

The number 10 represented concord, love, and peace to the sages, and when their 10 fingers would clasp hands, that was called "the Master's grip," a sign of union and good faith *(Morals and Dogma,* 634).

Pythagoras too, used the clasped hands as a symbol, for 10 was the number of Yods in the Tetractys. The 10 was the number in which all the preceding numbers were contained.

In the law of opposites, 10 is limited and unlimited, like 1. The 1 is found in every number, and every number has proceeded from the 0 and is contained within it.

The Kabbalists often wrote 10 this way:, unity in the middle of zero and representing God, man, and the Universe. It was not just a 1 and a 0, but a pillar and a circle; the Monad, or First Cause, creating and expressing through the circle of no beginning and no end and infinite in boundless space. It was completeness: the 1 being the masculine creative force and the 0 being the feminine uniting to form the Yod of creation. Later on the Yod became a phallic symbol of the Father, and the moon of the Mother aspects of the Godhead. In the Argian dialect, the 10 means "the moon."

The moon is related to mother and creation because woman's reproductive system is on a monthly 28-day lunar cycle. If we turn the "n" upside down in "month," it becomes "mouth." As you remember from the three views of creation, it is the Mouth of God that spake all of creation into existence. So the mouth is, in a sense, a womb. It is from "womb" that we get the word "woman," and it is from the Holy Creative Mouth that we get the word "mother" *(The Secret Doctrine*, Vol. 2: 463-4).

The 10th Sephira is the womb out of which all creation is born on Earth. It is called Malkuth, or Kingdom, and refers to Earth. The bounty of food, the beauty of nature, all come from the womb of Mother Earth for the benefit of her living beings.

"And God saw everything that he had made, and behold, it was very good" (Genesis 2:31).

CHAPTER 22

Prelude
to Numbers

Numbers are nine distinct vibrations. There is not a thing that exists that does not vibrate. Vibration is measurable, and to measure we must use numbers. Each number is a law unto itself, which never deviates from the principle behind the law that governs it, each one being a symbol for a type of influence or energy. "God created everything with weight, measure and number" (*Book of Splendour,* 41).

Pythagoras saw number as universal principle, and each number with a nature all its own. Scientifically this has been proven by modern physics: every manifestation has its own wavelength; a vibrational frequency of electromagnetic energy which is measurable.

This means there is a number that can be applied to everything that has existence, and that number includes its own qualities and characteristics, including its own opposites. So each number is like a balance rod with the positive qualities on one end, the negative on the other end, and the destructive on the reverse side, each number being a complete vibration of a type of energy or influence.

The destructive forces, called the "qliphoth," are brought into manifestation by the most negative thinking. In order for us to maintain perfect balance in our lives, we must avoid the destructive tendencies, the qliphoth, and walk the middle path. This where we find harmony in our lives, our health, and even our attitudes, which have a direct bearing on our success.

So this then is the secret that makes numerology work: letters are symbols for sound, sound vibrates and creates form and has its own traits, in order to know those rates of vibration, we need numbers. The letters' numbered place in the alphabet are their rates of vibration when either thought or spoken.

In numerology we always add the digits together until we come to one number, the root, e.g., 25 (full number) is 2 + 5 = 7 (root number), or 25/7.

CHART 3
LETTERS AND NUMBERS

Full Numbers			Root	Numbers
1-A	10-J	19-S	= 1	A,J,S
2-B	11-K	20-T	= 2	B,K,T
3-C	12-L	21-U	= 3	C,L,U
4-D	13-M	22-V	= 4	D,M,V
5-E	14-N	23-W	= 5	E,N,W
6-F	15-O	24-X	= 6	F,O,X
7-G	16-P	25-Y	= 7	G,P,Y
8-H	17-Q	26-Z	= 8	H,Q,Z
9-I	18-R		= 9	I,R

For deeper kabbalistic interpretation, the full number is important. In the Kabbalah, all words are totaled by their full number. Those that have the same word total have the same numerical rate of vibration and are related. So the Kabbalists substituted words of the same vibration (Gematria) in order to hide spiritual truths from the masses.

Since the full number is the one revered by the Hebrew Kabbalists, and it was used to decipher their holy writings, in English that full number pertains to the Source, the Divine Nature. The full word total reflects our personal level, and the word root number gives the rate of vibration and its basic attributes.

This is confirmed in Henrietta Bernstein's *Cabalah Primer* (34):

The beginning digits of the number would be its "face" (The God Self); and the final digits of the numbers would be its "back parts" (the human self). Reverse the one, and you have the other.

For example, for the word ART:

	Full Number	Number
A	1	1
R	18	9
T	20	2
Full Word Total	39	12 (Root Total = 3 (Root Number)

The full word total, 39, comes directly from the Source, the Creative Trinity (3), which created all in universal love with a great breadth of viewpoint (9). The vowel A is 1, originality, the number of the great artist.

On the human level, the word root total is 12. It is following the basic 1, 2, 3 or A, B, C, in order to accomplish the word root number 3, which is artistic expression.

Eliphas Levi calls this method of interpretation "the arithmetic of thought." He says:

The alphabet and the ten numerical signs are of course the basic elements of all sciences—each sign represents an absolute or essential idea. The form of each cypher and of each letter has its mathematical reason and hieroglyphic significance. Ideas, inseparable from numbers, follow their movement by addition, multiplication, etc., and acquire their exactitude. *(The Book of Splendours,* 136)

The words that are interpreted in this section are figured by their root totals.

Full word numbers are interpreted only in cases where they are especially significant.

Omnia in numeris sita sunt.
(Everything lies veiled in numbers.)

CHART 4

THE POSITIVE, NEGATIVE, AND DESTRUCTIVE ASPECTS OF NUMBERS

1

Positive: Active. Ambitious. Confident. Doer. Individual. Inventive. Leader. Thinker.

Negative: Aggressive. Lazy. Self-conscious. Selfish. Stubborn.

Destructive: A Bully. Antagonistic. Bigot. Egotistical. Puts self first at all times.

2

Positive: Cooperative. Friendly. Helpful. Modest. Neat. Tact and diplomacy.

Negative: Easily hurt. Indecisive. Insecure. Over-emotional. Subservient. Timid.

Destructive: Bad temper. Cruel. Deceptive. Lacks self-control. Liar. Sneaky. Sly.

3

Positive: Cheerful. Humor. The Entertainer. Enthusiastic. Good at writing, speaking, singing.

Negative: Bored. Dislikes responsibility. Impulsive. Moody. Vain. Wasteful.

Destructive: Gossip. Greed. Hatred. Intolerant. Jealous. Pedophile.

4

Positive: Disciplined. Family lover. Good worker. Honest. Organized. Patient. Patriotic. Practical. Reliable.

Negative: Argumentative. Dry. Humorless. Narrow-minded. Opinionated. Stern. Workaholic.

Destructive: Animalism. Crude. Hatred. Jealous. Violent. Vulgar.

5

Positive:	Adaptable. Adventurous. Brave. Charming. Clever. Freedom. Social. Super salesman. Witty.
Negative:	Impatient. Irresponsible. Restless. Thoughtless.
Destructive:	Debauchery: drugs, food, drink, etc. Dissipation. Gambler. Perversion. Self-indulgent.

6

Positive:	Artistic. Domestic. Humanitarian. Musical. Nurturer. Responsible. Serves. Teacher.
Negative:	Argues. Meddlesome. Mopes. Needs appreciation. Self-righteous. Smug. Sweet tooth.
Destructive:	Conceit. Domestic or sexual tyranny. Drudgery. Nosy and Interfering. Slavery.

7

Positive:	Dignified. Educator. Intuitive. Love of nature. Silent. Spiritual or Scientific. Studious.
Negative:	Aloof. Cold. Lives in the past. Melancholy. Peculiar. Skeptical. Sly. Unapproachable.
Destructive:	Cheat. Dishonest. Faithless. Gossip. Sarcastic. Evil intent. Secret motives.

8

Positive:	Ambitious. Athletic. Balance of energies. Efficient. Executive ability. Good judgement. Stamina.
Negative:	Impatient. Materialistic. Needs philosophic study. Not frugal. Pushy. Thoughtless.
Destructive:	Abusive. Cruel. Ignorant. Intolerant. Revengeful. Schemer. Temper. Uncultured.

9

Positive:	Artistic abilities. Brotherly love. Compassionate. Dramatic. Philanthropic. Unselfish.
Negative:	Aimless. Burdened. Frustrated. Over-emotional. Unfulfilled.
Destructive:	Bad habits. Bitter. Dissipates. Immoral. Liar. Morose. Possessive. Vulgar.

11

Positive:	Great artist: music, art, drama. Idealist. Inspired. Inventive. Religious leader.
Negative:	Aimless. Fanatical. Frustrated. Sets goals too high to reach.
Destructive:	Dishonest. Miserly. Wicked leader.

22

Positive:	Good at details. Master achiever. Powerful.
Negative:	Disapproval. Inferiority complex. Narrow. Uncultured.
Destructive:	Black magic. Gang leader. Reckless. Wicked. Ulterior motives.

CHAPTER 23

Numbers

1

ONE
"I'm Exclusive"

The 1 was the first and from it all things were made. Pythagoras called the 1 "Limited and Unlimited." This was part of his Law of Opposites, which he attached to every number. The 1 is limited to itself and is unlimited in other numbers, e.g., two 1's make 2, five 1's make 5, etc. So it is unlimited in all numbers but itself.

One is the line between Heaven and Earth, the creative power, the First Cause touching the Earth plane. The numeral 1, a straight line, is the first principle in geometry: an extension of the point and having length but no breadth. It is the sign of unity and good, and is represented by perpendicular lines, circles, spheres, upright columns, and openings.

In numerology, the 1 is a leader. It is the vertical line, which stands straight and confident. The 1 demonstrates creative abilities, originality, and is a trailblazer, an inventor, a style-setter. It is self-reliant, an individual, a doer, a thinker and planner.

In English there is one word that totals 1 and that is the word "A." A is an article meaning one, so it can be used to point out one of something, e.g., A car. A house. A person. In that way it is like Hebrew where every letter is also a number.

The cypher after any number intensifies the qualities of that number by its own amount, i.e., 20 is twice as strong as 2; 30 is three times as strong as 3; and 10 is 10 times more powerful than 1. This is because all Ten Sephiroth (numbers) are manifest in each 10.

Other 1 words (19, 28, 37, 46) total to 10 first, and differ in quality because of the numbers behind them.

\\ 10 //

The 1 is the self plus the strength and leadership abilities from the great I AM within every one of us. It is intelligence, pioneering spirit, and ambition, all in 1.

The 0 is the Cosmic Egg that contains the attributes of God in each of the Ten Sephiroth within that egg. The 0 is also a picture of a two-sided mirror that reflects the original thought from the spirit side into form on the material side. Together it is perfection.

The first man was ADAM:
$$1\ 4\ 1\ 4 = 10: \text{Perfected man.}$$

M A N
$$4\ 1\ 5 = 10: \text{Created perfect.}$$

M   4 — manifested presence
A   1 — individual; given breath of life
N   <u>5</u> — sensate being (five senses)
     10 — created perfect

The letters in MAN are significant. In numbers 1 through 10, man is considered as 5 because he has five senses. He is the exact middle of numbers, and created perfect.

Man comes from the womb of woman and the first stage of life is in amniotic fluid, or Water, of which M is the symbol.

The N is from Nun, meaning fish. Fish means "esoteric teachings," teachings that are very deep, just as an ocean is deep to hold many fish. Man has a very deep nature, for when he seeks truth he finds that he is eternal spirit.

In order for man to live in the physical body he must have the breath of life. That comes from the Hebrew letter, Aleph, which is the Element of Air. It is the A that, when inserted between the exact center letters of the alphabet, M and N, gives MAN life.

Without woman, physical life could not be generated. So the 0 is important; it is the Cosmic Egg of all creation. The woman has the egg physically and it shows in the word w0man; the "wom" points out that the egg is in the womb.

The W, being the 23rd letter of the English alphabet, consists of 2 and 3, the female 2 and male 3; male being the positive pole or active force, and female being the negative or receptive force. The union of these two impregnates the egg. The birth is shown by the full number of WOMAN: 66. Every body in this three-dimensional world has six sides: top, bottom, front and back, right side and left side. So the first 6 is the body of the woman and the second is that of the child. The ancients taught that the Father and Mother of nature are symbolized by 66, and its root 3, is the child (6 + 6 = 12 and 1 + 2 = 3).

When the child is born, the woman becomes a

MAMA, and the man, DADA:

4 1 4 1 = 10   4 1 4 1 = 10.

The 10 is synonymous with the Hebrew letter Yod, which is the germinal element of creation that makes up every one of the Hebrew letters. That means it is present in all of life, the perfection in every part of creation and regeneration.

\\ 19/10/1 //

This is known as a karmic number, for when it is on any of the major positions of the numerological chart, the individual feels a sense of urgency. Situations may push the person to stand on his own two feet. This is pictured by 19/1: that center 9 is the self (ninth letter is I) and the 1 on either side are its own two feet. There can be tests requiring boldness and initiative, but these are easily met when the person has gained confidence by use of his special abilities and individuality.

It is also called the number of initiation, for the 9 contains all the knowledge of the numbers before it and will be tested on them. When it finishes its exams it finds perfection in 10. Being alpha and omega, 19 always has a goal; it is ready to start a new project before the old is completed. Ideas constantly flow to them and 1's would love to get each one started, let the 9 take over the details and finish it up so 1 can get started on the next project.

Examples of 19/10:

BODY: 2647 = 19. The 1 refers to the self, and the 9 to humanity. Everyone in humanity has a body. The 1 and 9 add up to 10, which is perfection.

But we are not our body, for *body* begins with a B (2) and B comes second. We are first of all spirit and soul (they both start with S-1) clothed by 2, the body. Body comes from 0 (b*o*dy), the Cosmic Egg. It entered this world through D (bo*d*y), the Hebrew letter Daleth, meaning door or gate from which all birth must proceed. And Y is from the Yod of creation. The full number of BODY is 46: body made manifest (4) through love (6).

IDEA: 9451 = 19. Each one (1) of us has the ability to think. It is common to humanity (9) to have ideas. We achieve perfection (10) through the right use of ideas. You could say some come from the unconscious part of the psyche, the Id, the first two letters of *id*ea. And idea's full number is also 19. How can we accomplish our goals without them?

TEACH: 25138 = 19. There must be one to teach and one to learn. The 9 has the knowledge of all the other numbers (contains all the Sephiroth (numbers) before it, and it can teach others so that they can gain perfection in 10).

GRASS: 79111, CLOUD: 33634, and AIR: 199, are 19 words. Like alpha and omega they are constantly renewing themselves: fresh, new, and perfect.

GRASS begins with the 7th letter, G, a number of secrecy. We see only the green part above the Earth while its roots are hidden from view. Its full number is 64: artistic beauty (6) made manifest (4).

CLOUD: starts with the 3rd letter, C, the number of prettiness. 3's are nice to look at. The 3 is a number of travel. Clouds constantly move. The Cosmic Egg is in the center, the 0, which is also the center of God: primal substance. Its full number is 55, a master number of Directed Intelligence. In studying the function of clouds, we can see where this is true. They are a vital part of nature and our weather.

AIR: starts with 1: Aleph, the Element of Air. The second letter, I, is the Yod, germ of creation. Air is the necessary breath of life. It's full number, 28, shows pictorially the cycle of life (8) that must accompany (2) everything.

In the 19, as a karmic number, the 9 is highly emotional and the 1 must learn to be in control of these emotions. When we go against spiritual laws, there is CHAOS, STRESS, and sometimes we FAIL from being LAZY.

These words are all, by their root totals, the karmic 19. Each has a different full number. CHAOS = 46—disruption made manifest (4) for lack of harmony (6). STRESS = 100. Here we are 100 percent off course. It is complete lack of harmony.

\\ 28/10/1 //

When 28 is behind the root, the qualities of the 2 come first and are therefore stronger. The 2 is the peacemaker and the 8, the executive with good judgement. So in 28, 2 achieves leadership through diplomacy.

The 28 is known as "the breaking number." New experiences are in store, surprises and unlimited opportunity, because 2 + 8 = 10, which is a new beginning.

Both HEAVEN and HELL have the 10 root, but Heaven's root total is 28, new experiences and unlimited opportunity, while Hell's root total is 19, showing there is a karmic lesson to be learned. It cannot get away with anything. The full number of Heaven is 55, the same as Cloud. Clouds float in the Heavens, so we see a relation there. The 55 is a master number of Directed Intelligence.

Both words start with an H, which is the picture of a ladder, and a ladder can go in either direction: up or down. H is the eighth letter of our alphabet, the two circles of the 8 representing the above and the below.

The two L's in Hell are upside down 7's. The 7 is inner wisdom, occult knowledge, religious background. Hell turns that right around, stands it on its head, and empties it out. When inner wisdom is not used, the negative and destructive side of the L—selfish, critical, fault-finding, self-righteous, smug, and self-seeking motives—are traits that create their own Hell.

Heaven has a V in its center that is a pictorial symbol of arms up-stretched seeking higher knowledge and light.

GIRL, 7993, and GODDESS, 7644511, each total 28. The root, 10, is perfection. The 2 is feminine, has beautiful expression, and is the peace-maker. The 8 shows the roundness of figure, symmetry, and balance.

Girl contains two 9's, and the 9 is an emotional number. The 3 is prettiness and the ability to communicate. Both begin with a 7, a strong inner nature rooted in the spiritual. In the Kabbalah, the womb is sacred as it is the most secret place for life to begin. The creative force of the Cosmos is centered in the womb, and 7 is the number associated with all things sacred.

The full number of Girl is 46. Through her can be made manifest (4) the power of regeneration (6).

The full number of Goddess is 73: first spiritual (7) with creative intelligence and beauty (3).

The new experiences, surprises, and unusual events that 28 is known for are seen in the 28-words: MAGICAL: 4179313; CIRCUS: 399331; OPERA: 67591; and JUBILEE: 1329355.

It's interesting that opera begins with an O, a picture of an open mouth. O is a 6 letter, and 6 pertains to the voice. The first consonant, P, is a 7 letter, which demands deep study. And it does take a great deal of study to sing opera. Perhaps that is why its full number is 55: Directed Intelligence.

Negative 28's take action without thought, and impede their own progress by their attitudes. Some 28-words that reflect this side are:

Coward, Loner, Prude, Hateful, Crafty, Futile, and
Backwards.

Backwards has the full number of 82, which is a backwards 28.

Coward, Crafty, and Futile all share the full number 73. This means hidden motives (7) with intolerance and hypocrisy (3) in the first two. In Futile the 7 is a sense of despair while the 3 is worrying and whining. It starts with an F which is the upright man carrying a double load.

\\ 37/10/1 //

The 37 achieves perfection (10) through study (7) to develop talents (3). The 7 always seeks the perfection found in 10. This is seen mathematically. If you add all the numbers from 1 through 7: 1+2+3+4+5+6+7, they total 28/10. So the ancients say that perfection is hidden in 7.

PERFECT totals 37 and it begins with P, which is a 7 letter. The full number is 73, putting the perfectionist 7 first. The 3 suggests that whatever is perfect is pleasant to see and a joy to behold. The center letter F, on which the word pivots, shows that achieving something perfect takes care, time, and patience. F carries the double cross, and is the sixth letter that is a number of responsibility.

RAINBOW is a beautiful example of 37, for the 3 means beauty that brings joy, and the 7 is the seven colors of the spectrum that are present in the rainbow.

It is said that both business and religion appeal to the 37. Related words that vibrate to this number are: DEDICATED, whose full number is 55 (Directed Intelligence); RELIABLE and GUIDANCE, whose full numbers are 64 dependable (4) counselor (6); MOTIVATED and AMBITIOUS, whose full number is 109, the self (1) working with all the creative power within (0) to achieve its goals (9); PRODUCE is 82, a cycle of achievement (8) through cooperation (2); SPIRIT and GROWTH are 91, what it takes to start (1) and finish (9); REVERE is 73, a deep feeling from within, usually spiritual (7) and an appreciation for aesthetic qualities (3).

\\ 46/10/1 //

This is the body (6) working through organization (4) or by manifesting (4) itself. That refers to EVERYONE including CHILDREN. This is EMBODIMENT.

These qualities relate also to the following 46-words:

Producer. Ministry. Resurrect.

The negative side of the 46 vibration is reflected in the following 46-words which show a misuse (4) of the body (6):

Fighter. Sacrifice. Deception. Licentious.

\\ 64/10/1 //

When the 4 and the 6 are reversed, the body and voice qualities of the 6 are manifested:

Impersonator. Hummingbird.

\\ 73/10/1 //

The wisdom of the 7 comes first. The beauty of the 3 benefits greatly from one who has studied and applied (7) the self to achieve perfection. We see this in the 73-words.

Comprehension. Inspired-artist. Extraordinary.

In the final analysis, birth names that total 1 are people who are capable of leading an organization. They are natural inventors and exceptional planners.

When the 1 is missing from the name altogether, the person needs to develop self-confidence, ambition, and independence.

We need 1's for self-confidence.

ONE (1)

Positive: Active. Ambition. Creative ideas. Determination. Good mind. Individuality. Inventive. Originality. Self-confidence. Starts many projects. Willpower.

Negative: Aggressive. Braggart. Impulsive. Lazy.Self-conscious. Represses feelings. Selfish. Sensitive. Stubborn.

Destructive: A bigot. A bully. Antagonistic. Domineering. Extremely egotistical. Puts self first at all times. Tyrannical.

The 1 is androgynous—male and female in unity.

2

TWO
"Let's Be Friends"

Pythagoras called the 2 "Odd and Even" because 2 is an even number made up of two 1's, each of which is odd.

This is a number of partnership, companionship, and marriage. Eve was sent to be a helpmate for Adam. She came second, was 2. The 2 is a wonderful companion. The number faces and bends toward the 1 because the 2 wants to help. It feels incomplete by itself.

The 2 is associated with pairs of things, as is readily seen by the Roman two, II. That is also 11, which adds up to 2, but on a higher level. Where 2 is a follower, 11 stands on its own two feet, showing leadership ability. The 2 is stronger on Earth than the 11 for its base is straight on the ground: 2.

Many 2 words total 20. The cypher doubles the power of the qualities found in 2. Since 2 is "a pair," there are words that total 20 that have a mate:

Breast. Foot. Rib. Shoe.

Two of such things make for balance, and the word BALANCE totals 20.

Many 20-words signify a collection:

ARCANA:	A collection of secret mysteries.
OCEAN:	A collection of water.
FARM:	A collection of animals and food.
MUSEUM:	A place that preserves and exhibits collections.
MUSIC	A collection of harmonic sounds.
SUITE:	A collection of rooms.
TAROT:	A collection of mystical cards.
ZOO:	A collection of animals on exhibit.

An unbalanced collecting 2 may become a "collecto-maniac" (klepto-maniac). The word "kleptomaniac" has the Soul's Urge (vowel count) of 22, twice the power of 2, obviously in the negative side of the vibration.

If you look closely at 2, it is actually the upper half of a 3. It is like a plant with roots deep in the ground, showing only its outer self. This gives 2's great sensitivity. Their feelings go as deep as the roots of the plant and what they feel hurts keenly (*Morals and Dogma,* 362).

The 2 also gives a tendency to hide things. Negative 2's tend to be sneaky, and cover their acts with lies: LIAR (22). Like 3's, 2's are good talkers, except that the bottom half of the 2 is buried, so 2 hides the truth; the 2 may say one thing (upper part of 2) and mean another (buried part).

The 2 is a feminine and receptive number (Eve came second). Though it is not a leader, it does have an influence that is gentle, kind, and helpful. It is happy to go to work in the background; taking care to perform detailed work to perfection. And it does not mind not getting full credit so long as the work is admired and appreciated.

It is interesting that the word DEATH totals 20. If death were final it would total 7 or 9; but 20 denotes companionship—an angel at the cross-over. Often people who fear death, or have a strange attitude toward it, have a prominent 20 in their chart. The full word total is 38. The 3 is just an 8 that has the left side removed. The left denotes the past, so 3 is a cycle that precedes the 8, which is a new cycle that continues.

People who are 2's are known as peacemakers, for they are able to see both sides of a question and have the desire to BALANCE emotions on either side, and to keep the peace. They have an inborn tact to deter tempers from flaring. Those who have many 2's or a strong 20 in the name become our best diplomats.

Words that total 20 and reflect these qualities are KIND, WISE, SEER, and TACTFUL. The outstanding traits of 20 are:

- ✦ Tact and diplomacy; a peacemaker.
- ✦ Kind, gentle, and giving; a perfect companion.
- ✦ Urge to collect things.
- ✦ Gets along well with women (2 is feminine).
- ✦ With the cypher following, 20 loves women.

A true and amusing story appeared in the newspaper on March 6, 1987, about a man who was discovered to have at least five wives and fathered as many as 14 children in four states. He was able to maintain them for over seven years without suspicion because he was a flight engineer with a major airline and was regularly expected to be gone for weeks at a time.

He spent a few days at a time with each family as he flew from one destination to another, and was caught only because he was gone a little too long from his wife in Seattle who reported him missing.

All of his wives found it hard to believe that he had other families and were devastated by the news. Some decided to leave him, but he was always so kind and loving they all forgave him. He still loved them and wanted to do right by them, even after he was found out.

After reading the story I thought to myself, this man must have a strong 20 somewhere. Doesn't he have those outstanding traits just listed?

To my delight, his full name was in the paper. I saw right away that he had two T's in his last name, and T is the 20th letter. That alone was not enough, but would have influence. But there it was in the vowels: o ae ue = 20. How interesting that the 20 was in his name area of deepest desire: the Soul's Urge!

If a man's missing number is 2, he may have a problem relating to women.

The 20 loves and needs music, may have a foot fetish, and may fear death. This is because Music, Foot, and Death all total the same numerical vibration: 20.

The 2 tends to be neat, due to its inborn quality of attention to details.

One 2 is good at detail work. Two 2's (4) organizes and gets things done. Three 2's (6) teaches and performs, and four 2's (8) is the executive overseer.

The 20's are happiest when they can be of service to others. Those with a 20 Birth Path, or born on a 2, 11, 20, or 29 day usually find their success in life as part of a team, e.g., Bob Hope, 5-29, and Bing Crosby, 5-2.

Those whose full birth name has the root of 2 are diplomats. Others find their niche in the ministry, as dentists, private secretaries, and in some branches of medicine. 2's are our best speechmakers because 2 is sensitive to facts and knows how to use the right words.

We need 2's for tact and diplomacy.

Two (2)

Positive: Affectionate. A way with words. Beautiful expression. Better at continuing projects than starting them. Considerate. Cooperative. Diplomatic. Friendly. Good companion/business partner. Good with details. Helpful. Loving. Modest. Neat. Sensitive to self and others. Sincere. Tactful. Works well with others.

Negative: Conflict. Dissatisfied. Easily offended and hurt. Fastidious. Glib. Indecisive due to being able to see both sides of an issue. Insecure. Meticulous or careless. Occasional moods of depression. Over-emotional. Subservient. Tactless. Timid.

Destructive: Bad temper. Cruel. Deceptive. Demanding. Lacks self-control. Leans too much on others. Liar. Sly. Sneaky. Wants to control others.

The 2 is female and receptive.

3

THREE
"Let's Spread Joy"

Man is a threefold creature having spirit, mind, and body. Likewise, every system has a first, middle, and a last part; so 3 was considered the first perfect number.

Pythagoras called 3 "the One and the Many," meaning a limited expression of both 1 and 2, and a number of talents because 3 is the Creative Principle in the Godhead, the number of self-expression, the artist and entertainer.

The 3 is an 8 with the left side open, so 8 makes its own boundaries by organizing its affairs. The 3 is open to scatter its energies. Both are moneymakers, but 8 strives to keep money growing. The 3 doesn't want to think about organization, but do as it pleases. It wants fun, not work.

\\ 12/3 //

The basics are the ABC's, the 123's. This is the Creative Principle. A word that refers to many forms of creative expression is ART, and it totals 12.

DAY, 417 = 12, is recreated 24 hours for our use. It begins with D: Daleth, or door, and each day is like a new door opening for us.

It is human reproduction that is the creative expression we are given as lesser creators made in God's image. Mate, Sex, and Baby are 12-words that mirror this Divine gift.

BABY, 2127, starts with a B, a letter that needs companionship: 2 leans toward 1. Two B's show baby to be dependent. A is the breath of life and Y is Yod, the generative sperm. As 7, Y shows a spiritual nature, and that it comes from mystery into the world.

Both DAY and BABY have the full number of 30: the Creative Trinity (3) by the Cosmic Egg (0) from which all proceeds. It is a number of newness, great potential, and joy.

The full number of MATE is 39 (13,1,20,5 = 39). The 9 is a picture of the generative sperm and it stands next to the creative 3, both numbers of pleasure, fulfillment, and creative abilities.

SEX, 156, begins with a letter of directed wisdom, S. It refers to the 1 which is first the Monad, or God Center, and to the self which takes responsible (6) action (5). The X is open and vulnerable and can "X" itself out by hasty action.

As a full word number (19+5+24) it is 48: the act that keeps the cycle of life (8) constantly bringing forth manifestation. Both 4 and 8 are numbers that relate to physical production and to stability (4) and justice (8).

Whenever the Bible mentions "twelve nations," it refers to the whole human race, for it encompasses the 12 astrological signs of the zodiac.

\\ 21/3 //

The 21 is the mystical number of Cosmic Consciousness. It is renewal of mind and body and using them to express creatively. It is the self (1) putting the "2" qualities first: courtesy, cooperation, tact, and diplomacy. The 2 speaks well, is the peacemaker, and is also very sensitive.

The 3 is also verbally expressive, so 2 and 3 together enhance creative expression through the voice or the written word. Words that have 21 as their root are: Human, Actor, Salesman, Woman, and Bible.

Both HUMAN and ACTOR have the full word total of 57: a sensate being (5) with an inner spiritual and creative nature (7). The 7 also refers to the professional, and one who studies to better himself. SALESMAN has the full word total of 84, which shows he must strive (8) harder to set a secure foundation (4) for himself. Both 8 and 4 are numbers of work. (WOMAN is analyzed in the chapter about One.)

The BIBLE, 29235 = 21/3, is the story of creation, the Trinity. The 3 is the number for words and communication, so it is important as a root total for Bible, the Word of God. It has the full word total 30: the Creative Trinity (3) next to the Cosmic Egg (0), or "the Word made manifest."

Bible has two B's, showing it is meant to be a companion. It has no purpose by itself alone and unread. It contains the I, or Yod; the generative sperm, so it imparts life to its words.

Another 21-word that imparts renewal for mind and body is SLEEP. Its full word total is 57. The 7 signifies rest, but the 5 shows there is activity during sleep. While sleep may renew the body, it often gives us dreams that in turn give us mind activity and sometimes, creative ideas.

PEACE is 75135 = 21. The number of tact and diplomacy comes first: 2. It is the self (1) putting others first, a symbol of selflessness. There can be no peace when the self comes first, expressing greed and thoughtless acts. Also, Peace starts with P, a 7 letter—7 being at rest, thoughtful. The first vowel is an E, which is directed energy, and the pivot point, the center of the word is A: the breath of life, which is also (1) expressing through us individually. Together they total 3, a number of joy and fulfillment.

Every number has opposing qualities, each vibration is a balance rod with positive on one end and negative on the other. The 21 can be a number of unhappy events. It corresponds to the 21 letter, U, which is pictorially a cup on a rocker. It fills easily but can rock and empty out its treasures, for that rocker is built of emotion—the 2—which comes first, and is very sensitive.

The 21 is composed of three 7's, so it is the finishing of a cycle in three worlds (see figure 4 on page 71).

Yod:	ATZILUTH	(Spirit)	7
Hé:	BRIAH	(Mind)	7
Vau:	YETZIRAH	(Soul)	7 Takes form in
Hé:	ASSIAH	(Body)	21

The 7 is a time of rest after completion, but 3 (2+1) wants to perform, so it is impatient and will do things in haste. This makes 21 a great test for humanity. The 7's demand spirituality, which is needed for inner strength. We can see the negative expression of 21 in the following 21-words:

Lustful. Fool. Wild. Vile. Evil. Envy. Fear. Glib. Sneaky. Beastly. Clumsy.

\\ 30/3 //

The 30 is filled with artistic talents and expression. It is the God-Power of the cypher (0) behind the 3 of self-expression. It represents the completion of projects, celebration, and happiness.

Birth. Family. Genial. Happy. Humor. Kindly. Serene. Sociable. Strong. Thankful. Uplift.

The root total of ANCIENT is 30: (1539552). The most ancient of all is the Cosmic Egg (0) and the Creative Triad (3), called by some "The Ancient of Ancients." Its full word total is 66, which was known as Father-Mother God.

Since 3 has a way with words, spoken or written, the cypher following it will intensify those qualities:

Doctor. Lawyer. Lecture. Write. Savior. (With
the u, "Saviour" is 33, a number of spiritual service.)

A musical sound that is pleasant to the ear is CHORD (30).

A gem is pleasant to the eye is the AMETHYST (30).

When self-expression is hindered we see the negative side of the 30 vibration:

Dilemma. Fixed. Idiot. Nemesis. Sadistic. Strive. Stubborn.
Sulkiness. Thief. Tremble.

\\   39/12/3   //

The 39 is loving and caring. It desires to give loving service and help make the world a better place. It is easygoing. The 9 represents humanity and its emotions, feelings, and love of life, expressing itself in the 3 which is happiness, joy, and using one's talents to express life at its fullest.

Positive 39's:

Friends. Gentleness. Humanity. Quietude. Refine.
Romantic Wedding. Writer.

Negative 39's use words to hurt people:

Critical. Disgrace. Malicious.

Then there are negative 39-words describing actions that do harm:

Corrupt. Foolish. Slaughter.

\\   48/12/3   //

TREE is a 21-word by root, 2955, but 48 by its full number: 20-18-5-5 = 48: a reliable (4) and very productive (8) part of the cycle of life (8). The first letter is T, a letter that stands tall with a strong, protective overhang. Trees give us shade and protection. They furnish us with tools for many things: wood, paper, and their products. The T is the 20th letter, and 20 refers to collections and groupings, and trees have a collection of leaves.

The 48 is a number of searching for satisfaction and finding material success. It needs to be balanced by the spiritual:

Beneficial. Satisfying. Metaphysics.

The 4 comes first and it is a loyal supporter of home, family, and country. There are two 4's in 8; this makes 8 a strong leader. No wonder words like PATRIOTIC and DIPLOMATIC vibrate to 48. And yes, the basics still apply since 4+8= 12/3 (also true of 39 and 57).

A misuse of the 4's honesty, and the 8's good judgement, can be seen in the following negative 48-words:

Dishonesty. Hysterical.

\\ 84/12/3 //

In 84, the highly mental and intelligent 8 comes first. I found one word that totals 84: INTELLIGIBILITY. It starts with an I, the ninth letter. The 9 holds all the knowledge of the preceding numbers. The middle letter, G, and the last letter, Y, are both 7 letters, showing that the state of understanding clearly must come from within.

\\ 57/12/3 //

The 57 will work hard to make negative conditions better. It under-stands people's problems and knows how to seek help, for 5 wants to know how other people feel, and understands due to its own experience.

The 7 is spiritual. It does need to cultivate a sense of humor and an inner response to situations. The 7 always seeks perfection. Some 57 words are:

Perfection. Reverential. Cooperative. Omnipotence.
Prevention.

The negative 57 will Criticize, needs Correction, is often Negligent.

\\ 75/12/3 //

The 75 accepts challenges; it wants to do things right. It does get down to basics—1, 2, 3—in order to succeed.

FIREFIGHTER: The full word total is 111, the basic 3-in-1, all suffi-cient; the highest principle of the soul. The first letter, F, is a picture of arms outstretched to help someone at its side. The first vowel, I, is a 9, which is the number of compassion and service. The center pivot letter is also I, so its work is "around" compassionate service. There are 11 letters in the word, so its very traits point out that it is there to help humanity.

The negative 75 may fail due to procrastination.

Strive, Stress, and Strain all begin with STR = 12/3. When I first began studying this science, I understood the positive energies of 3: hap-piness, joy, talents expressed, and communication. Then one day I was talking with a young man about his numbers. His month of birth was March (3) and a month tells the main vibration of youth (to age 27). I remarked that his childhood must have been happy. Not so. He said he did not have a happy childhood at all.

I had failed to take into consideration that every number is a complete vibration, including its negative polarity. Though the 3 is expressive, it can dissipate and scatter its energies; is not practical like the 4, and will err for lack of boundaries. Also, 3 is the child, and the adult 3 loves children, while the negative polarity finds the child molester/abuser.

Strive, Stress, and Strain all start with STR=12/3, the negative side. (The letters that come first have a direct influence.)

Those who have a 3 root for their complete birth name will find their success in acting, oratory, dancing, painting, singing, all forms of entertaining, and writing.

One 3 is the performer. Two 3's (6) is the teacher. Three 3's (9) has performed, taught, and is now finishing up for perfection in 10. Here we see the importance of the numbers within a number.

We need 3's for self-expression.

THREE (3)

Positive: Artistic. Attractive. Charming. Good imagination. Cheerful. Creative. Enthusiastic. Expressive. Gift of gab. Good at writing. Good host/hostess. Good sense of humor. Optimistic. Outgoing. Singing. Sociable. Speaking. Talented. The life of the party.

Negative: Bored. Critical of others. Dislikes responsibility. Exaggerates. Hates work; wants only fun. Impulsive. Jealous. Moody. Scattered. Self-centered. Vain.Wasteful.Wears too much makeup or gaudy clothes. Worrywart.

Destructive: Cowardice. Deep jealousy. Dual-personality. Gossip. Greedy. Hatred. Hypocrite. Intolerant. Uses hurtful words.

The 3 is male and active.

4

FOUR
"Let's Get Organized"

The Sacred Trinity sent vibrations via the spoken word down into material form. The Trinity, or Godhead, is shown graphically as a triangle, which stands on the line depicting spirit descending into matter, making the symbol 4. Some see it as upright man carrying the Godhead Trinity. Pythagoras called it "Right and Left," the land to your right and left as you stand, or the four corners of the Earth. Geometrically, 4 is a square, the most stable of all forms. When a man is honest they say he is square with you." The 4 represents uprightness, honesty, and integrity. The 4 is devoted to family, community, church, and country.

The square is closed in on all sides, so the 4 will set up its own limitations and sometimes feel boxed in. But it does not mind working nine to five in an office room because that affords a feeling of security. The 4's will work hard for a secure future. They want to set a firm foundation early in life. Sometimes they get so wrapped up in their work that they forget to play, and then they can be pretty dull. The saying, "All work and no play makes Jack a dull boy" evokes the image of the 4. But 4 is an honest achiever and has material success.

\\   40/4   //

The active God-Power of the 0 making things manifest on Earth is the story of the 40. Going through four planes of creation, each a separate Sephirotic Tree, totaling 40 Sephiroth, makes this a number of completion.

Creation. Terrain. Biology. Fundamentals.

The first three of these words have the full word total 85. Constant change (5) is part of 85's life cycle (8). The full word total of Fundamentals is 130: the Creative Trinity (3) in the midst of perfection (1 and 0). In the Bible, 40 is associated with spiritual advancement and completion. Jesus fasted 40 days, and the great flood was 40 days and 40 nights. 40-words that relate are:

Awakening. Consecrate. Penitent. Victory.

All 4's work well and are good with their hands. The cypher after 4 also means working for perfection:

Artistry. Organist.

Both words have the full word total of 130, the same as Fundamentals. The active physical force expressed through the intellect has qualities of the 40:

> Reading. Thinker. Library. Politics. Calculations. Mathematics. Listeners.

The closed-in, four-sided square suggests limitations:

> Surround. Envelope.

The extremely negative 40 can be very dangerous. It lacks a sense of humor, takes everything too seriously, and can become violent:

> Demolish. Terror. Violence.

\\ 13 //

The 13 is not as unlucky as most people believe. It is the self (1) using its creative talents (3) to put ideas into form (4).

The 13 gained a reputation for being unlucky from the fact that Jesus and his disciples numbered 13, and one of his disciples betrayed him.

Another reason for fear of the 13 was the fact that witches were believed to have met in groups of 13 to receive orders from their master (*Why Do Some Shoes Squeak?*, 396). "Friday the 13th" became an ill omen because in old England the hangman was paid 13 pence for each hanging, and that always took place on Friday.

The negative side of 13 comes into evidence mainly through carelessness. The 13 must achieve balance between the creative and the material side. This is because the corresponding letter, M, is in the middle of the English alphabet (13th), and it has both feet firmly on the ground, maintaining balance between the spiritual forces at its right and the material forces at its left, as though it were on a balance board.

In the entire alphabet M is the only letter pronounced with the mouth closed. It corresponds with the 13th Tarot card, DEATH—a picture of a skeleton riding on a horse and carrying a flag with an image of the five-petaled rose that represents the life force. Its meaning is not really to die, but to change. This may be because the original pagan year consisted of 13 months. It is the aspect of the old dropping away so that the new can come forth.

As the birth date or name number, 13 says, "Here is someone who is courageous and willing to lead the way." Esoterically it represents the death of a man as a mortal and his rebirth as a disciple who reaches for the higher consciousness.

\\ 13/4 //

The 1 is First Cause, or Creator; it is also ourselves as creators in His image. It is originality, the inventor, the style-setter, the pioneer.

The 3 is creativity, self-expression, happiness, entertaining, writing, the artistic and decorative, and prettiness.

The 4 is where the ideas of the creator take form.

Here are a few words that total 13:

SOUL: The root of Soul is 4. This shows that the soul is a definite form, though not perceptible in this dimension. It was created by First Cause and is individualized, as evidenced by 1. It has self-expression, as evidenced by 3. The full number is 67, meaning spiritual (7) body (6).

ARTS: By individuals (1) using their creative expression (3), the Arts take definite form (4). The full number of Arts is 58: ideas from above becoming manifest below (8) in various ways (5).

ATOM: This is the basic material (4) of the creative (3) energy field put into action by the Monad (1), or First Cause. Its full number is also 58.

This is one of the elementary components of matter in all its forms, and the letters show that the elements come forth from the Cosmic Egg (0) in its center. A is Air, M is Water, and the T is a picture of spirit descending into matter. At the point where they cross creation takes place.

TABLE: This is an example of a creative idea made into form with 4 legs or with one central base as shown in the letter T. Some tables are ornate, which is another quality of the 3. It takes a creative person (1 + 3) to design such a table. Its full number, 40, is practical, and the cypher makes it all the more so.

CAR: This 13-word describes a vehicle with 4 wheels designed by a creator (1) and used for transportation and travel (3).

Lastly, 13 is not a good number for a gambler. The 3 scatters its energies and acts in haste, or impulse. But the 3 gives the otherwise-sober 4 a sense of humor.

\\ 31/4 //

This number is prevalent among good writers, interior decorators, artists, and homemakers. When the 3 comes first it often refers to creative writing, or something related:

Calendar. Covenant. Script. Sentence.

The 3 is a number of words, positive or negative. Someone who uses words in a negative way is a gossip.

GOSSIP: 761197 = 31/4. This word sounds like what it is—it gives a hissing sound like that of a snake about to strike. Numerically it begins and ends with a 7 letter, G and P, and the negative side of the 7 is fault-finding, deceitful, and sarcastic with words.

The Soul's Urge (vowels) of Gossip, O =6 and I =9, totals 6. Where the positive 6 is responsible and kind, its negative side is the opposite, hurtful, using the voice as a sword.

The personality (sum of the consonants) of the word, 7117 = 16/7, is the negative side of 7: cold, secretive, and unfeeling. The 7 gives the appearance of turning its back on the one spoken about. It first totals the karmic number 16, which shows it is outwardly doing something that will have a karmic effect. The total expression of Gossip is 4, which is manifestation. It may make something out of nothing by its unkind words (3), and cause someone pain.

The full number is 85. The number of continuity (8) comes first. The 5 is a talker. Here we see that 5 talks on and on, like the cycle that goes on and on, and the word continues to be told. That 8 also represents the Law of the Circle: what is given out will come back to the sender. No wonder its personality scores the karmic 16.

All 4's make good doctors, but the 31's and 13's are the best. The 3 makes them more reachable, willing to talk, and they appear to be more understanding.

The 31 is totally reliable and takes responsibility seriously.

SCIENCE: 1395535 = 31/4. This is a fundamental knowledge (4). Each science is individual (1) and governed by its own creative (3) laws. The first letter is the S that seeks knowledge. It has strong ideas. The first vowel is I, a letter that must learn to master the self. It is a 9 letter, and 9 is a number for serving mankind. Its full number is 58: continually (8) seeking answers (5).

\\ 49/13/4 //

This number refers to many talents and those who use them for great achievement, for it also has the qualities of 13 and 4.

- 4: Has ideas take form through organized skills. 4 is a tireless worker.
- 9: Considerate of other people; will work for the benefit of many.
- 1: Leadership ability and confidence to see things through.
- 3: Creative talents longing to be expressed.

Note these qualities in the following 49-words:
Prodigy. Inspired. Enlighten. Instructor. Phenomenal.

The 49 is very attached to home and family, for 4 loves security and the 9 has emotional attachment:

Appreciate. Patriarch. Pregnancy. Intensify.

The 49 must work for a balance between mind and emotions, for 4 works through the intellect and 9, through emotion. The negative 49-words that fit this description are:

Irritable. Criticism. Unemotional. Constricted. Pomposity.

When the mind permits the negative emotions to take control, there can be devastating effects because ideas take form in 4:

Destruction. Demolished.

Both words start with a D, which is a 4. This shows the destructive side of the 4 rather than the constructive. Note too, that Destruct begins with D-4, while Construct starts with C-3. And 3 is creativity. "De" always means "to take away from." It starts such words as Detract, Debit, Default, Defeat, Deface, Defame, Defer, Deficit, and Defraud. E is a 5, and the 4 and 5 are antagonistic to each other. 4 seeks boundaries and 5 must have freedom.

\\ 58/13/4 //

The 58 refers to very deep thinking subjects and intellectual pursuits; a number of insights.

5: Has mental curiosity. It seeks facts, is imaginative and good at analysis.

8: Shows executive abilities. Great organizer. Skilled. Has good judgment. Is physically strong.

58-words:

Realization. Imagination. Profundity. Forgiveness. Independence. Pythagorean.

On the opposite end of the spectrum are:

Profiteer. Self-indulgent. Opposition. Elimination. Competition. Licentiousness. Corruptible.

\\ 67/13/4 //

This number refers to things well thought of.

6: Cares for people, gives loving service, takes on responsibilities.

7: Is introspective, distinguished, looked up to for its wisdom. It is the professional.

Plus there are all of the creative abilities of the 13/4. We see these attributes in these 67-words: Administration. Distinguished. Practitioner.

All 4's are good in mental work, especially where hands and mind work together. Here we find outstanding engineers, mechanics, jewelers, electricians, mathematicians and musicians, teachers, managers, and foremen.

We need 4's for stick-to-it-iveness.

FOUR (4)

Positive: Accurate. Conscientious. Conservative. Disciplined. Good worker. Honest. Loves home, family, country. Loyal. Organized. Patient. Patriotic. Practical. Prudent. Punctual. Sincere. Studious. Stable. Wants the law enforced.

Negative: Argumentative. Dull. Forgets to take time out to play. Headstrong. Humorless. Intolerant. Jealous. Must see to believe. Narrow-minded. Not affectionately demonstrable. Opinionated. Overworked. Prejudiced. Too serious. Workaholic.

Destructive: Animalism. Antagonistic. Crude. Cruel. Hatred. Strong negative emotions. Violent.

The 4 is manifestation, for it follows the Creative Trinity: Idea. Planting. Growth. In 4 is the harvest.

5

FIVE
"Don't Fence Me In"

The 5 loves its freedom and wants to come and go as it pleases. See how the number is open at both sides? How its base is on a rocker? It is so adaptable, likes so much variety, that it sometimes doesn't know if it is coming or going.

The 5's are very restless under routine; they must have the freedom of adjusting their own schedules. A job in the same place every day, within four walls, is confining to the point of extreme uneasiness.

Pythagoras called 5 "Masculine and Feminine" for it is composed of 2 and 3, the feminine and masculine numbers. So 5's are very popular and get along very well with both men and women.

In travel they like to take the side roads and explore. They like to see how the natives live and speak their language. The lower half of the number 5 is like the top half of a 3. That gives it good speaking ability. Remember, the 3 has a way with words. This makes 5 a super salesman.

Having many 5's in a chart means changes and unexpected happenings. Basically 5's are curious. They want to know what makes things tick and what is going on. They will investigate everything.

The 5 is called the number of man because it is the exact middle of numbers and man has five physical senses. When we are born, the first thing we become aware of are our senses. We feel the warmth and cold. We see the light and are aware of faces—of our parents, of other people, and then of our surroundings. We touch various objects and feel the difference in texture. We develop taste for certain foods that we like better than others. We can smell the aroma of foods and of the changing air about us.

Discovering our five senses is surely the first lesson in life. As the child grows, any temptations that come affect one or more of these senses. The child learns that sweets taste good, but too much gives a tummy ache. And so it is with each of the senses. So discrimination must be learned.

We are all Adam and Eve. Adam is the active masculine energy represented by A. Eve is the receptive polarity represented by V, which is A reversed and with the "rib" removed. V, spelled Vee, is an anagram for Eve (*The English Cabalah,* Vol. 1:172).

Likewise, man begins with an M: the middle of the alphabet, just as 5 is the exact middle of numbers. M has two feet well balanced on the ground. Reverse the M and we have W, the initial letter of Woman. Negative polarity. Emotional. So Adam is representative of the masculine active force, and Eve, of the feminine passive force.

To be well balanced, we all have a small amount of the opposite force, in that man must have some negative receptivity to soften his nature and woman needs some of the positive force to give her strength.

We can see this in the letters M and W: the feminine force, V is clearly visible on the top middle of M. The masculine is the reversed V, or A without the rib, in the bottom center of W.

When man has grown to the point where he is in control of his five senses and has mastered them, he then has control of his body; he is well balanced in the middle of numbers. Because 5 is the exact center, it has been called "the balance board" and man is meant to have dominion, for MAN (415) totals 10. Perfection.

It is part of 5's lesson to learn the right use of freedom and not to overdo sensual pleasures.

Because 5 is not bound-in like the confining square of 4, it is apt to take chances, be the daredevil. It has no fear; wants new experiences; is willing to gamble.

\\   50/5   //

According to the Kabbalah, all knowledge there ever was and ever will be is included in the 10 numbers, the 22 paths which are the letters, and the 50 gates of knowledge which are a classification of all being into five series of 10 *(The Book of Splendours*, 134). This makes 50 an intellectual number. This can be seen in the following words that total 50:

> Concordance. Efficient. Engineer. Explorer. Fact-finder. Instructors. Investigate. Memorize. Organize. Professor. Prophesy. Physician. Technician. Theosophy.

The charming and popular aspect of the 5 is also heightened by the cypher:

> Admiration. Considerate. Delightful. Sincerity.

Remember we said that 5 will take chances? Is fearless? INTREPID means fearless, and it totals 50.

We also said that 5's are versatile and like change. A word for that is DIVERSITY, and it totals 50.

Destructive 50's are:

> Endangered. Ignorance. Instability. Intolerable. Revolting.

\\   14/5   //

This is a karmic number. There are lessons to be learned or there will be accidents, losses in business and in friendships. It is known as the number of experiences, for its possessor learns no other way.

The 14 must learn self-control of all physical appetites and temper. They can become too involved in physical sense pleasures and that could bring about health problems.

The 14's have sharp mental faculties and enormous energy. It helps them a great deal to study philosophical truths to balance out their emotional energies.

The 14's are enticed by anything they feel can bring them a moment's JOY (14) or FUN (14). They are too EASY (14), will WED (14) on impulse and later regret it. In Genesis it is the serpent who tempts EVE (14). To us, a serpent is a snake, and SNAKE totals 14. Its full number is 50, which shows it to be highly intelligent.

A SAGE (14) is one who has gained complete control of the senses, and is on the spiritual path. It begins with an S, which is a picture of the serpent of wisdom and shows the path to be anything but easy. It has turns in it, but it learns through experience. The first vowel, A, shows it is a leader with a good mind, and can put the material and spiritual differences into proper perspective because of the clear balance line across the center of the A that separates one from the other. G is the seventh letter, and 7 denotes spirituality and will seek it. But E is 5 of the five senses, and only he who learns self-control develops the powers of the true Initiate (14 is 2 × 7).

JOY: 167 = 14. At first this was a surprise to me. I expected joy to be a 23 because of the creative, talkative 3 with the 2 that loves to share. But no—real joy comes from within the individual (1) before it can be shared. Sometimes you and you alone can experience a joy.

And that joy is real to us when we WORK (22/4) toward and achieve fulfillment. That 4 is something we have earned, and that is what brings the individual joy in the real sense. Also, joy has the full number of 50, which is a number endowed with intellectual quality. Animals cannot experience joy in the same sense that man can. The root is 5: Curiosity. Freedom. Variety. All refer to man and the spice of life. All bring joy.

\\   41/5   //

The 14 and the 41 are numbers of nature. Nature is perfect organization (4) through intellect (1 and 5). It is form (4) created from ideas (1 and 5).

When the 4 comes first, the freedom-loving 5 is structured, as in these 41-words:

Astronomy. Geology. Universe.

The 4 is composed of two sensitive 2's, so when it comes first, that sensitivity is shown. At the same time, 4 solidifies character and makes the 5 more responsible:

Character. Emotional. Feelings. Generous. Giving.
Prudence. Purify. Respected. Sensitive.

Negative equivalents are:

Antagonism. Blasphemous. Brooder. Condemned. Dangerous. Fright. Pessimism. Prudish. Transgress. Wretched.

The 5 is a marriage number. It produces its own offspring. (5 × 5 = 25. 5 × 7 = 35. 5 × 9 = 45.)

In 41/5 the self (1) now puts the family (4) first and thinks of starting a family and having offspring of its own:

Married. Admirer. Promise. Pregnant. Existence.

MARRIED: 4199954 = 41, starts and ends with a 4-letter. This shows it intends to set up its boundaries. It starts out with M, two feet set firmly on the ground. M is the 13th letter and corresponds with the 13th Tarot card, Death; but instead of death, it means change—something new coming into one's life. It is the death of the old single self and the birth of a loving partnership.

The D at the end of the word is the Hebrew "Daleth," door, mouth, or womb. This suggests that Marriage is meant to be the means by which new life is conceived and regenerated. To some the door is a way out of the marriage.

The very center of the word, RRI, or 999, are three letters of loving service, giving of self without thought of return; the number of great emotion, the great lover, the understanding attributes that make the bond between two people so very special and valued.

The 41/5 is intellectual and a good talker. The 5 gathers facts and the 4 is made up of two 2's that are sensitive to details. The 5 consists of 2 and 3; both fluent speakers. No wonder then that the following words have the total of 41:

Collaborate. Counselor. Discourse. Research. Teachings.

The full number of RESEARCH IS 77, and 7 is the number of the analytical thinker.

\\   *23/5*   //

The 23 has much to do with LIFE: 3965 = 23/5. The 2 is the number of the female, and 3, the male, both with five senses and the desire for freedom to explore and enjoy life to the fullest.

ANIMAL totals 23/5. There are male and female animals, and they require their own freedom. The LION (23/5) is known as the King of Beasts. The full number of Lion is 50, which shows it to be quite smart.

The 23 corresponds with the 23rd letter of the English alphabet, W, a graphic picture of ups and downs, highs and lows, the good and bad we encounter in our experience.

The 5's are known for their bravery. And who takes more chances than the Hollywood STUNTMAN (23/5)? Many women are "stuntmen" too; 23 means both sexes.

Some negative 23-words are:

Maniac. Scream. Shoot.

SHOOT: 18662 = 23/5. This is someone (1) using his power (8) by using his body (6) to harm the body (6) of another person. The 2 is duality and the necessity of knowing the difference between good and evil.

The word begins with Sh, the Hebrew letter Schin, the Element of Fire. A gun is a firearm. The two O's are the eyes that take aim. The T is the cross of crucifixion or of responsibility. The one who shoots must carry that cross for the rest of his life. The full number, 77, is the Christ number (Jesus was the seventy-seventh in his lineage and CHRIST totals 77 by its full number). So Shoot is the direct polar opposite of the Christ-consciousness vibration.

\\   32/5   //

The 32 has the same basic qualities but shows mastery over the animal nature by its words:

Admire. Polite. Respect. Sanction.

This is also true of: Christ. Glory. Power. Those three 32-words each have the full number of 77.

AMERICA: 1459931 = 32/5. The full number is 50. Directed Intelligence, and a number of freedom. It begins and ends with 1, the individual. The very center has two 9's, the number of universal service and brotherly love. Its first consonant, M (4), is a number of the builder, the firm foundation.

CIRCLE is also 32/5 with the full number of 50. The circle pertains to life never-ending, for its root as a word is cycle, and its glyph is a continuous circular line with no beginning and no end. It is male and female, 3 and 2, the positive and negative forces that keep the cycle of life continual. And it is done by Directed Intelligence (50).

Knowledge, leadership ability, and intellect are all part of the 32 vibration; the Creative Trinity's (3) detailed (2) work:

Career. College. Cultured. Logical. Sagacious.

In contrast to the king of beasts, the Lion (23), where the sneaky 2 comes first, we have the Parakeet (32) where the pretty and talkative 3 comes first.

Negative traits that vibrate to 32 are:

Condemn. Despise. Fight. Oppose. Psycho. Quibble. Shrewd. Temper. Vandalize. Weird.

\\   59/14/5   //

This is the number of the person who has done a job well:

Cooperation. Experience. Professional.

The 9 means the lessons are coming to a close and there will be a change coming about, for after 9 comes 10, a new beginning.

The 9 contains all the knowledge of the numbers preceding it and is adaptable to change due to the 5 before it. So 59 completes, and 14 is the Sage.

Environment. Hierarchy. Precipitate. Scintillating.

PRECIPITATE, 59, in the occult sense, is to bring forth out of nothingness, as sages and magicians were known to do. The word starts with P, the circle of eternity high on the self (1) and enclosed to hold much knowledge. It is a 7-letter that refers to spirituality, scientific thinking, and the possible understanding of the mysterious arcana. Its very center letter is also P. The center letter is known as the *keystone* and is found only in words and names of an uneven number of letters. That center letter is a pivot point that helps to carry out the initial action of the first letter, also called the *cornerstone*. The last letter is called the *capstone,* and it shows the destination to be accomplished, or the aim.

So Precipitate sets out to bring forth out of nothingness (First P), is helped along by its arcana of knowledge (center P), and its destiny is to bring forth. The last letter is E, 5th in our alphabet, and 5 is variety so it can bring forth any variety of things.

The full number of Precipitate is 122, the one (1) who is master of accomplishment (22). Interestingly, the word COOPERATION had the keystone R-9, humanitarian. Its full number is 131, the great communicator (3) between the pillars (11) of the peace-loving 11.

\\ 68/14/5 //

This is the number of the well-educated. The 6 understands the law and knows what must be done. The 8 is the number of the executive, one who has good judgment and leadership ability.

CIVILIZATION (68) depends on education. Without it men are uncivilized. This is an interesting word to analyze kabbalistically. Keep in mind that civilization refers to all of humanity whose number is 9.

The total of Civilization by its full numbers is 149, so we have 14 9/14/5.

If we put letters to those numbers we get.............................N I N E, the number of humanity.

Those who have 5 for a total name number are natural salesmen, travelers, good in all occupations that call for versatility and adaptability. This includes actors, writers, scientific inventors, detectives, speakers, and promoters.

We need 5's for adaptability and desire for knowledge.

FIVE (5)

Positive: Adaptable. Alert. Analytical. Attractive to opposite sex. Charming. Clever. Courageous. Curious. Dynamic. Gets along with all types of people. Learns languages easily. Love of freedom. Loves to travel. Popular. Social. Super salesman. Wants adventure. Witty.

Negative: Careless. Discontent. Impatient. Impulsive. Irresponsible. Procrastinates. Restless. Takes dangerous chances (daredevil).

Destructive: Gambler. Overindulge the senses in sex, drugs, alcohol, or food. Perversion. Rude.

6

Six
"I Want My Voice to Be Heard"

The 6 is the vibration of home, family, and service. It is man (1), standing by the family circle (o), or 1o or 6. So it is a number of regeneration. Every body has six sides. Pythagoras called 6 "Rest and Motion" because these are important to all bodies for good health.

The 6 is known as the "Cosmic Parent" for four reasons:

1. It wants the responsibility to nurture and care for its family, pets, or those who need care.

2. The vowels of our home planet, Earth (E-5 and A-1) total 6.

3. All words that vibrate to 6 show an affinity for the body of persons, places, and things (six sides).

4. The circle of the 6 is on the bottom, denoting the womb. Womb's vowel, O, is a 6-letter.

The 6 corresponds with sex because Vau, the sixth letter of the Hebrew alphabet, is the "peg" or "nail" that connects the male Yod to the female Hé (IHVH) that there might be creation.

People with strong 6's love to eat; some are overweight. In this case, the lower circle indicates a full tummy.

Those born on a 6 day (6, 15, or 24) may have an unusual or outstanding voice. The 6 is open at the top to depict this. They talk well, sing, and teach. They make good counselors for they know just what to say, are calm and receptive in nature, and have a knack for making people feel at ease. They like to be comfortable and dislike dressing up.

The 6's are artistic. They like to have their surroundings reflect their good taste, artistically arranged and in their favorite colors.

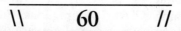

\\   60   //

This is a strong family vibration. The cypher shows the creative attributes of the Deity (0) being expressed through a body (6):

Grandmother. Re-embodiment. Thanksgiving.

TYPEWRITER (60), has creative attributes in that it gives birth to words. WORD, by its full count, is also 60 and proves their relation.

The 0 accentuates the speaking, singing, communicational side of the 6, and it has been found that strong 6's make their career around the voice.

In the following 60-words you can see where knowledge (0) and voice (6) are important:

Communication. Definition. Description. Investigator. Performance. Performer. Psychoanalysis. Understanding.

\\ 6 //

Anyone with a 6 prominent in the name enjoys the creative arts. Some make acting their profession. The word ACT totals 6. Its full number is 24: putting sensitivities (2) into emoting (2) that appears to be real and true (4).

The 6 is also a domestic vibration: love of home, garden, children, pets. CAT is a domestic pet and it totals 6. Its soul urge is A-1, meaning it has a mind of its own—typical of cats.

\\ 15/6 //

NAME: 15/6. Names are individual (1). Males and females have them (5), and they refer to places and things as well as people (6). The soul of name (A and E, or 1 and 5) totals 6. So it refers directly to the person, place, or thing to which it belongs.

The personality (consonants of name: N and M, or 5 and 4) totals 9 which represents all humanity, everything, so a name is meant to be attached to anyone or anything. Plus it is a spiritual gift. That is seen by its full number: 33.

ALIAS: 15/6. It can be described the same as a name.

1—Refers to the self, person, place, or thing.

5—Is male or female because it contains the 3 and 2. It is also variety.

6—Is domestic, artistic, vocal, has six dimensions and responds to love. It is associated with families.

Other 15-words are:

Boy. Castle. Lady. Self. Suit.

Basically, 6 is love, home, and family in vibration. At one end of the spectrum there is the caring and loving 6 that wants to be responsible. On the other end is the caring 6 that wants to be of help on his terms only. This is the meddler who causes more pain than joy and does not even realize it. This person is SMUG, another 15/6 word, but on the negative end of the vibration.

The opposite of love is hatred. These 6's are so sure they are right and everyone else is wrong that they will fight for their beliefs. The negative words that vibrate to this 15/6 force are:

Battle. Duel. Mean. War.

They are governed by MARS, which is also 15/6, and is known as the God of War.

It takes someone who is BOLD (15) to stand up for his own rights when dealing with the negative smug 6. No wonder Bold has the full number of 33, the master number of spiritual gifts and of loving sacrifice.

\\   51/6   //

In one aspect, this number leans toward the military. 51-words of this type are:

> Collaborator. Foolishness. Historical. Horrible. Negativity.
> Prisoner.

On the creative side we find these 51-words:

> Creativity. Horoscope. Individual. Masterpiece.

Some 51-words that reflect home, love, and family are:

> Expectation. Godmother. Traditional. Veneration.

The 5 shows an active mind present in the self (1). One side leans to the love side of the total 6 vibration while the other leans toward cruelty: two sides of the same whole vibration. That is why balance is so important in one's attitudes.

\\   24/6   //

This is the number of the successful person, an attractive personality; the 6 root referring to the "Cosmic Parent," the 2 revealing their loving ways, and the 4, their honesty, dependability, and respectability:

> Enjoy. Female. Husband. Justice. Lovable. Magic.
> Mature. Natural. Nuptial. Share. Succeed. Wealth.

Then there are the words that show the peaceful 2, the dependable, accurate 4, and the artistic 6:

> Artist. Costume. Dreams. Gift. Holy. Musical. Planets.
> Pray. Pure.

MUSICAL: Its full number is 78. The 7 is the inner experience; 8, the fine balance of rhythm and harmony with the root of the melodious, audible side of the 6. The word begins with M, a glyph of Water, which refers to emotions and movement. The pivot point (keystone, or middle letter) is I, or the self who is affected by the mood it creates. And the capstone is L which, besides ox-goad, means the outstretched arm in the act of accomplishing just as conductors outstretch their arms to lead the orchestra for the musical.

When the 24/6 works in the negative side of the vibration, there is the stubbornness of the 4, the sensitive and jealous 2, and the tyrannical 6 who either uses words to hurt—or uses silence as a weapon:

Crude. Deadly. Silent. Trial. Verbal. Vexed.

\\ 42/6 //

When the 4 comes first there must be a firm foundation.

4: Secure, honest, and just; manifestation.

2: Kind and cooperative nature.

6: The voice, artistry, persons, places, and things with size, shape, and dimension.

We see these reflected in the following 42-words:

Allegiance. Astrology. Compatible. Guaranteed. Investment.

The kind and loving nature is apparent in the following:

Benevolent. Cheerful. Glowing. Thankfulness.

The full number of CHEERFUL is 78: expressing the positive energies of the cycle of life (8) from within (7).

GLOWING is 87; also showing that it is from within (7) that the creative energy (8) is expressed.

THANKFULNESS has the full number of 150: Intelligence directed (50) by the self (1).

An ANNOUNCER, 42/6, uses his voice (6) in his career. The 4 is a number of work and structure, and the 2 does not wish to be the center of attention, but very ably calls attention to others, as an announcer would do.

JOURNALISM, 42/6, is the voice expressed through the writer.

An ACCOMPANIST, 42/6, lends solid support (4) to a soloist (6). The 2 desires to be of help to another.

The negative end of the loving, caring, family-oriented 42/6 vibration would be:

Frustrated. Neglectful. Reclusive.

\\ 69/15/6 //

REINCARNATION: 69. The 69 is identical to the astrological sign Cancer: the time of year when nature renews itself. This is a good description for the word Reincarnation.

This word is so interesting, lets analyze it more deeply. When we add 6 and 9, we get 15/6: 6 represents the body, 1 is the individual life force in the body, and 5 is the five senses. Its desire (vowel count) is 31/4: the 3 showing the desire to express the self creatively; 1, with individuality; and 4, in a form of physical manifestation.

Remember, 4 represents the beginning of form. Two fours produce the cube: a three-dimensional figure. The human body is, in a way, a package for the soul to inhabit, and the word PACKAGE has the full number of 44, which totaled is 8. The root number of REBIRTH is also 44. The 8 is a pictorial symbol of the life cycle and of the orbit of planets.

The picture of two circles, one above the other (8), is the path of all living: circles or cycles. The root of CIRCLES is 33, the number of spiritual gifts. Its full number is 69, again the germ of life, the same as reincarnation. Therefore, reincarnation is a gift to us as a part of the cycle of life. The full number of Reincarnation is 141: 1 is A, 4 is D. So we have Ad A, or "add A." What is meant by "Add A?" A is the Element of Air, the breath of life that is necessary to live. It is also spirit—the conscious inhabitant.

Reincarnation is defined as "a rebirth of the soul in successive bodies." Procreation is the physical act that will create the body for the incoming spirit. The full number of PROCREATION is 134/8, MD, or Mid-8. Consider it as the union of the upper circle to the lower circle at the midpoint and you see where the cycle begins a new life.

PHILOSOPHER has the same full number (141) and the root number (69) as Reincarnation. So a philosopher is an old soul, one who has lived before.

The soul or desire of Reincarnation is 31/4 while that of Philosopher is 26/8; 4 being material existence or matter, and 8 being the "above" of the four, or having been here be-4 and completing a cycle (8). Since God - 26 by its full number, it is the philosopher's desire to seek God. Do you not see how, by knowing the meanings of numbers and letters, we can interpret the relation of words to each other?

There are 13 letters in the word Reincarnation. The number of letters tells the special traits of a word. The 13 refers to the 13th letter, which is M. M is the exact center of the English alphabet just as 5 (the five senses) is the exact center of numbers. Interesting that the center of each refers to man, and man begins with M. After M comes N, and if Air, the breath of life, is inserted between M and N, MAN appears.

Man's life-giving fluid, blood, is 90 percent Water, and the ancients' symbol for Water was M. It is in the waters of the womb that the fetus takes form and becomes the baby that is to be born. M is life and death, renewal and regeneration. It is the end of the old and transformation into the new. And isn't this fitting for a trait of reincarnation?

Those whose name totals 6 are our artistic workers, teachers, philanthropists, organizers, doctors, nurses, and politicians. Many of our presidents have 6 for a Birth Path or total name number.

We need 6's for being responsible and caring.

Six (6)

Positive: Adores family, home, children, pets, garden. Advice-giver. Artistic. Comforter. Cosmic parent. Gives loving service. Good education important. Harmonious. High ideals. Honorable. Humanitarian. Just. Lawful. Musical talent. Poised. Protective. Responsible. Sympathetic. Teacher. True friend. Understanding. Uses voice in career: teaching, singing, speaking, acting, politics. Wants to nurture.

Negative: Anxious. Bossy. Cynical. Egotistical. Domineering. Expects too much of people; easily disappointed in them. False pride. Interferes. Jealous. Meddlesome. Mopes. Needs to feel appreciated. Outspoken. Self-centered. Self-righteous. Smug. Suspicious. Sweet tooth.

Destructive: Conceit. Domestic tyranny. Martyr. Nosy and interfering. Slavery.

The 6 often refers to the body of something, since Adam was created on the sixth day and since all bodies have six sides.

The 6 refers to the voice because God spoke forth the creation in 6 days.

7

SEVEN
"Give Me Time To Think About It"

The 7 is the number of spirituality, mysticism, wisdom, and success. Pythagoras called 7 the "Crooked and the Straight."

God made the world in six days and rested on the seventh. The 7 turns its back on the upcoming numbers, does not start the fervent work of the 8. It looks back in retrospect on all the lessons it has learned in 1 through 6, or to reflect on work well done, just as God looked upon His creation and saw that it was very good. We were told to do likewise. We were told to keep the Sabbath holy, meaning that it has spiritual and moral worth. By resting we build up our energy for the work we do in 8. The 8 has physical stamina, good health due to proper rest on the seventh.

The word SABBATH is 17/8: the self (1) resting (7) to renew strength (8).

Those with 7's prominent in their charts need more rest than other people. They can't take loud music, crowds, noise, or commotion. They maintain their balance through serenity. The 7's stand straight, tall, and dignified. They are usually conservative in manner, thinking, and dress. They don't talk much but when they do they have something of substance to say, for 7 is an intellectual number. They read a lot and think deeply about things. They seem to be secretive.

The 7 is a number of faith. They seek spiritual wisdom unless they are negative. Then faith is replaced with fear and the strong, quiet person is, instead, an incessant talker. In general, negative 7's will express faith or fear, alertness or laziness. The 7's continually seek perfection. Whatever type of work they decide to do, they must be the best. If doctors, they will specialize. If musicians, they will compose and perform. The 7's will dig for facts and analyze everything. They work best alone. Also, the 7's prefer quality to quantity. They want to share their life with someone they admire or they would rather be alone. They are very private people and can be hard to know. Only when they know and like you will they open up and be friendly. They need understanding, love, and compassion. They may seem cold but they do like to do things for people.

The 7's are very intuitive. They are the ones most apt to remember their dreams and dream in color.

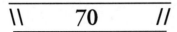

The cypher accents the introspective nature of the 7. Both LISTEN and SECRET have the full number of 70: the strong, silent, mysterious 7 amplified 10 times.

The cypher seems to capitalize on the negative aspect of the 7 in the following words that total 70:

Imperfection. Procrastinator.

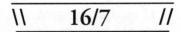

This is a karmic number. It corresponds with the 16th Tarot: the Lightning Struck Tower, equating with sudden experiences, losses, and accidents. The bearer of this number can overcome anything through silence and meditation, qualities of the 7. This number shows a talent for speaking, singing (6), writing, performing (6 and 7). The 7 is the professional, a number of ideals and values. Words that vibrate to 16/7 are:

Altar. Ballet. Book. Plan. Solo. Value. You.

BALLET: 16. The initial letter B (2) means it is performed by more than one. The 2 refers to groups. Ballets are cultural, an aspect of 6. Costumes, too, are 6. It takes a great deal of study (7) to be able to perform ballet.

In politics, 16 is the self (1) wanting law and order (6). It wants its voice (6) to be heard. The 7 will study, take exams, and know the statutes. Related 16-words are:

Book. Exam. Statute.

There is a need for all karmic numbers (13, 14, 16, and 19) to develop the spiritual side of the nature. That is the strong, loving force that balances out all negative conditions.

\\   61/7   //

This number stands for ACCOMPLISHMENT (61/7).

The 6 always seeks to complete projects. (God created the world in six days).

1 is creative: the doer who initiates projects.

7 has the inner serenity to be in control. It will analyze and probe for facts. This applies to the following 61-words:

Concentration. Intelligence. Tranquillity. Visualization.
Wholehearted. You.

GRAPHOLOGY: 7917863677 = 61/7 loves to write, and graphology is the study of handwriting. Being analytical, 7 can easily find the hidden meanings in handwriting.

6 will study things quietly. It will take the responsibility of accurate appraisal.

6 refers to the body of something, and handwriting is the tangible "out-picturing" of the soul.

1 refers to the uniqueness of each writing specimen and to the individual to whom it belongs.

The word starts and ends with 7-letters: G and Y. Y is always attracted to things of a mystical nature. G is very intuitive and draws in knowledge. See how the letter turns in on itself? It is usually wise and spiritual or analytical.

Negative 61-words are:

Transgression. Irritation.

IRRITATION: 9999212965 = 61. The interesting thing here is the fact that the most emotional number, 9, dominates the first four letters, and to feel irritation is definitely an emotional response. Those four 9's are followed by the highly sensitive 2, which surrounds the self (1). It's full number is 133, which can be translated as "death (13) of creativity (3)," or "the self (1) martyred (33)."

\\   25/7   //

Talented musicians and painters are born on the 25th.

This number shows a bright, inquiring mind.

7 thinks deeply about things and will analyze and decide for itself. Much comes through intuition. 7's appear wise for they speak only when there is something worth saying. Psychic.

5 has curiosity, will probe for facts. It wants to know how others feel and think; is interesting and changeable.

Both 5 and 2 are good talkers. See the resemblance between the bottom curve of 5 and the top curve of 2? They are both open on the left, the side that faces the past. This means that both have good memories, remember facts, and are open to talk.

The 5 is open on the material plane (lower), so is concerned more with things of a sensual nature.

The 2 is more cautious about its words, for it is open on the very top or mental/spiritual plane, so it uses discretion and tact.

With this in mind, consider the following 25-words:

> Apostle. Charm. Listen. Messages. Pleasant. Relate.
> Secret. Silent. Story. Words.

WIFE and SOULMATE are 25-words: the feminine 2, sensual 5, and faithful 7.

Other 25-words bring out the collective aspect of the 2 and its love of detail, 5's diversity, and 7's inner feeling:

> Brook. Create. Earth. Galaxy. Heart. Nature.

DEVIL is 25/7. It is said that the Devil deceives because of his fine appearance. The 7 stands tall and proud. The 2 appears kind, helpful, and cooperative. But behind the dignified appearance of the 7 lurks a cold and calculating negative aspect, for 7 puts its back to the higher numbers to "lord over" the lower numbers. And 2, in its negative aspect, is sneaky and a liar. The 5 knows how to get along with everyone and is popular. But 5 is also the five senses and temptation. And the Devil is highly skilled as a tempter.

The Devil inspires the following 25/7-words:

> Abusive. Felon. Odor. Panic.

And is often found in the:

> Despot. Fatalist. Zealot.

\\ 52/7 //

This is a number of wisdom, high ideals, and values. There are 52 weeks in a year and 7 days in each to grow in wisdom.

5 is a perceptive mind that seeks answers.

2 is the peacemaker; kind and giving.

7 is the deep thinker, dignified and correct unless negative. One side is faith, the other, fear.

Qualities expressed by the 52 are:

> Apologize. Discernment. Expectations. Expressive. Independent. Persistence. Reference. Religious. Taciturnity. Transformed.

ARITHMETIC, 52/7, is the science that Pythagoras valued as the first and most important because it is the basis of all things and necessary in creation. Through the knowledge of numbers he found wisdom, high ideals, values, and the reason we are here. 5, 2, and 7: numbers of study, analysis, and curiosity satisfied.

PROPHECY: 79678537 = 52: A prediction. The 7 root shows this is a word of mystery. The 7 goes within for answers, uncovers secrets. Not only is 7 the root, but the word begins and ends with a 7 letter. The first letter, P, locks much within itself. See the enclosed circle on top in the mind area? This shows it has great foresight, but it is not on a stable foundation. P needs to be balanced with philosophy or it can be mentally too "material-minded."

Y is known as the mystic letter, and when in a name, the person is drawn toward things of a mystical nature.

The numerical adjectives before the root, 5 and 2, tell us that this 7 seeks answers (5) and desires to give facts and details as part of its service (2).

The full number is 106: 10 is the complete picture that is seen and 6 is the voice that describes it.

CONFERENCE: 3656595535 = 52. Here again we can see where the qualities of the 5, 2, and 7 apply. All the numbers in the word are communicative numbers. 3's and 5's talk a lot. The 5 is good on many subjects. The 6 is the voice that must be heard, and near the center is the humanitarian 9 that represents the voice of the people.

The first letter is a C, which means, "open to talk." The 3 is the number of self-expression and is good with words. C is open on the side toward all the other letters, so it wants to get its point across to everyone.

The last letter is E (5), so it will discuss a variety of subjects. The 5 seeks answers and is adaptable to any subject. E represents both animal and spiritual forces for it is open on both planes. E must be confined to the subject at hand or it will ramble on.

The full number of Conference is 88, and 8 is the never-ending cycle. Conferences can go on and on. The 8 is also skilled as the executive, and is the vibration of good judgement; all necessary to a good conference.

The negative sides of 5, 2, and 7 are:

5: Rude. Impulsive. Ready to fight. Takes dangerous chances.

2: Easily hurt. Glib. Over-emotional. Shy. Sneaky. Takes everything personally.

7: Deceitful. Fearful. Sarcastic. Sly.

Some negative words that total 52 are:

Frightens. Indiscreet. Retaliation. Revolution. Self-conscious. Treacherous.

\\ 34/7 //

All 7's have to do with the hidden mysteries of life and nature. When the 3 is first, it is usually a word that describes something attractive, pretty, decorative, or ornate, such as a FLOWER (34/7).

The 4 tells us that the thing has form and is something of substance.

These qualities of 3 and 4 can be seen in the following 34-words:

Beautiful. Church. Elegance. Swimsuit (supposedly hides the mysteries of life).

The 3 also refers to words written, spoken, or sung. The 4 adds the form on which the words are seen:

Calculator. Concerts. Diploma. Handbook. Material. Notebook. Refer.

The 3 is a bringer of joy. It can be the joy of giving or of entertaining. But whatever it does it means using its gift of self-expression to bring pleasure to others. The 4 with it makes it practical:

Benefit. Pleasure. Present. Thrill.

Some negative 34/7 words are:

Anguish. Burglar. Contempt. Drench. Poison. Putrid.

The words POISON and PUTRID have the full number of 88. In the negative side of this strong cycle-of-life number is the power to take away life-giving properties. Where the positive 8 is good judgment, the negative side has none. Numbers don't lie.

The 7 is the "day of rest" number. Work is finished, so it is an ending number. On the positive side it means completion and perfection. But on the negative side it shows aloneness, and on the destructive side, finality, as in the 34/7 words:

Morgue. Murder. Venomous.

Both MURDER and MORGUE have the full number 79. Both are finishing numbers. VENOMOUS has the full number of 124. 24 refers to the letter X, so here X crosses out the self (1). The 52-word RETALIATION also has the 124 full number; it will cross itself out by its own negative action.

The positive side of the full number 124 does not "cross out." Being a 6 number of service and love, the X, if used in a loving way, will always benefit the X greatly.

\\ 43/7 //

This number has a strong sense of justice because the honest and reliable 4 comes first.

ARISTOCRAT: 1991263912 = 43/7: This appears to be successful, and like the A that starts its name, has both feet stable on the ground. The 4 shows solidarity and strength. The 3 stands out in a crowd and the 7 is dignified. There are 10 letters in the word, so it tries to attain perfection. Other 43/7 words are:

Champion. Compassion. Defender. Dignity. Nobility.
Proper. Refined. Sweetheart.

Both PROPER and DIGNITY have the full number 88: good judgement, good health. Leadership ability. Strength. Strong cycle of life. COMPASSION and SWEETHEART share the 124 full number, the loving side of the vibration that benefits the self.

The 7 is the thinker, the analyzer. It faces the past (left) so it is proud of its heritage, loves history, and has a good memory. It strives for perfection (numbers 1 through 7, when added, total 10). The 7 works well alone:

Brilliant. Memories. Secretive. Subconscious.

The negative side of 4 is the opposite of honest and reliable. It is extremely opinionated and untrusting. It also refers to a condition or thing of poor judgement. Negative 43-words are:

Criminal. Perilous. Suspicious. Temptation.

ENTERTAIN: 552592195 = 43/7, is interesting. The 3 likes to perform; the 4 gives it a strong base for self-expression, and the 7 shows that inner creative talents are used. Those being entertained respond from what they feel within (7). All the 5's are doers, the 2's are helpers, and the central 9 is the audience that enjoys. R (9) is also the great actor in the heart of the word.

When 7 is the root total of the full name, the person has natural talent for scientific analysis, spiritual work, inventing, and all professional lines that take a great deal of study. Here are the scientists and mystics.

We need 7's for spiritual growth and independent thought.

SEVEN (7)

Positive: Analytical. Book-lover. Deep thinker. Dignified. Educator. Faith. Good mind. Great inner strength. Inspired. Intuitive. Knowledgeable. Logical. Loves history, antiques, and the arts. More spiritual than religious. Musical. Nature-lover. Peaceful. Perfectionist. Poised. Refined. Scientific. Silent. Spiritual. Wise.

Negative: Aloof. Argumentative. Broods. Cold. Confused. Either says nothing or doesn't stop talking. Fearful. Haughty. Hermit/loner. Lives too much in the past. Melancholy. Nervous. Peculiar. Represses emotions. Sly. Secret motives. Skeptical. Stubborn. Suspicious. Unapproachable. Unpredictable.

Destructive: A cheat. A gossip. Dishonest. Evil intent. Faithless. Resentments. Sarcastic. Slyness. Thief. Unreasonable.

8

EIGHT
"I'll Work Hard For Nice Things"

The 8 represents the law "As Above, So Below." This vibration understands the Earth (o- lower circle) and the intellectual plane (Ο-upper circle). This means it can take an idea and make it work on the material level.

Both 8's and 3's are strong personalities, but 3's are more extroverted. They are the performers, while 8's are more conservative and are the business people. The 3 is 8 with the left side removed. It is like two half-moons letting their light shine. Personality plus. Humor. Fun-loving. The 8 is enclosed, self-contained power. The 3 will spend on impulse; the 8 will save, and is good with money.

On its side, 8 is a picture of the balances: ∞. This means it has good judgment and a good dose of "common sense."

The 8 balances good health, strength, and stamina, and is found in the name total of many athletes. Many musicians also have this number as it reflects their fine sense of rhythm. But anyone with an 8 for a name total will find it is a better name for business than for the performing arts.

Some people are aware that the number 888 refers to Jesus, but few know why. The numerals that correspond to the letters of Jesus' name in Greek are 10, 8, 200, 70, 400, and 200 which, when added together, total 888.

The 8 is also a number of resurrection because Jesus arose on the eighth day, and 8 is a picture of "the below that rises above." It came to represent the law "As Above, So Below," for by studying man and the world around us, we come to understand the worlds above—the Universe and spiritual man.

Ancient man discovered the shape of the 8 to be the orbit of planets. It has since been proven that it is the natural path of activity for people and animals as well. In 1928 a professor of zoology at the University of Kansas, Asa A. Shaeffer, observed that people who have been lost in the woods or blindfolded really do travel in the pattern of the figure 8. So do swimmers and drivers who have been blindfolded, and pilots who are lost in a fog; all will travel in spirals. Shaeffer concluded after many experiments which included animals and even amoebas, that spiral motion is a universal property of living matter in form (*Why Do Some Shoes Squeak?*, 221).

Pythagoras called the 8 "Light and Darkness." The darkness is the selfish material-minded moneymaker, and the light is the spiritual-minded who offer light to those in the dark. This knowledge of spirit and matter gives the 8 inspiration, leadership ability, and even genius. It is 4 plus 4; the organizational abilities of the 4 doubled—44: Mastermind. Prosper. Unlimited. (See Master Numbers for more on 44.)

\\   17/8   //

The 17/8 is a staunch individualist: the scientist, researcher, intellectual. The 1 and 8 are the mental or intellectual numbers, and 7 is intuitive and logical in thinking. Because 8 is the number of good judgement (the balances) with the 1 and 7 preceding it, there must be success. The 17 has great hopes for the future, as seen in the following 17-words:

Exact. Goal. God. Sense. Smart. Study. Success. Mason.
Monk.

It is interesting that GOD vibrates to 17/8 while CREATOR is 35/8. We perceive God as being one (1) Original Cause, unseen and mysterious (7), whereas Creator brings to mind the many and varied (5) types of creation in all its beauty (3). We could also say that God (1) breathes the breath of life (7) into man: "As Above -o, So Below -o."

The 8 relates to justice. If a law is broken, the debt must be paid, for this is the Law of the Circle: what goes out must return to the sender. Occultists have long known that the thoughts and deeds of man are moral (or immoral) forces that affect the world around him. Earthquakes, floods, all so-called "acts of God" are not acts of God at all, but nature's balancing of the scales of justice. All that we send out must return to us.

This is easier to understand now that we know the power of the vibrations that are set up through thoughts and words. And there will always be those who will travel far to be where disaster takes place, as though it were a self-appointed destiny. *(The Bible and the Tarot,* 238-9).

\\ 71/8 //

When the 7 comes first, great inner strength (7) is within the self (1) to accomplish (8). The 7 seeks perfection and often becomes skilled at his craft. This inner strength that ultimately reaps success is reflected in such 71-words as:

Rehabilitation. Representation. Wholeheartedly.

There are other 8-words that have 71 as their full word number (root totals are in parenthesis):

Athlete (26). Builder (35). Daydream (35). Hallow (26). Smart (17). Temple (26).

When we fail to use the positive side of this beautiful 71 vibration we see the outcome in the following words that have 71 as their full number:

Apathy (26). Dreadful (35). Frantic (35). Ruined (35).

\\ 26/8 //

The 26 is a physical number. The 8 root gives strengths to the physical 6, and since the 2 is sensitive, the 26/8 can be a passionflower. It can be impulsive in love and must learn self-control. The 2 desires partnership and enjoys being with people in work or marriage.

The 6 gives physical dimension: it wants to nurture and take responsibility. The 8 appears successful and is strong, athletic, and vital. We see this energy in the following 26/8-words:

Athlete. Action. Backbone. Grand. Majestic. Sports.

Someone who takes responsibility in an executive way befitting the 8 is a Queen (26).

Money is a form of energy: Capital. Dollar.

As inner strength we see it in: Faith. Hallow. Joyful. Mystic. Pleased.

There is a great strength in ideas and the spoken word. The 6 represents the voice and 2 is good with words and communication:

Answer. Crystal. Spoken.

Crystals are used in instruments of communication as natural batteries. Different types of crystals give off beneficial vibrations for different things.

TEMPLE: This refers to the body as well as a place of worship, and there are those who worship the body. The Soul's Urge (vowels) of temple, EE (5 and 5), total 10, the number of man. This shows kabbalistically that the motivating force of temple is man.

The 26 is a number that has need to prove physical or inner strength; it will learn through experience. Negative 26-words are:

Abhor. Amnesia. Apathy. Fiasco. Pseudo. Pushy. Riot. Ruin. Scheme. Stupid. Tyrant.

\\   62/8   //

When the 6 precedes there is a responsibility toward the person, place, or thing. Very intelligent; knows more through intellect than reason:

Administrator. Commissioner. Contributions. Exercises. Information. Intelligible. Philosophy. Procreation.

The full number of CONTRIBUTIONS is 179: the self (1) giving secretly (7) for the benefit of others (9).

The 6 refers to a body (anything with six sides). In Contributions, that which is contributed is the body. In Procreation a body is given its beginnings in form, and Philosophy is a body of knowledge.

PROCREATION: (62/8). Here the root, 8, shows that the cycle of life continues here. The 6 is the womb of life (lower circle) and it is the domestic number of home and family. The 2 desires marriage and family. The full number is 134. The 13 is M, or Water, from which life arises. It is also the thirteenth Tarot card, Death, which means the old dying away to make room for the new; not an ending, but change. The 4 is Daleth, or door; the mouth of creation. So 134 is birth (4) from the waters (13) of the womb.

PHILOSOPHY: 7893616787 = 62/8. This word begins and ends with the 7 of inner wisdom: P, having the good head on its shoulders for perception, and Y that seeks to know the mysteries.

The 6 is the Cosmic parent; it understands much and gives of itself. The 2 knows good and evil; it sees both sides on an issue so it understands people's beliefs and inner needs. The 8 has excellent judgment, great strength, and leadership ability.

\\   35/8   //

This is the most fortunate number. Many blessings are associated with it, including inheritance and physical and spiritual vitality. The 3 is attractiveness, popularity, and expressiveness. The 5 shows varied interests, freedom, and versatility. It also has to do with unexpected happenings and change, as well as diverse assortments. The 8 is success through effort. Strength. A good sense of rhythm. Perfect order.

Words that vibrate to this fortunate number are:

Audience. Builder. Carnival. Country. Creator. Daydream. Degree. Flattery. Flowers. Leisure. Memory. Merlin. Miracles. Moralist. Mountain. Movement. Musician. Royalty. Vegetables. Vitamins. Weather.

Then there are traits aptly described by 35/8:

Achieve. Goodness. Observant. Sanitary. Steadfastness. Transcend.

Some negative 35-words are:

Critic. Dreadful. Glower. Infamous. Misery. Pillage. Ruined. Tragedy.

See how "critic" begins and ends with an open-mouthed C? How "tragedy" starts with a cross and ends asking Y?

\\ 53/8 //

When the 5 comes first there is more assertiveness required in order to attain the goal. More attention is paid to detail:

Articulation. Examination. Fellowship. Illustration. Microscope. Musical comedy. Religion.

Some negative 53-words are: Competitor. Demolition.

The 8's make good doctors. They see the overall picture, but dislike details, so they seldom specialize. Those whose name totals 8 may be in science, analysis, technical work, big business, music, or athletics.

We need 8's for good judgment.

EIGHT (8)

Positive: Ambitious. Capable. Dependable. Efficient. Executive ability. Fine leadership abilities. Good at starting projects and getting others to finish. Good judge of character. Good judgment. Handles money wisely. Likes nice things. Makes a good boss. Musical and/or athletic ability. Organized. Physical stamina. Practical. Prudent. Realistic. Sets goals. Successful.

Negative: Careless with money. Hard. Impatient. Materialistic. Needs philosophical study. Pushy. Represses feelings. Thoughtless.

Destructive: Abusive. Cruel. Demanding. Ignorant. Intolerant. No feelings for others. Revengeful. Schemer. Temper. Uncultured. Unscrupulous.

9

NINE
"I'll Help You Any Way I Can"

Hermes was considered to be the wisest of all philosophers and brought light to this world in the form of wisdom. The 9 is a reflection of his lamp that lights the way; so 9 holds the knowledge of all numbers before it. This endows 9 with understanding and a feeling of brotherly love. So it is a humanitarian number.

A 9 in the Birth Path or total name number is a sign that the person is born to give loving service in a profession or in the arts. It is able to draw from the attributes of the preceding numbers and therefore understand and form any character desired. So 9 is called "the stage where the drama unfolds." This is also because 9 is emotional, hence, "emote." This is the vibration of actors and some politicians. This is why some actors aspire toward politics, and why politicians are great orators. Both serve the public and appreciate the applause.

Turn the 9 upside down and you have the 6: the voice that must be heard, the vibration that has interest in its home and community.

Many actors, and probably politicians, have a big EGO (18/9). There is a big head on the 9 and a strong 8 after the 1 (self).

That same circle that applies to an inflated ego is also a mind filled with knowledge. The 9 has a natural bent toward LAW (9) and it likes law and order.

Pythagoras called 9 "Good and Evil." Being enlightened, 9 should know the difference between the two. Because the 9 understands love in its highest sense, it sees only good, even in faults *(Vibration,* 63).

The 9 is the circle of continuity, the tail being the life force that propels it. This is seen mathematically. Take any numbers and subtract them in a reversed position from each other. The remainder, when reduced, will always be 9.

Example: 864
 - 468
 396 = 18/9

If you add the digits 1, 2, 3, 4, 5, 6, 7, 8, and 9, the total is 45, which totals to 9 *(The Key to the Universe,* 323-4).

\\ 9 //

The 9 is the unlimited soul expression of all things, of humanity and its law. Its by-word is "universal service." Some 9-words are:

I. Job. Law. Me. Sun.

The 9 is a finishing number, for after 9 comes 10; a new beginning on a higher plane. Some 9-words that really can finish us are:

Blast. Fat. Lack. Mad. Tax.

\\ 18/9 //

The 18 is sensitive and friendly. It always has a goal to be completed in 9. It has been called "the goal-setting number."

The 1 refers to the self, its accomplishments and feelings.

The 8 refers to physical endurance, rhythm and movement, music and athletics.

The 9 is very dramatic. Music is strong in 9's. Here we find opera stars, musicians, and people who do professional or creative work. The 9 is 3 × 3, so its talents are multiple:

Baseball. Care. Cool. Dance. Diva. Ego. Goals. Play. Sweet.
Talent. Venus.

The opposite end of the vibration are uncultured people with negative habits and attitudes:

Awful. Bully. Foul. Tactless.

\\ 27/9 //

This is a number of deep affections, spiritual insight, creativity, and love of beauty and the arts.

The 2 adds a loving and cooperative quality; it is ever the peacemaker who works quietly in the background.

The 7 adds poise and reserve, and a desire for study and perfection.

The 9 represents humanity, people, and brotherly love.

Advanced. Agree. Breath. Educated. Gentle. Honest.
Public. Quiet. School. Whole. World.

See how one letter makes a difference in the words breath and breadth?

BREATH (27/9) is invisible like Air. First Cause descended into matter (2) and breathed into man's nostrils the breath of life, and man became a living soul. The soul is the unseen center of the body, or 7. The body with a soul is common to humanity (9).

When the D is added and the word becomes BREADTH, or "distance from side to side," it is no longer invisible air, but something measurable. It has taken form. The letter added here is D-4, the number of manifestation, and now the word totals 31/4, the total being 4 also.

The 3 behind the number is a number of travel. If the distance is great it is necessary to travel in order to go from one point to the other. Do you see now how numbers describe the words they relate to?

WORLD is 27/9. The Bible tells us the world was formed by the Word. What makes the Word (24/6) into a world? It is L: 12/3, The Creative Trinity.

The 27/9 has to do with those who have a concern for the public: the performers who need an audience, the law officials who deal with public laws, and those who give CARE (18/9) and COMFORT (36/9), as in the following 27/9-words:

> Buyers. Chapel. Gentle. Lover. Money. Pilot. Satisfy.
> Stardom. Steward. World.

The full number of SATISFY is 99, a master number of complete fulfillment.

The 27/9's like to either travel or stay put:

> Limit. Quiet. Restless. Search. Trip.

Negative parts of humanity are the following 27/9's who must get their spiritual (7) house (2) in order (2): Cynic. Vulgar. Witch.

\\ 72/9 //

When the 7 comes first, that which is felt deeply inside comes first—keen, analytical powers: Improvisation.

Those who seek help (2) by reaching the subconscious mind (7) sometimes try Hypnotherapy (72/9).

\\ 36/9 //

This is the creative trio where all the arts are represented: The 3 is the writer, 6 is the voice, and 9 is the stage of drama; loves to hold the pen, can copy and improve articles. Some 36-words that express these traits are:

> Aesthetic. Editors. Enthrall. Poetry. Singer. Violin.

The one who enjoys what these performers have to offer is the Spectator (36/9).

People with this number make money easily: Fortune. Revenue.

This is a number that requires perseverance, strength of character, and the ability to overcome problems with good faith and patience.

The 3 has a caring attitude and does everything with kindness.

The 6 takes on responsibility, even burdens itself.

The 9 believes in honesty and justice.

We see these qualities in the following 36-words:

> Cashier. Charisma. Comfort. Consumer. Co-pilot.
> Diplomat. Discern. Florist. Popular. Surgeon.

The 9 loves to travel. When the 3 is behind the 9, the travel may be longer because 3 is the number of long distance travel. Journey (36/9).

In the Kabbalah, all comes from Ain Soph Aur: AIN—three letters meaning "negative existence"; with three more letters, SVP "unlimited wisdom" = six letters; and AUR, another three letters meaning "light." Together they are 3-6-9, symbolizing all nine Sephiroth in the One Source. This is the genesis of 3, 6, 9 as the Creative Trio (*777 and Other Qabalistic Writings*, 6).

Negative 36/9's are easily upset, and burdened with obstacles to overcome. They experience more trying times than most people and seem to have more problems:

> Argument. Barbaric. Combative. Despised. Dogmatic.
> Failure. Immoral. Problem.

The 99 is a master number of complete fulfillment. The full number of ARGUMENT is 99, the negative side of this vibration.

The extreme destructive side of 36/9 is seen in the word TORTURE. The full number here is 117: wrong use of power (11) in a sadistic (7) way. Note, too, the first and middle letters are T, the cross, carrying the load.

The 9 is emotionally affected by people and surroundings. It lets its deep feelings affect it adversely. It becomes restless and dissatisfied, forgets its high standards and lofty ideals, and sinks into self-indulgence where it dissipates its energies. The 9 is indeed a testing number. It must forget the self, the "I" (which is the ninth letter), and think more of others.

\\   63/9   //

The 63/9 wants to work for everyone's good. Here are the humanitarians and missionaries. Both 6 and 9 are humanitarian numbers.

The 6 cares for family, friends, the old, and the young.

The 3 wants to do good, bring a smile.

The 9 gives to humanity in general; seeks no reward; is inspired.

Words that total 63/9 are:

> Corporation. Experienced. Inspiration. Introduction.
> Millionaire.

If destructive, there is ANNIHILATION (63/9), for 3, when it is negative, represses itself, and 9 brings things to a conclusion.

The 9 can find fulfillment when it is an INSPIRATION (63/9) and of service to others. Numbers 8, 9, 11, and 22 must consider other people. They have learned the lessons of self—1, 2, 3; of family—4, 5, 6; and the introspection of the 7 that is the bridge to 8, 9, 11, and 22, who are concerned with the good of all mankind. The true expression of the 9 is to use its talents on behalf of others.

\\   45/9   //

This number combination presents a mystical aspect. The intuitive and psychic abilities can be at their peak, making the bearer of the number outstanding in some way.

The 4 gives a firm foundation.

The 5 gives powers of communication and freedom of movement.

The 9 holds the knowledge of all the numbers before, is dramatic, the great lover, the humanitarian.

Some 45-words with these characteristics are:

Accomplish. Befriend. Communicate. Conscience.
Fortify. Marriage. Mountainous. Outstanding. Painting.
Symphony.

For the negative 45 there can be emotional dissatisfaction:

Cowardice. Difficult. Mediocre. Unreliable.

Destructive 45-words are:

Catastrophe. Malefaction. Tyrannical.

MALEFACTION and UNRELIABLE have the full number 99, the reverse vibration of complete fulfillment—the opposite of the feeling of good will.

\\   54/9   //

When the 5 comes first there is verbal eloquence, gifted intellect, and a probing mind that seeks and finds answers.

The 5 satisfies curiosity; has many new experiences; is popular.

The 4 is very well-organized; gets things done; is reliable, conservative.

Some 54-words are:

Cheerfulness. Conservative. Conventional. Incredible.
Politician. Popularity. Trustworthy.

The 9 shows that the curiosity of the 5 and the detailed study put forth by the 4 can lead to fulfillment for the 9:

Certificate. Instruction. Prosperous. Recipient.

The 5 applies to the five senses, marriage, and procreation. This leads to GENERATION (54/9).

In contrast to generation there is the ending of life as in the destructive 54/9 word: SACRIFICIAL.

The 9 as the total for a name denotes those suited as musicians, actors, orators, artists, teachers, and preachers as well as lawyers, doctors, and advisors.

We need 9's for appreciating people.

NINE (9)

Positive: Broad-minded. Brotherly love. Caring. Love for humanity. Compassionate. Creative. Dramatic flair. Generous. Great artist. High ideals. Philanthropic. Romantic. The great lover. Unselfish. Very considerate.

Negative: Aimless. Burdened. Extremely sensitive. Fickle. Frustrated. Impolite. Overly emotional. Resentful. Tactless. Thoughtless. Unfulfilled.

Destructive: Bad habits. Bitter. Dissipates. Immoral. Liar. Possessive. Vulgar.

CHAPTER 24

Master
Numbers

There are nine basic numbers. All the following compound numbers, when added together, always return to one of the basic nine. However, there are several compound numbers that are considered numbers of mastery and are usually not reduced in numerology or astrology. It is said that these numbers are bestowed on "old souls" who are here to be of service to mankind. People who have these numbers prominent in their names or Birth Path are aware of a tremendous amount of nervous energy in their lives. Some can channel it into constructive projects that benefit many. Others use the energy in its negative aspect and never really realize their full potential. Still others use the destructive side and cause great harm.

Children with master numbers have more nervous energy than other children and must be kept busy or given special projects to work on. It is extremely helpful for parents to know if their child's energy is due to the high vibration of their name or birth number.

People with these numbers do not always work in the high velocity of this energy or they would feel depleted in a short time. Instead, they often work and live in the root digit of the master number, but the achievement potential is always there.

The numbers considered to be master numbers are mainly 11 and 22. There are others: 33, 44, 55, 66, 77, 88, and 99, though these are rarely mentioned.

The 11 is the first and is the "As Above," as is every alternate master number: 11, 33, 55, 77, and 99. The others are the "So Below": 22, 44, 66, and 88.

The "As Above" numbers are more intuitive, psychic, and spiritually sensitive. The "So Below" numbers are better adapted to the material world. All are meant to be of service: the "As Above" in a spiritual or professional way, and the "So Below" in a material or physical way.

All master numbers are powerful because they accentuate themselves and their root number, e.g., 11/2, 22/4, 33/6, and so on.

11

ELEVEN
"The Psychic Master"

The ancient temples of mystery had a pillar on either side of the entrance looking very much like the figure 11. The one on the right is called Jachin and means, "He shall establish." The left is called Boaz, which means, "In it is strength" (*Morals and Dogma*, 9).

They represent the positive-negative, masculine-feminine, active-passive forces—that by walking between the two of them we bring a sense of balance into our lives. So the 11 who enters the temple by the center between the two pillars has chosen the positive, upward way. Once on the right path, his success is assured.

Where 2 is a follower, the 11 likes to stand on its own two feet. It has the natural abilities of the 1 and is artistic, spiritual, and inspired.

All 11's are meant to be professional people for they cannot be happy in mundane work. Here are the inspired artists, painters, teachers, philosophers, ministers, musicians, composers, performers, and decorators. Their desire is to uplift others through the beauty of their creations or with their inspired thoughts.

They are an "As Above" number because of their highly intuitive and inspirational thoughts. They can mingle freely in the world and yet not be a part of it. They have a charisma, a mysterious glamour that makes them stand out in a crowd, and they easily draw followers.

The 11 is known as "The Psychic Master"—a messenger of God and a master among men, for it is the nature of 11 to delve into the mysteries of life.

Jesus was such a master and his name total is 11. He desired to bring his light to the world, and LIGHT is the same vibration. He said: "I am the light of the world. He who follows me shall not walk in darkness, but he shall find for himself the light of life" (John 8:12).

An 11 who does not pursue a spiritual or religious vocation is either artistic, musical, or politically inclined. Irving Berlin, who brought us hundreds of America's best loved songs, was born on May 11. And an inspired pianist and brilliant entertainer who thrilled us with his performances was a man with a name totaling 11: Liberace. All 11's need music in their lives. The root of 11 is 2, and music is a strong 20 whose root also is 2 but with the power of the spirit (0) next to it.

All master numbers are filled with greater energy than single numbers because they include the vibration of the root number. The difference between 2 and 11 is that the 11 prefers to stand on its own two feet and take the lead rather than be the modest, willing follower that the 2 is.

The 11 strives for perfection and will study hard to achieve it. They don't feel fulfilled unless they can give something to the world. Many become famous.

On the other hand, they are easily disappointed in people for they expect the same perfection in those they look up to.

ABLE is an 11-word that vibrates to this energy. It begins with A, the letter of action and initiative. All 11's are able.

LAUD means to praise highly, and often 11's are praised for their talents, their abilities, and their spiritual strength.

On the opposite end of the vibration are the destructive 11's. Rather than uplift humanity as the positive 11's do, these 11's want to rule and enslave others. They become despots, wicked leaders such as Mussolini and Hitler (name totals of 11), who were blinded by and misused their powers.

Negative 11's lack the practical aspect because they are not in tune with material matters. They become neurotic from not being able to make their brilliant dreams work for them on the material plane, and they have trials and hardship.

Like 2, they must learn to choose between good and evil, the opposite ends of the vibration. When they turn toward the light, which is the Yod of Divine Light within, it will illuminate the way. Then the darkness of confusion will be replaced with the light of understanding and 11 will reflect that light. When that happens, we see the special glow, feel the charisma, and sense that something special which radiates from the 11. "If we live in the light as He is in the light, we have fellowship with one another" (1 John 1:7).

\\ 29/11 //

The 29 behind the 11 stands for spiritual power.

➤ The 2 is peace, cooperation, loving service, fluent speaker.

➤ The 9 is humanity, completion or "job well done," universal service, and brotherly love.

Words that total 29 are:

Abundance. Associate. Author. Beloved. Bride. Force. Forest. Grail. Guides. Light. Messiah. Parent. Risen. Wisdom. Ultimate.

In English, the word LIGHT is spelled rather strangely. Why not lite? If we analyze the spelling we can see where the letters are absolutely perfect for its meaning. The word itself tells us it is first, last, and always because it begins with L, our 12th letter; 12/3 = the Holy Trinity. In Hebrew L is Lamed, number 30: the Trinity (3) by the All (0) of God.

Light ends with a T which is Tav, the final letter in Hebrew, thus first and last. T is also a plus sign (+) meaning "add more," so it continually adds warmth from Light and that is necessary for continuing creation.

The very center is G, the first initial of God; God at its center. It is our seventh letter and 7 is spiritual and mysterious. G is also for geometry, the science that governs the shape of every letter, number, and physical manifestation.

In Hebrew G is Gimel, the third letter, and 3 again is the number of the creative Holy Trinity which governs creative ability and communication.

Then there are the I and H, the masculine Yod, I, meaning "the creative hand of God." The I also refers to the great I AM, the eye that sees and comprehends all. H is the feminine, receptive, magnetic force known as the "childbearing letter."

In English H is 8, a picture of the above becoming manifest below. In Hebrew H is Hé, the fifth letter, connected with the fifth house of astrology that is the "giver of children."

In the Bible, Light is the first principle of the awakened consciousness. In man it is necessary for life and intelligence. When we understand something we see it clearly; we have "the light of understanding."

Jesus came to enlighten the multitudes. He said "I am the truth and the light. None come to the Father but through my teachings...." He was the light personified as the Son (sun) of God. So 11 has come to mean Light. According to biblical scholar and researcher of ancient religions, Max Freedom Long, this pure and correct translation was misinterpreted by the church fathers to read "only through me" and "in my name," and these misinterpretations became the convictions and tenets of the Christian religions (*What Jesus Taught in Secret*, 8).

Negative 29/11 words are opposite of light:

Angry. Fever. Fiend. Hatred. Unaware. Weapon.

\\ 38/11 //

This means "a gift of vision." It requires a lot but the rewards are worth it.

➤ The 3 is self-expression, creativity, and sociability. It can be attractive, ornate, showy, talkative.

➤ The 8 is organization, leadership, success, application, a good sense of justice; it will strive to attain and is always practical.

The 11 always brings light when positive.

Words that total this 38 vibration are:

> Admirable. Agreeable. Ambition. Articulate. Authentic.
> Christmas. Conserve. Creative. Delight. Diction. Educa-
> tion. Emanation. Energy. Friend. Healing. Heavenly. Il-
> lustrate. Immortal.Oration. Practical. Prayer. Prince.
> Psychic. Purpose. Rejoice. Splendid. Winner.

"Christmas" begins with the two letters Ch, which is called Cheth, or Heth in Hebrew and is its eighth letter, meaning "field." It refers to two worlds: the spiritual and the material. In this sense it means that man is born of dust and then evolves out of dust into the spirit.

The letter Cheth is a picture of two columns with a crossbar (ח) over the top and resembles a doorway or opening between two pillars. In Egypt, Initiates would walk through the pillars of the temple to reach the sanctuary. Before they could enter the Holy Place they were required to walk through two more columns. These inner two columns signified that the Initiate was able to balance his own dual natures and was therefore worthy to proceed (*The Bible and the Tarot*, 70-1).

Christ and Christmas show the worthiness of entering the Holy Place. The full number of Christ is 77, showing it is the Christ-consciousness achieved. The full number of CHRISTMAS is 110, or the self (1) seeking perfection (10) or Power (11) from the Godhead (0). Truly they are "a gift of vision."

There is a negative side to even the most beautiful vibrations. We can see that side reflected in the following 38-words:

> Abominable. Blasphemy. Braggart. Bullheaded. Cowardly.
> Frustrate. Narcotic. Negative. Reverse. Traitor. Vexation.

\\ 47/11 //

A 47 behind an 11 means "inner wisdom reflected through organization."

➤ The 4 is honest, true, and dependable. Organized. Traditional values.

➤ The 7 is wisdom from inner knowing. It is either faith or fear. It reflects on the past and what it has learned. The 7 is always introspective, analytical, and mysterious.

As a root, the 11 always points out a leader who is quite intuitive and inspirational.

Some 47-words are:

> Authority. Christian. Director. Enduring. Foundation.
> Graduation. Grandiose. Historic. Incentive. Inspector.
> Mastership. Meditation. Mysterious. Preacher. Tradition.
> Training. Vibration.

Negative 47-words are:

Chilling. Frivolous. Horror. Impossible. Probation.
Retaliator. Terrify.

The Ch in "chilling" is not the letter Cheth that is in "Christmas," for the sound of Cheth is a k sound (guttural) rather than a "chi" or "cha" sound made with the tongue behind the teeth.

\\ 74/11 //

When the 7 comes first it means outer manifestation (4) is first felt strongly within (7) or comes from the invisible (7). The full number of Mastership is 74. Two words that total 74 by their root number are:

Irrepressible. Precipitation.

Their full number is 155, the self (1) that cannot be held back (55). In the *English Cabalah*, 74 (GD) refers to God.

\\ 56/11 //

This number shows a need for self-control and balance. There is nervous energy because the 5 comes first.

→ The 5 seeks knowledge and often learns by experience. It is male and female (3 and 2), and represents change or travel and new happenings.

→ The 6 refers to the body of something or a group. It is artistry, generosity, loving, and giving.

Liberace's name total was 11 and he was a magnificent (56) entertainer at the piano-forte (56). His costumes were a phenomenon (56). He showed generosity (56) in his lifetime. It's interesting that he was so in tune with those 56-words since his own name totaled 65.

Negative 56-words are:

Transgressor. Unfriendly.

\\ 65/11 //

When the 6 comes before the 5 it means "a talent for leadership," and it also refers to things that are systematic and orderly:

Christianity. Coordination. Enlightenment.
Investigation. Relationship. Science of Mind.
Stenographer. Transportation.

ELEVEN (11)

Positive: Artistic leanings. Creative. Dignified. High ideals. Highly selective. Inspired. May be religiously or politically inclined. Not a physical laborer, but a professional. Persuasive. Quiet. Reserved. Teacher. Witty. Wants to uplift people (as a whole, not necessarily individually).

Negative: A daydreamer: it's far easier to dream about great things than to accomplish them. Aimless. A loner. Can't always put ideas into constructive form. Confused. Emotional. Expects too high a standard in others. In the world, but not a part of it. Miserly. Not at all practical. Prejudiced. Represses feelings. Repressive leader. Self-centered. Self-love. Shiftless. Unfair.

Destructive: Devilish. Dishonest. Wicked. Lacks understanding. May unconsciously antagonize others. Self-indulgent. Religious fanatics.

If there are two 11's in a name, the person may have very little tact.

22

TWENTY-TWO
"The Master Architect"

The 22 came to be known as a master number for several reasons. It has always been the characteristic number of any circle, and the circle is associated with the Monad, or God. The original Hebrew alphabet consists of 22 letters that are the creative basis and attributes of all that has been created. So 22 represents the whole circle of creation.

The 22 is the "So Below" for it makes manifest on the material plane. It is known as the Master Architect because it is capable of building the great roads, waterways, and buildings of the world.

The 22 knows how to unite the inspirational idea with the physical manifestation. Yet 22 is less spiritual than the "As Above" numbers 11 and 33. It is more adaptable to the Earth plane; it can make manifest because of its root of 4.

The energy with this vibration is very high. In childhood the child is often hyperactive and must keep hands busy. This is the child who enjoys Erector Sets and building blocks.

When working in the positive energy of this number, much good is accomplished. Many constructive ideas come to 22's and they have the innate ability to make their ideas reality.

Words that add up to 22 reflect the attitudes of success:

Aglow. Capable. Gallant. Heed. Ideal. Modest. Nice. Noted. Pro. Smile.

Negative attitudes of the same vibration are found in these 22-words:

Aloof. Biased. Bore. Dismal. Fret. Jumpy. Rage. Storm.

The 2 pays attention to detail and likes detailed work; so 22's are masters of detail. As a result they are valuable (22) to society:

Actress. Chef. Clerk. Clown. Crafts. Master. Model. Sleuth. Statesman.

Other types of masters are:

Angels. Buddha. Guru.

A GURU has the full number of 67: a spiritual (7) teacher (6). The full number of BUDDHA is 40, the number of someone who is admired for his honesty and integrity. It is a number of completion and manifestation.

ANGELS have the full number of 58: great activity (5) on the mental level (8).

On the opposite end of the spectrum are those who lack these traits:

Dope. Hobo. Liar.

These all share the full number of 40. They definitely show the opposite of honesty, integrity, and completion.

Most 22's have weak bodies in contrast to their strong minds. It is important for them to have good nutrition. One end of the vibration is starve (22) and the other is food (22). It is invaluable to good health to laugh (22).

Laughter makes the body organs move in a harmonious rhythm that is beneficial.

In Hebrew the 22nd letter is Tav, (ת) the sign of the cross. This makes the negative side of the vibration extreme, so negative 22's lack fulfillment and feel oppression. They become destructive materially and spiritually and they are inclined to go to extremes, even against their own judgement. They often have a hard struggle with themselves. These type of people are in sympathy with the negative end of the spectrum which includes the following negative 22-words:

Clip. Crash. Damage. Flop. Hurt. Harm. Lethal. Pain. Spend. Stolen. Stoop.

Adolf Hitler is a prime example of a leader on the negative side of the master numbers. His total name is an 11 and he was born on the 22nd of the month.

Since 2 is a number of sensitivity, 22 is doubly so. Safecrackers, whose unusually sensitive fingers pick up the inner clicks of the combination locks, have been found to have a strong 22 in their charts. TOUCH is another 22-word. People with these master numbers in their name or birth date have an unusually high amount of nervous tension. This means potential for good, and when channeled into constructive projects they become the benefactors of society by building what is most needed by the people.

But those who become frustrated for lack of an outlet for these energies, either through lack of education or misguided direction, become a grave burden on society.

The strength of 22 is seen in nature, as in the following 22-words:

Muddy. Pond. Pool. Water. Woods. Stream. Trees.

The backbone of a mountain range is called a MASSIF (22) and one of nature's strongest forces is found in a STORM (22).

The 22 is the entire circle of God and His creation, and the spiritual qualities that are to be developed for unfoldment. This number is equated with major Water forces such as tidal waves and energy derived from Water. People with this name number benefit from living near Water.

Water also equates with our emotions, so 22's are extremely sensitive. Feelings go as deep as the ocean, and when aroused, they "make waves." They can be one extreme or the other: calm and deep, or raging fury.

The 22 is 11 + 11. It has the vision of the 11 but is able to put it to practical use. It completes work. It is very strong because it is the double of both 2 and 11.

TWENTY-TWO (22)

Positive: A doer. A hard and tireless worker. A master of accomplishment. A very capable leader. An acute sense of touch. Dynamic. Great achievements. Known as the Master Architect. Organized. Practical.

Negative: Aimless. Fanatic. Feels inferior. Frustration. Indifferent. Nervous tension.Talks big. Service with ill will.

Destructive: Black magic. Criminal. Crooked. Evil. Gang leader. On edge.

33

THIRTY-THREE
"Selfless Giving"

This is the master number of spiritual giving. It is the "As Above" for it benefits the spiritual needs of others. The root number 6 is the vibration of home, love, family, service, and responsibility. It must make its voice heard in its family or career. "No greater love has any man than to lay down his life for his friends" (John 15:13).

One who will do this is experiencing the 33 vibration. Jesus was 33 years old when he gave his life for humanity. The word SAVIOUR vibrates to 33, so this is known as the love vibration in its highest form—compassion.

Another aspect of the master 33 vibration is the experience of the Kundalini force making its way upward through the 33 segments of the spine, opening the chakras as it rises, and causing a tingling sensation in the body from the movement of the petals of each lotus-like wheel.

Positive aspects are seen in the following 33-words:

Ability. Angelic. Blessing. Inner. Inward. Peaceful. Potence. Unique.

The diamond was chosen to be the spiritual gift a man gives to his betrothed to show his love. Diamond vibrates to 33.

Hawaii is considered by many as Heaven on Earth. It totals 33.

Our great spiritual gift is the Genesis (33) of life. The opposite side of the vibration is Doomsday, Holocaust, and Calamitous, all 33-words that are the negative side of the spiritual.

Persons with 33 in a name or Birth Path number are highly sensitive to the needs of others, and through their occupations they will give of themselves in caring and comforting:

Broker. Costumer. Customer. People. Person. Pillow. Police. Priest. Salesclerk. Selling. Teacher. Victor. Waitress.

Occupations are the same as for 6, which is 33's root number.

Some 33-words connected with love and family are:

Believe. Desire. Romance.

The 6 root represents the voice. When it is elevated to the 33 vibration we find it at its height in the great orator and in the teacher. 33-words that have to do with the voice and sound are:

Announce. Concert. Dramatic. Dynamic. Preach. Quality. Resound.

The opposite end of the 33 spectrum is the negative voice that is Shrill (33) and Unpleasant (33) to the ear; voices that speak Untruths (33).

It is the negative 33's that are the Martyrs (33). Other negative 33-words are:

>Cheater. Helpless. Phantom. Robber. Selfish. Torment. Unpleasant.

Both Cheater and Robber have the full number of 60 which is a vibration of power, and in these cases, in the negative use of power.

"33" Facts

➤ The first temple of Solomon stood for 33 years in pristine splendor.

➤ King David ruled for 33 years in Jerusalem.

➤ The Masonic Order is divided into 33 symbolic degrees.

➤ There are 33 segments in the spinal column.

➤ Jesus was crucified in the 33rd year of his life.

➤ The name of God appears 33 times in the English translation of the first chapter of Genesis.

➤ The Tree of Life contains 22 paths and 10 globes plus the one invisible Sephira, Daath, totaling 33 steps of wisdom.

THIRTY-THREE (33)

Positive: Compassion. Deep understanding. Empathetic. Gentle. Kind. Loving service. Nurturing instinct. Selfless giving with no thought of return. Unpretentious.

Negative: Burdened. Careless. Sweet tooth.

Destructive: Martyr. Meddlesome. Slave to others. Slovenly.

44

FORTY-FOUR
"Master Therapist"

The 44 is the master who solves the material needs of the world. It is the "So Below" that makes manifest on the material plane.

Two 4's make this number doubly practical. The 44's are very resourceful. They can take valuable ideas and put them to work helping people build or rebuild their lives. Some help through Medicine (44). The full number is 62: help (2) the body (6).

Edgar Cayce provided solutions for seemingly unsolvable, insurmountable physical problems, and his Birth Path was 44.

Dr. Jack Ensign Addington of the Abundant Living Foundation had a 44 Birth Path, and he gave spiritual insight, hope, and rehabilitation to countless prisoners and others through his radio ministry, "Peace, Poise and Power," and *Abundant Living* magazine. Minister is 44. Its full number is 107: spiritual help (7) on Earth (10), or, seek perfection (10) through spirituality (7). The 10 is the 10th sphere on the Tree of Life: Malkuth. This is where spirit descends into matter.

The 44 is a very special kind of Therapist (44), one on a Spiritual (44) level. These people usually have a foundation in Theology (44).

Edgar Cayce did his work while under self-imposed Hypnosis (44). As his conscious self, his knowledge was ordinary. But when he had these Tremendous (44) Encounters (44) with his Mastermind (44) while in a trance-like state, his knowledge was Unlimited (44).

The church, throughout the ages, has been a powerful Therapist in showing how spiritual ideas can be used for our benefit. There are quite a few words that total 44 which are associated with the church and the ministry, such as:

> Benefactor. Ceremony. Contentment. Eternity.
> Happiness. Improve. Influence. Minister. Rebirth.
> Respectful. Reverent. Spiritual. Theology.

It is interesting to see the esoteric difference in meanings between certain words. Both Happiness and Contentment total 44, so they are important to the spiritual-material balance. But Happiness has the full number, 107: completeness (10) from within (7), while Contentment has the full number 143: ease, joy, and comfort (3) worked for and earned (4) by the self (1).

Certain 44-words also show some problems that must be handled:

Dependence. Discordant. Disturbance. Eccentric. Hysteric. Ignorant. Shrewdness. Suspicion. Stupidity. Unpopular. Wrongful.

Sometimes an extraordinary type of person will have a name that totals 44, such as Houdini. His Influence (44) in illusion was such that people could not tell Appearance (44) from Realities (44).

The 44 also relates to persons, places, and things of beauty:

Beauty contest. Gorgeous. Shangri-La.

Two 4's make this number doubly limited, for 4 sets up its own boundaries, as is seen by the four-sided square. There can be boundaries such as the infliction of Pollution (44), which is Poisonous (44). By disobeying basic laws we cause our own misfortunes. But we can Improve (44) our lives with proper Exercises (44). Swimming (44) is particularly beneficial.

Where exercises can be used for therapeutic value physically, harmonious music is of like value to us emotionally. The Orchestra (44) is a dynamic medium for balancing our energies through musical sound.

We can group certain 44-words together and come up with powerful ideas that total 88:

Marriage-ceremony. Marriage-happiness. Respectful-appearance. Spiritual-therapist. Unlimited-diplomacy. Tremendous-influence. Tremendous-masterwork.

People with a 44 Birth Path or name total find themselves involved in helping themselves and others in physical or emotional therapy. It is a master commitment.

FORTY-FOUR (44)

Positive: A leader. Confidence. Knows what needs to be done and how to do it. Mental Control. Strength of conviction.

Negative: Inconsiderate. Overworked.

Destructive: Self-destructive.

66
"Creative Power"

55
"Intelligence"

77
"Christ-consciousness"

88
"Success"

99
"Fulfillment"

These master numbers are rarely found in the name or birth date. But words that add up to these numbers correspond with the qualities of the numbers themselves.

FIFTY-FIVE (55)

The entire scope of all knowledge is contained within the Ten Sephiroth, or numbers. When 1 through 10 are added to each other, their total is 55, so 55 is known as the number of intelligence. Since 5 plus 5 is 10, the number of perfection, 55-words strive for perfect answers:

> Aristocratic. Dictionary. Discipline. Intelligent.
> Numerology. Omniscience. Orchestrated. Picturesque.
> Profession. Refinement. Researcher.

The basic meanings of 5 are sexuality and the senses, freedom, curiosity, and adaptability, so the 55 is both a physical and a mental number. Its 10 root is a new start, on a new cycle:

> Generations. Grandparent. Personality. Rejuvenation.

The negative vibration is found in: Braggadocio. Condemnation. Counterfeit. Profligate (reckless spendthrift).

Some 55-words that have 100 as their full number are: Discipline. Lightning. Researcher.

The 100 is the power of 10 raised to the Cosmic level: 10 multiplied by itself. It has been described as the Ten Sephiroth of the Tree of Life accomplishing by self-contemplation (*The Book of Tokens*, 172).

These are strong words. Lightning is unharnessed primal energy. Discipline makes us strong, and it is the researcher who finds the answers.

SIXTY-SIX (66)

There are six-dimensional aspects of matter as we know it—height and depth, right and left, back and front. This corresponds to the vowels of EARTH: E-5 + A-1 = 6. So Earth's desire (vowels) is to bring forth matter and to be our Cosmic Mother.

Where 6 is representative of matter, 66 refers more to the higher spiritual perspective, as in the following 66-words:

> Discipleship. Personified. Religionists (A body of believers). Resurrection. Spiritual work. Transformation. Venture-inward.

Something pertaining to purely renewing the body is RECONSTRUCTIVE (66) surgery.

The 6 is the number of the voice, for that is a creative tool to bring forth words. Two 6's double the strength behind this creative power. The words CURSE and SWEAR both total 66 by their full numbers and they do give body to negative feelings.

It is interesting that WOMAN is 66 in its full number, and it is from the body of woman that the child is born. The 6 is known as the Cosmic parent. The 66 is both father and mother, and 6 plus 6 is 12/3, so 66/3 is father, mother, and child. There are several words that are 66 in their full number which relate to the family:

> Family. Happy. Sociable. Wedding.

SEVENTY-SEVEN (77)

The 77 is known as the number of the Christ-consciousness because CHRIST has 77 as its full number, and Jesus was the 77th in his line of ancestry. Related words that total 77 as the full number are: Abundant. Disciple. Glory. Power. Stamina. Stars.

Three ideas that total 77 by their root are:

> Intensification. Psychoanalytically. Spiritual-quality.

77 is the analytical thinker—as can be seen by the "77-word," RESEARCH. True 7's are spiritual. The more spiritual, the more they radiate that "spiritual-quality," an "intensification" of inner wisdom.

EIGHTY-EIGHT (88)

The master numbers 88 and 99, I have found, exist in words by their full totals only. The 88 is a number of the master executive. By full word total it has such words as:

> Agreement. Apostle. Conference. Dignity. Excellence. Exercise. Pianist. Pleasant. Proper. Vision.

To me it is particularly interesting that Pianist should have the full number of 88, for the instrument played has 88 keys. Excellence (88) is achieved by Exercise (88) resulting in Pleasant (88) sounds.

8 and 8 = 16/7, and 7 is the root that represents analytical study, spirituality, and perfecting the self. The words above reflect the positive side of the 16/7 vibration. The 16 is known as a karmic number and corresponds with the 16th Tarot card, the Lightning Struck Tower, that depicts ruin unless the spirituality of the 7 is sought. When the mind is kept on a purely physical level it becomes Poison to the body (Poison's full word total is 88/16/7). But when consciousness is raised to the spirituality of the 7, the great power of the double eight blossoms forth in the full-fledged Apostle with his Vision, the Pianist who reaches Excellence through Exercise, and all is Pleasant and Proper.

Since H is the eighth letter, 88 = HH. Each H is a ladder up to success or down to failure. The 8 is a picture of the cycle of all life, and success is due to continual application of the governing laws.

Ninety-nine (99)

The 99 represents complete fulfillment. By full word total it has such words as:

> Accomplish. Answers. Ascension. Comforted. Fortune.
> Poetry. Physics. Satisfy. Thought.

The ninth letter is I. So 99, or Ii, is the I of the Higher Self and the i of the ego. When the ego is in tune with the Higher Self, complete fulfillment is possible.

PART FIVE

Keys *to* Self-Knowledge *and* Word Analysis

CHAPTER 25

The Keys to Personal Vibrations

W e are all here to learn certain lessons. Those lessons are found in our personal names. Every letter, every number contains divine attributes of our Creator, talents, and qualities that are given to us at birth. They are our incoming vibration along with the birth date, and we act and react according to its vibrational content. It is our Higher Self that is responsible for and has decided upon our personal numbers, and tunes into the vibration of the birth name and date in order to fulfill it *(Vibrations, 11).*

Pythagoras taught that everything in nature consists of three parts. Man himself has three planes of life, each governed by its own principles: Soul found in the vowels, Body found in the consonants, and Spirit in vowels and consonants combined. All three planes must be in harmony if man is to achieve success, happiness, and good health.

Once we understand the meanings of the letters and numbers we can apply them to our names for this deeper awareness. (See chapters 22, 23, and 24.)

To find your name numbers, write your complete birth name, for that is the vibration you came in on, which tells your inborn character and talents. Using Chart 3 (see page 158), put the root number of each vowel above its letter and the root number for each consonant below it, for example:

$$6\,1 \quad\quad 5 \quad = 12/3$$

J o a n n e

$$1 \quad\quad 5\,5 \quad = 11$$

(The letters W and Y are considered to be vowels by some people, and consonants by others. I prefer to consider them vowels, but also to chart them as consonants to see the difference this makes. Perhaps there will seem to be a double soul urge. (See Chapters 26, 27, and 28 for a discussion of the treatment of W and Y).

To the right of the name, write in a vertical column a V for the Vowel total; beneath that, a C for the consonant total, and beneath that a T for the total of vowels and consonants combined, that is:

$$V — 12/3$$

$$C — 11$$

$$T — 23/5$$

Reduce all but the master numbers (11, 22, etc.) to their root number, 1-9. Add a B.P. under the T for your Birth Path number, which is your birth month, day, and year reduced to one number, for example,

January 23, 1967 = 1 + (23)5 + (23)5 = 47/11.

This is the way to find your four major numbers.

Vowels tell you the basis of your motivation, which is your animating spirit. This is called your *Soul's Urge* or *desire*. You desire all that number has in its vibration.

Consonants are active in you by their individual letters. The consonants' number total is the "real you" as you perceive yourself in your dreams. This affects the way you act, react, and dress, and becomes the you that others see. It is your personality. It has been called *mind, quiescent self*, and the *secret self*.

Vowels and consonants combined tell you your expression, what your natural abilities and talents are. This is called the *total expression* or *destiny*.

The Birth Path is found in your birth date: month, day, and year added and reduced to its root number, except for the master numbers 11, 22, 33, and so forth. These, however, often also work in their own root number: 11/2, 22/4, 33/6, 44/8. (This is also true for master numbers in the name.) The Birth Path shows *what you are here to do*. Other important factors are:

➤ The First Vowel and First Consonant, separately, are the keys to reveal your natural approach and initial reactions to life's experiences.

➤ Your first name tells a lot about you personally.

➤ Your last name gives your inherited tendencies. These, too, are analyzed three ways: vowels, consonants, and total expression.

➤ The number of letters in your birth name tells what your individual traits, habits, and idiosyncrasies are.

➤ The birth day, exclusive of the month and year, is the "real you" at maturity.

There is also much more in your birth date and name, such as your challenges and opportunities in life, karmic lessons (missing numbers in your name), and the planes of your expression: the mental, physical, emotional, and intuitive areas. This is a most revealing character study, and is covered in Chapter 16 of my book, *Numerology & the English Cabalah,* as well as such books as: *Your Days Are Numbered* (Chapter 6) by Florence Campbell; *Helping Yourself with Numerology* (Chapter 13) by Helyn Hitchcock; *The Romance in Your Name* (Chapters 8, 9) by Dr. Juno Jordan; and *The Complete Guide to Numerology* (Vols. 1, 2) by Matthew Goodwin.

The roots of numerology go back to antiquity and the principles of numbers and letters have been kept alive in Freemasonry and other secret orders. But it was not adapted for our personal names until the beginning of the 20th century when it was "rediscovered" by a Mrs. L. Dow Balliet of Atlantic City.

Mrs. Balliet was a music teacher who specialized in musical composition. She found in her study of harmony that the letter name of a musical note and its sound had the same vibration. This correspondence between the letter number and rate of vibration led her to the ancient study of numbers.

Before Balliet, Isadore Kozminsky of Australia used old systems of numerology, tying in English letters with the Hebrew letter values, and also using the Chaldean alphabet, which some still use with success today *(Numbers, Their Meaning and Magic,* 94).

But it was Mrs. Balliet who set numbers to the English alphabet. It was her feeling that the alphabet of each language expressed the culture's thought-world. She proceeded to write several books on the subject, which she called "number vibration," around 1903.

Among her students were Florence Campbell, who later wrote *Your Days are Numbered*, which has remained one of the main handbooks on the subject, and a woman dentist, Dr. Julia Seton, along with her daughter Juno.

It was Julia Seton who gave the science the new name, numerology, and through her worldwide lectures it became well-known. Dr. Seton's dentist daughter, Dr. Juno Jordan, carried on the work by writing several books of her own, lecturing, and founding the California Institute of Numerical Research.

One of the best known numerologists was Matthew Oliver Goodwin, whose remarkable two-volume book, *Numerology the Complete Guide,* was first published in 1981. His testimony on the accuracy of numerology for character analysis has appeared in newspapers all over the country and a great number of people have had their charts done by him. His wonderful two-volume set adapts each number to each category, so it is not necessary to repeat here what has been done so masterfully. The focus of this book is primarily on the spiritual and scientific laws that work in conjunction with these symbols.

CHAPTER 26

W:

Double-You

The W is a controversial letter among numerologists. Some recognize it as a vowel only when it is preceded by another vowel: aw, ew, ow. Others consider it a consonant at all times. Actually it is a vowel when it gives its delicate "oo" sound.

As explained in the *Reader's Digest Great Encyclopedic Dictionary*:

> The sound represented by the letter W is a voiced bi-labial velar (back vowel formed near the soft palate) semi-vowel before vowels (we, wage, worry) and a U-glide in diphthongs (how, allow, dew, review).

And, in the *American Heritage Dictionary*:

> The only time a W is a consonant is when it has no phonic value, which is before R, as in wrist, wrong, wrote, write, and when used internally as in answer, two and sword.

W before a vowel adds an "oo" sound. Without it, William would be Illiam and Walter, Alter. This delicate vowel sets a high vibration into the ethers that is more subtle than open vowels, and it changes the overall vibration to the extent that the whole feeling of the name changes—which is what a vowel accomplishes.

In Esoteric Science we learn that every sound is accompanied by a color that is sympathetic to the same vibration as the sound. The "oo" gives the spiritual purple-violet color, which is imbued with the qualities of responsibility and gentleness. Because of this, W has been known as "the spiritual letter," that when rightly oriented brings wisdom, the wisdom of the sages. (Note that wisdom begins with a W.)

W stands for "I AM." In *The English Cabalah*, letters of a word are totaled by their full numbered place in the alphabet. M is the 13th letter, so we keep it as 13 rather than reduce it to 4. For I AM, we have: $9 + 1 + 13 = 23$. And W is the 23rd letter of the English alphabet (*The Cabalah Primer*, 138).

I find that persons with a W in their names have two Soul's Urges; reading such a chart with the W first as a consonant and then as a vowel gives a truer reading. It shows the change in consciousness as the person matures.

When the W (23) person realizes that the true meaning of 5's freedom is responsibility for one's actions (2 + 3 = 5), the W is raised in vibration five degrees on the soul plane and takes on the qualities of responsibility and gentleness (*Harmonies of Sound, Color and Vibration*, 66), giving it a second Soul's Urge.

It is the double-you!

CHART 5
ADDING THE W (5) TO THE SOUL'S URGE

Soul's Urge

1 becomes 6:   It thinks less of self and is more caring for others; it may consider having a family.

2 becomes 7:   It is no longer a follower and now desires to specialize in a career to achieve perfection through study, or to grow spiritually.

3 becomes 8:   It has more power, is better organized, and no longer scatters energies.

4 becomes 9:   Once its own foundation is secure it seeks to help others and becomes more aware of others' needs and feelings.

5 becomes 10:   The senses are under control. It now has a spiritual mission to fulfill.

6 becomes 11:   It becomes more intuitive, artistic and/or spiritual, and tends to daydream.

7 becomes 12/3: From introvert to extrovert, the inner knowledge bursts forth into beautiful self expression.

8 becomes 13/4: From striving to manifestation.

9 becomes 14/5: From tests well done, to seeking knowledge on yet a higher plane.

CHAPTER 27

Y: Vowel
or Consonant?

There is question among numerologists as to when the Y is to be considered as a vowel.

Some always use the final Y as a consonant; others always use it as a vowel. Some say it is such a letter of indecision that it is not fit to be considered as a vowel in the Soul's Urge expression at all. Indecision occurs because Y asks "Why?" and because it is a symbol of a crossroads where a decision must be made.

Some use Y as a vowel only when it sounds like E, as in the name Betty, but not as a vowel when it is next to another vowel, as in May. And so the confusion. Who is right?

Mrs. L. Dow Balliet did not recognize the Y as a vowel, and I feel she was in error on this point.

In her book, *Number Vibration in Questions and Answers,* she explains the meaning of the master numbers by their own "spiritual urge": her name for the vowel count that we call the Soul's Urge. On page 23 of that book is the question: "Which is the higher vibration, 11 or 22?"

Her answer is that the 11 is higher, as the vowels of "twenty-two" make 11, showing the 22 wants to make 11. The vowels of "eleven" are EEE, or 555, which totals 15/6, or 6 value, showing the eleven wants to be a Cosmic Mother.

To me, that answer does not add up. She is counting only the E and O in the 22 as vowels (5 and 6), thereby making the pronunciation, "tent-two." The "ee" sound is gone, and that is definitely an aspirated vowel sound.

Also, the W gives the "oo" sound, so I feel it is a vowel. In "two," where the W is silent, it is a consonant.

Here is what happens when we include the W and the Y in the Soul's Urge of "22":

$$5\ 5\quad 7\quad 6\quad = 23/5$$

T w e n t y-t w o

This number, 23/5, is accurately defined in *The Divine Triangle*, by Faith Javane and Dusty Bunker, as "...strength in material ideas, intelligence in action and wisdom in control." And this is the true essence of the master number 22. It is known as "the material master," or " the great architect."

To be absolutely accurate we should give the W two Soul's Urges, the first recognizing it in its consonant position, which would make the first Soul's Urge 18/9. This number is the goal-setter (1) working hard (8) to complete (9) projects. It's only natural that the master architect would first set the goals, and then in 23 complete them with intelligence in action.

From the time of its inception into the alphabet in the first century B.C. the Romans used the Y as a vowel (*American Heritage Dictionary*). According to the *Reader's Digest Great Encyclopedic Dictionary*:

> The initial Y represents either a vowel pronounced as in honey, pretty, steady; a diphthong pronounced I as in fly, my, or the final glide of diphthong as in gray, obey and annoy.
> Internal Y represents a vowel I as in lyric, myth, syllable; a diphthong I as in lyre, type, psychic, and an **R**-colored central vowel, ur, or er as in myrtle and martyr.

Further indication that Y is a vowel can be seen in the Soul's Urge of the word *numerology*. Without the Y (7) the soul is 20: a collection. It *is* a collection of numbers; but 27/9 is truer because the 7 adds the most important part of numerology—the spiritual essence which is the beginning of understanding. The 7 wants to dig down deep to get to truth. The 9 root represents humanity, so the spiritual truths are there for all who seek. And it is true that through the study of numerology people are led to great spiritual truths. Here you can readily see how much more accurate the Y reads when used as a vowel.

So the rule is the same for Y as it is for W and any other vowel: "A vowel is a speech sound produced by the relatively unimpeded passage of breath through the mouth." And, "consonants have no phonic value."

There may be such words where the Y gives no phonic value, but I could find no name whose sound was not changed by it. Henry would be "Henr" (No "ee"). Shirley and Yvonne would be "Shirle" and "Vonne" (No "ee").

But in names like Yolanda, Young, and York, where the first letter is Y and it precedes a vowel, the Y is a semi-consonant, just as the W is a semi-consonant when it precedes a vowel, as in William and Walter.

Normally Y before R, as in Ayres, is considered a consonant. But notice the change of phonic sound; with the Y it is pronounced "Airs." Without the Y it is "Ares." Here, too, the Y is really a semi-consonant.

People with a Y in their names have a leaning toward the mystical; a desire to study the mysteries of life. And since Y is the 25th letter (25/7), there is a drawing power of the 7 vibration to a deeper inward reflection.

The W has its ups and downs; the Y, its crossroads where a decision must be made. The W has its subtle "oo" sound and the Y, subtle "ee." In every case where this subtle vowel sound occurs I have found that more significant information can be gleaned when the Y, like the W, is used first as a consonant and then as a vowel, giving a double Soul's Urge.

CHAPTER 28

Double Soul's Urge Example: Walt Disney

				1st Soul's Urge W as consonant		2nd Soul's Urge W as vowel
6	15	21	**V:** Soul's Urge	42/6		47/11
1 5	5 91	9 57				

WALTER ELIAS DISNEY

5 32 9	3	1 4 15			
19	4	10	**C:** Mind	33	28/10
			T: Total Expression	75/12/3	75/12/3

In "Disney" the Y gives the E before it an "ee" sound, so we use the Y as a vowel.

Since the W is the first letter of the name and is generally considered a consonant in that capacity, and because it does give a phonic, subtle "oo" sound at the start of the name, it is considered a semi-vowel and thus constitutes a double Soul's Urge.

Soul's Urge 6: Disney came into this world wanting responsibility of a family. He had an idealistic and artistic nature and a desire to do good in the world.

Mind* 33: The 33 thinks in terms of service to more than his family; he thinks of humanity. He may have often felt unappreciated in this growing period because of the self-sacrifice aspect of the 33.

Total Expression 3: The total expression of 3 shows that Disney had a great deal of artistic talent and that his career had to be along the creative, imaginative, entertaining lines. (In a 3 these talents also can be— and often are—latent.)

*Mind is also called "personality" or "quiescent self."

Soul's Urge 11: When the W raises its vibration five degrees to give him the second Soul's Urge of 11, he does not lose the original urge of the 6. Instead it is either satisfied, and a new desire develops, or it comes to fruition through the new concepts perceived in the raised vibration.

Disney used the signature Walter E. Disney throughout his early years. He began as a cartoonist in 1920. It was not until 1929 that he achieved fame, and that was due to his animated cartoon "Steamboat Willie" that introduced his most beloved character, Mickey Mouse. That was the point when his second Soul's Urge took effect. Because the W is raised five degrees from the 6 to the 11, and 11 is a master number, the psychic master, Disney's creative imagination was at its peak and he became even more sensitive to details.

Mind 10: Disney's dreams became reality because his mind number becomes 10 when the Soul's Urge is raised to 11. The 10 is the same as his Birth Path: 12 + 5 + 1910 (10). The 10 is the pioneer, the inventor, having the rare leadership quality with the resources to follow through, for it has the perfection of the cypher (0).

Disney invented the concept of animation, making a new cartoon for each movement. It was also his first attempt to use sound. Few realize that it was his own voice that was used for Mickey. That same year, 1928, he made his first attempt at color in his animated film, *Silly Symphonies.*

Disney made *The Three Little Pigs* in 1933. His next project was the largest one attempted up to that time: *Snow White and the Seven Dwarfs.* That film took three years to make and was the first full-length animated cartoon. It was released in 1938. His inventive abilities continued to grow. In 1940 he desired to interpret beautiful music through the animated cartoon and the result was the entertaining, delightful phenomenon called *Fantasia* (1940). It is a one-of-a-kind, as no one has attempted anything like it since.

Next he came to interpret emotions in the beautifully animated cartoon *Bambi,* complete with color (1942). In 1946 was another innovation in *Song of the South,* using animation and real people together.

Disney did not change his signature to Walt Disney until he was well on his way making movies, probably in the late 40s. The vibration he worked in as Walt Disney reflected new goals: Soul's Urges, desires.

			1st Soul's Urge W as consonant	2nd Soul's Urge W as vowel

1	21	= 22		
1	9 5 7		**V:** (Vowels–Soul's Urge) 22	27/9
WALT	**DISNEY**			
(5) 3 2	4 1 5	= 20	**C:** (Consonants–Mind) 20	15/6
10	10		**T:** (Total Expression) 42/6	42/6

He had his ups and downs due to the peaks and valleys of the W in his early career, and again in major changes made later. His friend and co-worker, Carl W. Stalling, was a musician who worked on *Silly Symphonies.* Together, their ideas brought life to the animated cartoon.

Then Stalling left Disney and went to Warner Brothers, making *Merrie Melodies*, the Warner cartoons which were a treat for children of all ages, and which preceded the main feature at movie theaters in those days.

This was an upsetting time for Disney (in the pits of the W). But he pulled himself out (climbed the peaks) and used knowledge he had gained from Stalling's work in his new productions. His frustrations at the time showed up in his then-exaggerated signature. (Numerology and graphology tend to confirm each other.) He hired an artist to design the famous Walt Disney signature used in all his advertising.

World War II came and Disney's cartoons were used as a medium of propaganda. But during this time, the new Soul's Urge of the letters in his new signature was taking effect. He had fulfilled the old desires and he now wished to do something bigger and better than he had ever done before.

Soul's Urge 22:   His first Soul's Urge as Walt Disney is 22, a master number of the master architect. This was reflected in his motivation to make movies that would appeal to the whole family.

After 1950 he produced *Treasure Island*. Following that were many adventure stories. In 1953 he began producing documentaries on nature, one of which was *The Living Desert*.

Mind 20:   Along with the Soul's Urge of 22, Disney's mind was working on the 20 vibration. The 22 urge has so much energy it has to be directed wisely. The 20 mind indicates that there were many decisions to be made. The 2 represents the law of opposites, of duality. Disney's decisions were extremely important for they meant the failure or continuing success of his work. Changes were being made and it was an emotional time, for 2 is a sensitive vibration as well.

There was a new destiny number (total expression) of 6. His artistic talents had to be put to use so others could appreciate them more fully.

Soul's Urge 9:   Some time during this period, the W raised the vibration of the Soul's Urge five degrees to 9 (22/4 + 5 = 9). A decision had been made. The nervous energy of the 22 was put aside, and a super-achievement of his life became a reality, Disneyland.

The 9 shows loving service to others, high ideals, and a sense of perfection. Disney desired to reach more people (9), bringing his kingdom of happiness to mankind. The 9 is the humanitarian who wishes to benefit as many people as possible. It is a finishing number and this was the last of his great projects.

Mind 6:   At this time, the mind number is 6, another humanitarian vibration. The 6 mind is creative and understanding. It is what gives the fatherly appearance, and Disney saw himself, in a sense, as a universal father. The world was his family (information about Walt Disney is from *The Illustrated Columbia Encyclopedia*, Vol.6).

So we can see by the two Soul's Urges of the birth name and the strong vibrations of his professional name, the sequence of desires and modes of expression that took place in Walt Disney's life.

CHAPTER 29

Prelude to Word Analysis

W hen I first discovered that the letters and numbers of each word describe the word itself, I was beside myself with excitement. I would wake up in the morning analyzing words and thrill to the new meaning I found behind them.

I wondered if words, like names, showed their animating spirit in their vowel count. They do. For over a year I analyzed them by their root numbers, for example, A, J, and S are all 1's. Then I tried something new. I totaled them by their full numbers, i.e., A-1, J-10, S-19, and discovered that if I put a number to each letter in a word, I would often arrive at a homophone, anagram, or direct spelling of a related word, e.g.:

```
S  —  19
A  —   1
N  —  14
C  —   3
T  —  20
U  —  21
A  —   1
R  —   9
Y  —  25
     122/5
     AVE
```

The first letter of our alphabet is A, the 22nd is V, the fifth is E: AVE. A prayer. Isn't that what a sanctuary is used for?

This was all too exciting to keep to myself, so I decided to share it in this book. When I had it half written, a book title in a catalogue caught my attention. It was *The English Cabalah* by William Eisen. I had never

The Secret Science of Numerology

heard of the English Cabalah before, but I knew by then that "Cabalah" (or Kabbalah, or Qabala) meant letters and numbers as symbols of mystery, so I ordered the book.

The very next weekend I attended a lecture on letters and numbers at the Philosophical Research Society, and to my astonishment, the lecturer was no other than the author himself. And there on a table was not only *The English Cabalah,* but his other books as well: *The English Cabalah,* Vol.2; *The Cabalah of Astrology*; *The Essence of the Cabalah*; *Agasha: Master of Wisdom*; and *The Agashan Discourses.* His lecture was exciting because this man already knew and understood all the revelations and enlightenments I had been experiencing on my own, plus some more. And he understood higher math to such a degree that Pi and Phi and the pyramids were no mystery to him at all.

Eisen said we lose information when we don't analyze our names by their full number as well. I tried it with Disney and was amazed at the results.

Walter Elias Disney

79   46   76   = 201/3

This total can be analyzed two ways:

2 0 1 / 3 or 20 1 / 3

B O A C   T A C

BOAC = Be complete (0) AC (ace). Ace is Number 1. In Tarot it is the magician who has the power to create. TA C = CAT. Here is the cat that caught the mouse and made it famous.

Mr. Eisen was definitely onto something. Since his retirement from the Jet Propulsion Laboratory he founded the Cabalah Research Foundation in Los Angeles. His background gave great credibility to this science, and the Kabbalah definitely is a science. The English language follows the same rules as the original Hebrew, as though our alphabet were as divinely conceived as was the Hebrew.

Few know it, but Aramaic was the spoken language of the Semites, while Hebrew was sacred and used only for scripture. The basic laws on which our Universe was built are: "As Above, So Below," and "What is true as a whole is also true in part." The Hebrew Kabbalah follows these basic laws.

If a letter appears twice in one word, the first one begins a mission that relates to that letter and the last one completes it. In God's name, Yod Hé Vau Hé (IHVH), the first Hé (H) is the appearance of the feminine force and the second Hé is regeneration or, her powers to give birth. The first is the mother, the second, the child.

There is a great significance to the arrangement of letters in a word, and in shorter words extracted from them. Words that have the same numerical value have a relation to each other. And, if in related words other words can be found, they, too, have a special meaning.

For example, Binah, the second Sephira on the Tree of the Sephiroth (Understanding), and the feminine part of the Godhead, is the Mother of us all. In that aspect, she is called in Hebrew, "Aima." Aima totals 52 in Hebrew. This makes Aima "the desirable one" or "the precious thing" because the noun that means just that, khamad, Ch-M-D, also totals 52. The root is 7.

They say the son is hidden in the mother because the value of the word for son, BN (Ben), is 52 again. And those letters (BN) are in Binah (BINH). The Yod (1), is a masculine force present in Binh, so within Binh is the Trinity: I—Father, H—Mother, and Bn—Son *(The Book of Tokens*, 47-8).

English corresponds well with Hebrew in this way. We call Earth "Mother Earth," and the full number of Earth is 52. Binah has the power to Create (52); it created the Planets (52), and gave us Form (52). Plus we have, on our planet, 52 weeks in the year. In English, Binah's root total is 25 and the root is 7, which are the same numbers.

Another example is in Genesis 3: 20, "So Adam called his wife's name Eve because she was the mother of all living."

There is no E in Hebrew, but it is the fifth letter in the English alphabet. In Hebrew the fifth letter is H. Eve would be HVH, the last part of the tetragrammaton, IHVH; H—Mother, V—Vau, the connecting link causing fecundity so there can be birth in the final H. So Eve means "the mother of all living."

Now we see how English corresponds so well with Hebrew. All of this is really about vibrations. When we see how we vibrate in sympathy with our own note wherever it is found, then we can understand how the relationship exists between words of the same number. This is all part of physics: the science that deals with matter and energy and their interactions.

CHAPTER 30

The Keys to Word Analysis

We saw how "sanctuary" spells AVE. Through calculations and knowing the deeper meanings behind numbers we can learn all a word is meant to convey. Incredibly, English words prove to do the same as the Hebrew were designed to do: reveal these deeper meanings.

Here is the word EYE, by its full numbers and by its root numbers:

	Full Numbers:	Root Numbers:
E	5	5
Y	25	7
E	5	5
	35	17/8
	CE (See)	

The full number tells us that with the eye we see. The total root number states that I (I) see (CE) from within (7). And the root, 8, on its side is ∞, a picture of the eyes. The eighth letter is H, pronounced "each," so with CEH we have "see each." And we do see through each eye.

In some cases the full word total must be reduced if it is to make sense:

C	—	3
H	—	8
U	—	21
R	—	19
C	—	3
H	—	8
		61 /7

FA G = ef-a-gee, or effigy, meaning "a crude image."

This is amazing, because the original churches were built in a circular design to represent the all-seeing eye of God. So they were really an effigy, a crude image.

The ancient Hebrew Kabbalists saw that the words with the same total were related. So they would further hide truths by substituting a word here and there for an important word, and the substitute would have the same numerical value. Only the wise would understand the meaning behind the veil.

The interesting thing is that the words that are related by total *do* have a relation to each other. For example, "great fish" in Hebrew is dag gedul, DGGDVL, which totals 50. The word for sea is yawm, IM, and that also totals 50. The fish belongs in the sea and together they are one (*The Book of Tokens*, 132).

Another useful tool for extracting hidden meanings is to read the interpretation of the Tarot card that has the same number.

For a long time I would not be concerned with the Tarot because of my mistaken notion that they are just fortune telling cards. But I soon learned that they are filled with symbolism that goes back to biblical times, symbolism that reveals man's true nature and his relation to the world.

The Savant Count de Gebelin was the first to discover that the Tarot is the great key to the hieratic hieroglyphs. The prophecies of Ezekiel and of St. John have these symbols and numbers. Solomon was aware of them and had 36 talismans engraved with these 78 figures.

Later they were found in the Egyptian Book of Thoth, one of the few books saved from the great fire in Alexandria that destroyed the world's greatest library. This library contained thousands of original manuscripts written on papyrus—irreplaceable treasures of ancient wisdoms, knowledge, and thought. Wisemen of the day knew the medieval church would destroy any such knowledge if it were again put in writing, so they set about re-creating it solely in pictures, letters, and numbers on a group of 78 playing cards. The true seeker could learn and the unenlightened could play games. Eliphas Levi said that if a man were imprisoned with only these cards, and meditated on each one, he would gain knowledge and wisdom on every possible subject.

The major arcana consists of 22 cards, the same number as of letters in the original Hebrew alphabet, and each card has a corresponding letter. Each letter originally represented spiritual ideas whose vibratory rate was the number of the letter. These ideas were drawn in symbolic forms that tie in with the attributes of the letter. So each Tarot card's symbols are scientifically accurate in terms of vibration.

The Tarot meanings add insight to words that have the root number corresponding to the Tarot number. The more we understand the meanings behind the symbols and colors of each card, the more information we receive.

The methods of discovering dogma from sacred words are numerous and important, one of which is: finding the least number of a word by adding (and re-adding) the digits of its total number and taking the corresponding key of the Tarot as a key to the meaning of the word. (*777 and Other Qabalistic Writings of Aleister Crowley*, 14).

Every word can also be analyzed the same as a name:

- Vowels: The Soul's Urge, animating spirit, or desire.
- Consonants: The personality, or the way it appears to be.
- First letter: The nature of the person or word.

Background numbers (full numbers, for example, the 25 of the 25/7) are the adjectives which describe the type of expression the root number takes.

An easy way to see everything at a glance is to write the word vertically, put the full number next to each letter, then its root number further to the right of each full number, and repeat the vowels in the next column.

For the word LIFE:

Letter	Full Number	Root Number	Vowels	(Desire)
L	12	3		
I	9	9 ——————— 9		
F	6	6		14/5
E	5	5 ——————— 5		
	3 2 / 5	23/ 5		
	C B E			
	(See, Be)			

Life's desire is 5: to use the five physical senses, and to be free to come and go, to travel, to learn.

The 14 behind the 5 means it wants to experience living and gain control of the physical appetites, or simply enjoy them.

The total expression of the root number of LIFE is 23. That is significant because 2 is the female number and 3, the male. All of life is made up of male and female, positive and negative. It is necessary for the continuance of the species. The 5, as the five senses, shows life to be sensate, a world of feeling.

The full word total is 32/5, which, when the letters are attached, gives us CBE, or See, Be. And that fairly well describes life, doesn't it? Life is what we see and be.

For the word LOVE:

Letter	Full Number	Root Number	Vowels	(Desire)
L	12	3		
O	15	6 ——————— 6		
V	22	4		11
E	05	05 ——————— 5		
	54 / 9	18 / 9		
	ED I			

Love is an important life force. When we face adversities with love we find that it is a great neutralizing factor. It makes our whole being light up.

The beginning letter to both life and love is L, 12/3, or the Holy Trinity. It is 1, 2, 3 or A, B, C, or fundamental essence. Love's desire is 11, and 11 wants to uplift mankind. The 11 understands the spiritual better than the material. It is happiest when it can let its light shine (Light = 11).

The root total for LOVE is 18, and the root, 9, the number of humanity. It is a number of deep emotion, and is the great lover, the romantic.

The root total digits (1 and 8) are adjectives that define the 9 even further. The 1 refers to the individual expressions of love, and 8 is a picture of the continuing cycle of life. Love makes the world go 'round.

The full word total of LOVE is 54/9. This gives us ED I, or eddy. An eddy is a whirlpool. So LOVE is a whirlpool force that draws all to itself. What it gives out, comes back.

Anything we love we direct our energies to. Where does energy come from? Its full number is:

E —	5 ——————— 5		
N —	14		
E —	5 ——————— 5	17/8	
R —	18		
G —	7		
Y —	25 ——————— 7		
	74		
	GD (God)		

It is interesting that ENERGY spells GOD, and its desire is 17/8, the root total and root numbers of God.

G —	7	7
O —	15	6 —— 6
D —	4	4
	26 / 8	17 / 8
	BF H	

The full word total and word root number, 26/8, spells BFH, or "be of each." The ancients believed that a part of God was in every part of His creation, so He really could "be of each." It can also be read as BF8, or "be fate," as letters and numbers, in Kabbalah, can be combined to reveal even deepẽr meanings.

The desire is 6, a picture of the sperm of regeneration, and the number of the Cosmic parent and wise counselor.

In the Kabbalah, the letter O can remain as the number 0 (zero). In that case GOD would read:

$$
\begin{array}{ll}
\textbf{G} & - \quad 7 \\
\textbf{O} & - \quad 0 \\
\textbf{D} & - \quad 4
\end{array}
$$

The Cosmic Egg is in the center, and the Cosmic Egg is all. Energy totals 74. It is as though energy comes directly from the Cosmic Egg, the symbol of First Cause, or God.

In the Kabbalah, as in India, the Deity was considered the Universe (depicted by the circle) and was not, in His origin, the God made in man's image as He is now (*The Secret Doctrine*, Vol.1, 92).

In Hebrew, God is Yod Hé Vau Hé.

$$
\begin{array}{lll}
\textbf{Yod} & \textbf{(I)} & - \quad 10 \\
\textbf{Hé} & \textbf{(H)} & - \quad 5 \\
\textbf{Vau} & \textbf{(V)} & - \quad 6 \\
\textbf{Hé} & \textbf{(H)} & - \quad \underline{5} \\
& & \quad\ 26/8
\end{array}
$$

The total is equal to the full number of God in English.

The TAROT is an anagram for Jewish law minus one T: Rota.

T — 20	2		
A — 1	1 ——— 1		
R — 18	9	> 7—(spiritual and secret)
O — 15	6 ——— 6		
T — <u>20</u>	<u>2</u>		
74/11	20		

Tarot is a collection of cards, and 20 is the number that refers to collections. But by its word root number, Tarot is 11. What does 11 signify? It is light:

L — 12	3	
I — 9	9 ——— 9	
G — 7	7	
H — 8	8	
T — <u>20</u>	<u>2</u>	
5 6/11	29/11	

EF K = effect.

The desire of light is 9 and 9 is the number of humanity, so it is there for all people, to serve and enlighten them. The 9, remember, is a reflection of the lamp of Hermes.

The desire of Tarot, however, is 7—desire to hold secret spiritual knowledge. Fewer people will seek light through the Tarot.

Someone once asked me if I would define God and dog the same since they have the same letters and same numbers. The answer is no, for the sequence of the letters and numbers is different. The first letter gives the nature of the word. God begins with a G, the seventh letter. The 7 is a spiritual number. God is first of all a spiritual nature.

Dog begins with D, the fourth letter, and 4 is a physical number. A dog has a physical body with four legs. Its fun to see what the difference is by taking the word "difference" literally. I subtracted one from the other and an amazing thing happened:

$$
\begin{array}{ll}
\textbf{GOD} \;— & 764 \\
\textbf{DOG} \;— & 467 \\
& \overline{297} \\
& \text{BIG}
\end{array}
$$

There is a BIG difference between God and a dog!

Actually, in several mythologies dogs are the guardians of Hell, the opposite end of the polar spectrum from where all emanates from the God of Heaven.

Something very interesting happens when we analyze the Hebrew name for God, Yod Hé Vau Hé, by the letter numbers in English:

Y —25	**H** —8	**V** —22	**H** —8	
O —15	**É** — 5	**A** — 1	**É** — 5	
D — 4	13	**U** —21	13	
44 +	4 +	44 +	4	= 24/ 6

BD F (Be Deaf)

1. Yod is the male, positive force.

   Hé is the female, negative force.

   Vau (peg or nail) is the factor that joins Yod and Hé.

   The second Hé is the womb from which all becomes manifest, the result of the union (Vau) of Yod (masculine) and Hé (feminine).

2. Each part totals to 4's, the number of material manifestation: the four corners of the Earth, the beginning of form; all is Yod Hé Vau Hé.

3. The fourth letter of the Hebrew, Greek, European, and English alphabets is D. The Roman numeral for 50 is D. There are six D's, or $6 \times 50 = 300$; the Holy Trinity (3) and its infiniteness.

4. That Trinity is 3, and the third letter of our alphabet is C, which is the scientific symbol for the speed of light which is 300,000 kilometers per second. To hear the sound of light traveling through the Cosmos would be deafening: loud. Hence, "BD F." Be deaf.

5. C, meaning light, is apropos, because the ancients perceived God's body to be of light.

6. All those 4's are doors. Remember, D in Hebrew is Daleth, which means door. Only a door separates us from our Creator. "Behold I stand at the door and knock; if any man hear my voice and open the door, I will come in to him and will sup with him, and he with me" (Revelation 3:20).

Sometimes there is an alternate word used in different Bible translations where the word "door" is used instead of the word "words." George M. Lamsa caught this in his direct translation from the ancient Eastern manuscripts in the following verse: "Trust not your friends, put no confidence in your neighbors, guard the words of thy mouth from her that lieth in thy bosom" (Micah 7:5).

In all other Bibles the word "door" is used, as in this translation from the King James version: "Trust ye not in a friend, put ye not confidence in a guide: Keep the doors of thy mouth from her that lieth in thy bosom" (Micah 7:5).

As we can see, other words are translated differently also. But the interesting thing is the substitution of door for words, and the expression "door of the mouth."

Yod Hé Vau Hé is then a series of doors which, when opened, will bring forth words; words that establish creation. This is significant to us for we are made in His image and likeness, as lesser creators. But few of us realize our words are creative tools, and our mouth is the door that keeps them in or lets them out.

Daleth also means mouth, or womb. This refers to the entire circle of the Deity from which all creation is given birth. How appropriate then that Yod Hé Vau Hé be composed of 4's, or doors, or various birth channels.

This brings us to the word BIRTH:

```
B  —   2          2
I  —   9 ——————— 9 —— 9
R  —  18          9
T  —  20          2
H  —   8          8
       5 7 /12/ 3  30
       EG  L C
```

It is appropriate that BIRTH starts with a B, for it is pronounced "Be."

B is said to be the explosive sound from the lips suggesting the primal explosion that spewed the planets from the Creator's mouth as He spoke them into existence.

On close inspection, the letter B is graphically composed of 1 and 3 attached: 13: B. And 1 + 3 = 4, the number of manifestation. This is where form takes place in the outer world, after birth. Following the "Be" is I and R, or "I Are." It is after we are born (be) that we come to the self-realization that we exist (I are).

The only vowel is I, so the activating spirit is the individual. I is the ninth letter, the number of humanity, emotion, and feeling; it is a picture of the generative sperm, the Yod of creation—a part of the light from the Creator Itself that is within each and every one of us.

The root total is 30, the number of the Creative Trinity (3) next to the Cosmic Egg (0). The cypher always refers to the Source of all and all the God-Power within it.

The full word total is 57. Kabbalistically that spells EG, or "Egg." How appropriate for a correspondence with birth.

The 5 + 7 = 12, and 1 + 2 + 3, so we have the 12th letter, L, and the third letter, C. Viewed together this is EGLC. Immediately the eye sees the word LEGACY, which means anything passed on by an ancestor—again, a perfect description for birth.

We saw how IHVH, the Hebrew spelling for Jehovah, reveals its many doors that give birth to all forms of creation:

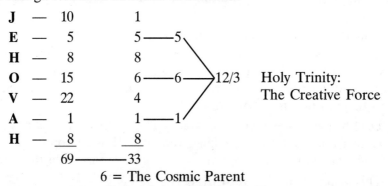

The 69 is a picture of the generative sperm.
The 33 is the number of spiritual gifts.
The vowels = 12/3, the desire to create.

Once we understand the meanings of the letters and numbers, and learn to read between the lines, not much can remain hidden from us. And with the meanings of the corresponding Hebrew letters, nothing remains hidden, for the word itself, HIDDEN, has a window (H) and two doors (D). By opening the right doors and having the windows of our soul unobstructed, mysteries are revealed.

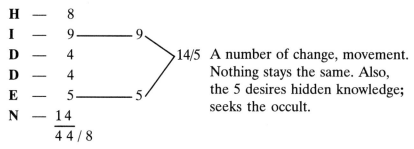

14/5 A number of change, movement. Nothing stays the same. Also, the 5 desires hidden knowledge; seeks the occult.

DD H The two doors and a window are revealed here also.

H is a picture of a ladder, or a window with a sash across its center. On its side it is a big I. I see through the windows of my soul, which is my understanding. If my understanding is good, I see clearly. My beliefs color my viewpoint and affect the depth of my understanding.

If I climb the ladder and observe from the upper window, my viewpoint will be much brighter and broader than it would be from the limitations of the basement window, which is the physical eye, or limited understanding.

"For there is nothing hidden which will not be uncovered; and nothing done in secret which will not be revealed" (Mark 4:22).

CHAPTER 31

Solving the Mystery of the 666

What is the beast? The mark is 666. The 6 letters are F, O, X, a sly and cunning animal sometimes to be feared. Where is the beast? Since 3 × 6 is 18/9, and 9 is the number of humanity, there is a beast in every one of us. It is important to add here that the exact translation from Greek is "Count the number of the beast, for it is the number of man," not "the number of a man." In Greek there are no indefinite articles and "a" was added in the English translation. (*Theomatics,* 178).

Because the lower loop on the 6 represents the womb, the full tummy, the material world, the mark of the beast is nothing more than man's lower nature. The 6 is the hieroglyph for the knowledge of good and evil. The encircling of the material world emphasizes all the worldly desires of the body, all that is part of the animal nature and not the spiritual counterpart.

This counterpart is the Christ-consciousness, which is centered in Tiphereth, the sixth Sephira in the center of man. This is a vertical line that comes down directly from the Source to become manifest in the center of man, which is designated, by the small circle (*The Key to the Universe,* 196).

There is a vast difference between love and sense gratification, which can be understood only when the spiritual consciousness from this center is developed (*The Bible and the Tarot,* 66).

The 6 is powerful because it is composed of two sets of 3 (Holy Trinity), and this power can be used for either good or evil since it is a complete vibration with both polarities. On the negative side, 6 is preoccupied with base emotions and drives. So man must learn to control the beast.

We release that beast any time we force our intentions on others, raise our voices in anger, speak negative words, and commit negative deeds. It is also found in the negative 6 who goes beyond being responsible and tries to run other people's lives.

The root number of 666 is 9, which, besides being the number of humanity in general, is the number of initiation. When man, nations, and humanity as a whole, conquer every lower force within by letting the raised consciousness of each 6 triumph, the beast is vanquished.

$$
\begin{array}{rl}
S & - \quad 19 \\
I & - \quad 9 \\
X & - \quad 24 \\
& \quad\;\; 52
\end{array}
$$

So, **SIX, SIX, SIX**

$$
52 \quad 52 \quad 52 \quad = 156/12/3
$$

$$
\text{O F L C} = \text{folc (folk) or floc(k).}
$$

So the 666 is concerned with many people—a flock or folk. When we think of a flock, we think of sheep, which are followers. They don't think for themselves but do what all the others do.

In Tarot, the 12th card is The Hanged Man. The meaning is that man must surrender self to Divine Wisdom, for there is too much preoccupation with physical things.

The third Tarot card is The Empress. This is marriage, fertility, wealth, and contentment. When reversed, it is infidelity, instability, psychological problems, and destruction.

Now lets analyze the full number of—

THE MARK OF THE BEAST

$$
33 \quad 43 \quad 21 \;\; 33 \quad 47 \qquad = 177/\mathbf{15}/\mathbf{6}
$$

$$
\text{Q G O F}
$$

Read backwards, this sounds like one of today's expressions used by the unenlightened vulgar. That is indeed a sound of the beast, which lets himself be known by his words as well as his deeds. Let's see what the Tarot has to say about this. The 15th card is The Devil, meaning potential bondage to the material, the dominion of matter over spirit.

The sixth card is The Lovers, the choice between vice and virtue. When we turn that 6 upside down we have 9, the card of The Hermit. Its upside down or negative meaning is rejection of one's own maturity, and having foolish habits.

When does maturity come? Some say it is when we become 18 or 21 and are called ADULT:

$$
\begin{array}{rl}
A & - \quad 1 \!\!-\!\!-\!\!-\!\! 1 \\
D & - \quad 4 \\
U & - \quad 21 \!\!-\!\!-\!\! 21 \\
L & - \quad 12 \\
T & - \quad 20 \\
& \quad\;\; 58/13/4
\end{array}
$$

$$
\Big\}\,22
$$

EH AC D—each a seed.

The Kabbalah tells us that we are "each a seed." Seeds produce after their own kind. We are not just a seed, but EACH a seed. In other words, we have individuality; some good, some not. The desire of Adult is 22, the master number of the Great Architect, or the Master Builder; one who desires to do something of value for more than just a few, but for all of humanity.

The negative side of 22 is found in the most deranged criminals and other nuisances to society. Jails are full of those with misguided 22 energies.

So here we see both extremes of an adult. The important thing to realize is that we do have a divine nature within us all. The spiritual antithesis of the beast, the principle of highest love, will overrule the selfish nature and tame the beast.

It takes MATURITY to be a fulfilled, well-balanced adult.

$$
\begin{array}{rcl}
M & - & 13 \\
A & - & 1 \\
T & - & 20 \\
U & - & 21 \\
R & - & 18 \\
I & - & 9 \\
T & - & 20 \\
Y & - & 25 \\
\end{array}
$$

127 / 1 0

LG   AO = Anagram for GOAL.

PART SIX

The New Age Inner Guidance Number

CHAPTER 32

Introducing the Inner Guidance Number

T he inner guidance number is the frequency we tune to when we go about solving our problems.

It is well-known that our brain waves emit frequencies during our thinking process. In our waking moments they emit beta waves and in sleep they are delta. In that time between wake and sleep, in the meditational state, they are in the alpha frequency, which is the border-line between conscious and unconscious activity that precedes sleep.

When we work on our problems consciously, we are in the beta state. But when we relax and enter the calmness of meditation for problem solving we reach the alpha state, where we have access to our Higher Self for answers.

Our Inner Guidance Number pinpoints our personal use of these energies that help us decide how to handle problems.

To find your Inner Guidance Number you either double your total name number (Total Expression or Destiny) or add that total name number to the vowel and consonant numbers. Check both ways, for one may give a master number that would otherwise be missed, i.e.:

Double Total Expression Root		OR	Add Total Expression to Vowel & Consonant Roots		
Vowels —	23/ 5		V—	23/	**05**
Consonants—	38/11		C—	38/	**11**
Total Expression—	61/ 7		T—	+61/	**07**
7 + 7 = 14/5				**23/5**	

We double that number because our Higher Self vibrates at twice the rate of our personal expression. That is the law of our being. "The vibratory rate of the Holy Spirit is doubled, making it an octave higher...." (*The Sacred Word and Its Creative Overtones*, 60).

Inner Guidance Number
(Beta State)

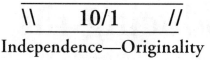

\\ 10/1 //
Independence—Originality

You solve your problems yourself. You know your own abilities and trust your own judgment.

(Negative 1: Every decision is entirely selfish. May be aggressively impulsive.)

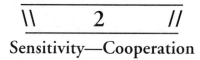

\\ 2 //
Sensitivity—Cooperation

You don't always trust your decisions because of your talent for seeing both sides of a question. You will often go to others for advice and then decide. But when you do decide, you make sure every detail is considered.

(Negative 2: You are too pessimistic to think clearly. It is too difficult to make your own decisions so you lean on others.

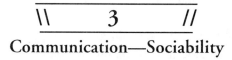

\\ 3 //
Communication—Sociability

You don't always take your problems seriously because you have an optimistic outlook. You come up with creative solutions and you enjoy discussing them. You are enthusiastic.

(Negative 3: Too self-centered. Scatters energies. Worries and frets. Has lack of direction. Talks more than thinks.)

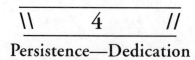

\\ 4 //
Persistence—Dedication

Unlike the 3, you take your problems seriously, face them squarely, and work them out in an organized way. You handle them with honesty and expect honesty in return.

(Negative 4: Too serious, argumentative, and stubborn. Unwilling to bend because of set opinions. You think you are right at all costs.)

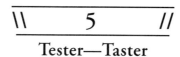

Tester—Taster

You are willing to try different solutions and are not afraid to take chances, and you often learn through experience. You will gather much information in order to make the right decision.

(Negative 5: Too restless to take time to apply self. Will procrastinate. Can be totally irresponsible and thoughtless until emotionally mature.)

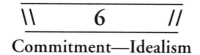

Commitment—Idealism

You are very concerned; you want to take the responsibility and do it right. You consider the feelings of your family and others close to you. You will nurture and protect.

(Negative 6: Inclined to meddle in others' affairs. Can be smug and self-righteous. Controlling. In own problems can be obstinate and slow. Will worry and complain.)

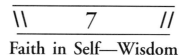

Faith in Self—Wisdom

You analyze the facts and work out your own solutions. You wouldn't dream of asking for someone else's advice. Answers often come through meditation, books, and within yourself.

(Negative 7: Suspicious and unreasonable. May have hidden motives—even consider cheating to get results. Will find fault with everything and thereby find it difficult to make a rational decision.)

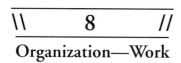

Organization—Work

You have innate good judgment and can formulate your own plans. If unsure, you will pay for expert advice.

(Negative 8: Will strain for material things. Can be overly ambitious with motives for self-gratification. Will not consider others' feelings; on a power trip. Tension will cause overreaction. Desires money; needs to look prosperous.)

\\   9   //

Compassionate—Emotional

You won't do anything that will hurt anyone, so your decisions take other people's feelings into consideration.

(Negative 9: Wants to please everybody in order to look good. Easily depressed and held back by daydreaming rather than deciding and doing. Becomes too emotional to think straight.)

\\   11/2   //

Intuitive—Inspired

You are very intuitive and will often rely on hunches and inspiration.

(Negative 11: Can be very dishonest. Thinks only of self and what can be attained. Completely lacks understanding. Loses through carelessness, apathy, or timidity.)

\\   22/4   //

Brilliance—Ingenuity

You are a master of accomplishment. You can figure out solutions when no one else can. You check the fine print and catch details that others miss. You have much nervous energy until you solve your problems.

(Negative 22: Cunning and underhanded. Can plan detailed schemes for self-attainment. Not to be trusted.)

Reduce master numbers 33 and higher to 1-9.

The Meditation Inner Guidance (Alpha State)

In addition to using our Inner Guidance Number on a conscious (beta) level, we can also draw directly from the creative principle of the Tree of Life by using our personal-number ray. This is the same number vibration but holds a clearer answer because we are open to hear our inner counsel. Each ray is a state of consciousness, and we can use it for effective meditation.

The following attributes pertain to the Inner Guidance Number on the higher, or alpha level:

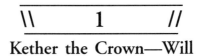

Kether the Crown—Will

Concentrate on one desire or problem at a time. Seek the Will of your Higher Self and you will be directed to the Crown; the great center from which all ideas originate. When you tune in to this first ray your awareness is raised, perception is keen, and all options are clear. (See below, 10. Malkuth: Kingdom.)

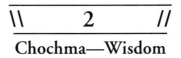

Chochma—Wisdom

Meditate first on Wisdom. This is the area of pure intellect. Your Higher Self is in tune with this ray, and by meditation you become one with this active force. By keeping your goal in view you will see, with your inner eye, the result of any conscious action. This will enable you to make the wisest choices for the action you will take. Wisdom takes form in intellectually controlled activity.

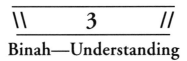

Binah—Understanding

Seek Understanding. In meditation your Higher Self connects you with insight into any problem. Leave behind any preconceived opinions and be open to truth and true purpose. You will become aligned with it. The right answer comes clothed in a feeling of peace, a sense of knowing. Understanding makes the way clear for you.

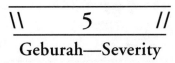

Chesed—Mercy and Gentleness

This is a ray of manifestation that wants to make your desires into reality. In meditation it is reached with deep humility and honesty and by desiring an answer that is fulfilling and due us by divine right. Having an attitude of kindness and gentleness lightens our load, lessens our stress, and gives us a brighter outlook. This attracts peaceful solutions, which are the balanced center of Mercy.

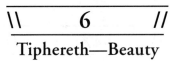

Geburah—Severity

This fifth ray is not as harsh as it sounds. It is a protective force that helps us maintain our balance by setting up boundaries for direction. Remain detached from the problem. View it impersonally, coolly, and calmly. Ask for Divine Order and meditate on right process so that the actual steps you must take will be revealed. Then firmly follow through each step with the feeling of the fifth ray's strength behind you. It is disciplined action.

\\ 6 //
Tiphereth—Beauty

Approach meditation in a state of joy and it will connect you with the sixth ray of Beauty—the ray of the Christ-consciousness whose reflection is in the solar plexus within us all. This is the ray that holds every true answer. Love and beauty are the route to satisfying every need. Any problem can be solved in a loving way. This is a state of consciousness that radiates beauty of expression and right, loving action. When we call on Beauty, we are one with peace and reap peaceful solutions.

\\ 7 //
Netzach—Victory

Approach meditation in the consciousness of having already accomplished the goal in spirit, and ask for the proper physical steps to fulfill it. Have a pencil and paper handy to list the steps received by your Higher Self, which is the seventh ray of Victory. Let the energy of the word Victory fill you with a feeling of accomplishment through Divine Order. When we focus on our goal in meditation, we are given the steps and the courage to follow through to victory.

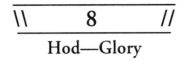

Hod—Glory

To enter this eighth ray, we meditate on the glorious feeling that comes with self-respect and knowing that those with whom we associate also respect us. With this sense of self-worth we reach up to our Higher Self, which is in tune with this eighth ray of Glory, and present our desire or problem in the spirit of "feeling good about it," and knowing we are worthy of fulfillment. Then we must see ourselves as having the talent to bring it about in all its perfection and glory. When we approach a problem with self-confidence, that energy field of self-worth is sensed and respected by others.

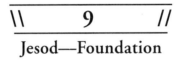

Jesod—Foundation

Foundation is the sphere of Yetzirah, world of formation¾the fourth dimension where our desires take form before being clothed in matter. Whatever we meditate on and see clearly with our mind's eye is where our answers take form, in the silence. To reach your ninth ray, breathe slowly in and out until you find that center of strength and poise within you. Meditate on balancing those energies on a firm foundation of strength. As you consider your desire or problem, know that you have the foundation of intelligent reaction to opposition, and the self-control to handle any resistance.

Keep your eye on your goal and feel as though it were now a reality. Bathe that reality with your calm inner strength, and with a sense of peace and acceptance. See the details that unfold during your step-by-step process for fulfillment. Realize that the strength of that peaceful energy will be with you as you physically take the steps toward accomplishing your goal, and the stability of the firm foundation will remain with you.

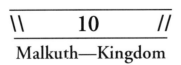

Malkuth—Kingdom

It is said that Kether finds its completion in Malkuth. There is a direct tie between the two, starting as Will to manifest all ideas necessary to do so in Kether, and the completed result in the world of action, Malkuth: the manifested world as we know and see it.

To realize the answers to problems and to achieve desires, we must tune in to the energy field of supply, which is brought about more quickly by working through all 10 spheres of the Tree of Life (Sephiroth), where it finds its perfect manifestation in 10: Malkuth.

1—Exercising will.	6—Joyful expectation.
2—Wise choice.	7—Seeing victorious completion.
3—Insight and understanding.	8—Feeling worthy of it.
4—Gentleness.	9—Balance energies; stand firm.
5—Discipline.	10—See it through to perfection.

(Reduce master numbers to 1 through 10.)

In my meditation I saw how this Inner Guidance takes form from its roots in our desires (vowels), our emotions/personality (consonants), and our total expression (vowels and consonants combined).

There are three interlocking circles of energy, Auric Circles, that constitute our aura, the emanation around every person which is formed by a semi-visible electric force which pours through the surface of the skin. Those who have the gift of clear seeing are able to tell at a glance a person's soul qualities and physical health by these emanations (*The Secret Teachings of All Ages*, XLVI).

I was shown how the three wheels interconnected, and observed the Dove of Peace take form in the center. It raised itself high above the wheels, emitting its glorious white light as the multicolored wheels turned below, changing colors with our desires, emotions, and moods.

The three main points of our being: the Soul's Urge, or deepest desires, our personality, and our total expression of talents are the three intertwined circles that fill with light and color as they turn.

Circle 1:

This first circle represents the Soul's Urge-energy of desire. It is influenced by the vowels in your name. This circle takes on the colors of all your desires, likes, and dislikes from the material to the spiritual.

A. Physical desires: Red spectrum.

B. Mental desires for knowledge: Yellow spectrum.

C. Prayer and healing: Green spectrum.

D. Spiritual unfoldment: Light Blue and Violet.

E. Desire to help others: Rosy Yellow with tinges of Violet.

Circle 2:

This is the mental energy expressed in emotion through the personality (the consonants of your name). These colors, too, run the gamut from the physical to the spiritual, from red to violet.

Figure 6
Auric Circles

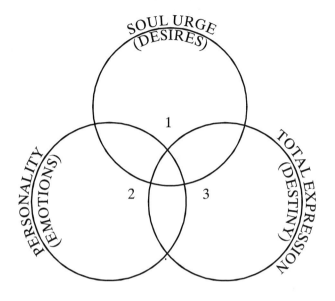

Dove of Peace

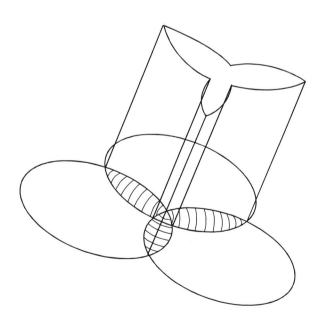

Negative emotions cast a shadow over the colors. Basic, uncontrolled passions are scarlet, while hatreds ooze a muddy brown with streaks of blood red running throughout. Jealousy and greed are dark greens with reddish brown or reddish black flecks. Dark and somber greys, browns, and blacks show depression. Grey is fear.

Happy sunny feelings emit rosy and clear yellow colors. A feeling of comfort and peace gives forth a lovely sky-blue. Feelings of deep friendship and love are a rosy hue. Lavender shades show spirituality. Light green is sympathy and understanding while the slightly darker but still clear green is healing.

Circle 3:

This is analogous to your total expression, or destiny (the total of the vowels and consonants combined). This takes on a little from desires and from emotions and blends the two.

Inner Circles:

In the center of the three wheels are the three loops that form the Dove of Peace. Picture it as being raised high above the outer wheels (Figure 6). This is the Higher Self, the source of guidance of our inner being.

The Dove of Peace remains high above the other three circles in its white-light God-energy, while the wheels are constantly turning and changing color with our desires, emotions, and moods—dark and somber when negative, and clear and beautiful when expressing the positive side of the same numbers. Altogether they constitute the aura of a person.

These colors have been photographed, and the true mystic is able to see them clearly. The rest of us sense them in our feeling world.

We all emit light according to our level of consciousness. The more spiritually aware, the more the face will shine and the more glorious the colors of the aura.

Some mysteries teach that a Christ seed is dropped into each person's heart where it is nurtured by mother-love and spiritual food. When sufficiently nourished, the seed becomes a dove that spirals upward and reaches the heavenly world where it continually supplies a life force to the physical self below. Through meditation this high consciousness can be reached and wisdom revealed (*The Key to the Universe*, 43).

And we must listen! Listening is the beginning of wisdom. How can we be sure it is really the voice of the Higher Self, the God within? We read sometimes of despicable acts committed by people who say that "God" told them to do it, for that was the voice they heard in their head.

The true test is to ask ourselves, "Is this a loving answer?" If the voice tells us to do something that will harm anyone, it is not God that we hear.

Always, the true voice of God will uplift and heal every circumstance. Love is the keynote. Never are we told to harm another or ourselves in any way. Never are we told to destroy property or to condemn anyone. The perfect law of the circle always metes out exact and right consequence without our conscious help. It is our responsibility to respond with love.

The inner Dove of Peace is the highest center of our being, which is in constant contact with us if we turn within and listen. It is the spark of Divine Light of Christ-consciousness direct from the Kether the Crown where Ain Soph Aur abides, a light that is in every living thing. It is the Creative Principle: the first three Sephiroth of the Sephir Yetzirah and of the Tree of Life, and of the top triangle of the Pythagorean Tetractys. It is this that our Higher Self touches upon.

When the three wheels constituting the aura fill with spiritual light, spiritual teachers who are ready to guide the Initiate into higher perceptive awareness see it. From then on, the still small voice becomes very clear.

There is a special feeling that comes with enlightenment. There is a lightness in the solar plexus area, exactly where Tiphereth, the sixth Sephirah, is centered in man—the area where the Christ-consciousness waits to be awakened, the location of the third Chakra of 10 petals that is associated with feelings and emotions. When those 10 petals unfold and vibrate, they send waves of cooling energy from that center, which undulate outward through the pores. That energy is felt as though we had walked into an "electrical" area. Later on, the actual enlightenment is often confirmed in other ways.

For me, one confirmation of these three intertwining circles occurred when I found that exact picture in Manly Palmer Hall's *The Secret Teachings of All Ages (CXLVIII)*. There, it is defined as "The Triune Divinity of Will, Wisdom and Understanding."

I feel that the Inner Guidance Number has not been revealed before because so many people had never sought it. It is and will be in this new millennium. More and more people are seeking enlightenment. They want to get beyond the age-old opinions and find the truth, which can only be found by the true seeker.

When I reflect back on my research, I realize how much I depended on my Inner Guidance. It was on tap for me just as it is for all of us. Most of us use it at one time or another and are not even aware of it. I know I was not aware that I was on a definite wavelength, one that I could put a number to, but I have called on it often in my life and learned that I could depend on it. In fact, this book is the result of my listening to that inner voice. It was amazing to me to learn that my approach is exactly as given in the number 7, both on the conscious beta level and in the alpha meditational usage, and that number 7 is my Inner Guidance Number. But the point that really matters is this: We all have the ability to tap that source. In fact, the full intent of the mysteries, for us all to know, is this one gem of truth: God dwells in man; within the soul of each and every one of us there is that abiding light which is a ray from the Divine Being, just as Yod appears in every letter of the Hebrew alphabet with its light of Wisdom from its Source. All of our God-like qualities—love, compassion, understanding—emanate from this light.

I am an earnest seeker of truth. Opinions and emotionalism mean nothing to me, only truth. I have studied all religions and have found good in each one and I embrace their truths, but I found something in the study of numbers that I could not find anywhere else: insight, answers, tolerance and appreciation for others—for what they are, what they believe, and why they are here.

When you know the meaning of numbers you have the key to understanding.

The light of understanding is within. The magic word is:

Listen!

Bibliography

Abraham, Karin Lee. *Healing Through Numerology.* 1st ed. Euclid, Ohio: RKM Publishing Co., 1985.

Alder, Vera Stanley. *The Finding of the Third Eye.* 7th ed. New York: Samuel Weiser, Inc., 1976.

America Heritage Dictionary of the English Language. New York: American Heritage Publishing Co., Inc., 1969.

Apel, Willi. *Harvard Dictionary of Music.* 8th ed. Cambridge, Mass.: Harvard University Press, 1953.

Balliet, Mrs. L. Dow. *Number Vibration in Questions and Answers.* 2nd ed. Albuquerque, New Mexico: Sun Publishing Co., 1983.

———. *Vibration.* Mokelumne Hill, California: Health Research, 1969.

Bernstein, Henrietta. *The Cabalah Primer.* Marina Del Rey, Calif.: DeVorss and Company, 1984.

Blavatsky, Helen P. *Strictly Private E.S.T. Instructions.* Glasgow: William McLellan and Company, 1921.

———. *The Secret Doctrine, Volume I: Cosmogenesis,* and *Volume II: Anthropogenesis.* Pasadena, Calif.: Theosophical University Press, 1977.

Cannon, Alexander. *The Power Within,* 4th ed. New York: E.P. Dutton and Company, Inc., 1960.

Capt. E. Raymond. *Our Great Seal: The Symbols of Our Heritage and Our Destiny.* Thousand Oaks, Calif.: Artisan Sales, 1979.

Case, Paul. *The Book of Tokens: Tarot Meditations.* 10th ed. Los Angeles: Builders of the Adytum, 1983.

The Illustrated Columbia Encyclopedia. 6th ed. New York: Columbia University press, 1969.

Curtiss, Harriette August, and F. Homer Curtiss. *The Key of Destiny.* 6th ed. North Hollywood, Calif.: Newcastle Publishing Company, Inc., 1983.

―――. *The Key to the Universe.* 6th ed. North Hollywood, Calif.: Newcastle Publishing Company, Inc., 1983.

David, William. *Harmonies of Sound, Color and Vibration.* 3rd ed. Marina del Rey, Calif.: DeVorss and Company, 1984.

Edwards, D.D. Tryon, comp. *The New Dictionary of Thoughts (A Cyclopedia of Quotations).* Standard Book Company, 1957.

Eisen, William. *The English Cabalah, Volume I, The Mysteries of Pi.* 1st ed. Marina del Rey, Calif.: DeVorss and Company, 1980.

Gaer, Joseph. *How the great Religions Began.* New York: Dodd, Mead and Company, Inc. 1956.

Guthrie, Kenneth Sylvan, comp. and trans. *The Pythagorean Sourcebook and Library.* Grand Rapids, Mich.: Phanes Press, 1987.

Hall, Angus. *The Supernatural: Signs of Things to Come.* Spain Danbury Press, 1975.

Hall, Manly Palmer. *The Philosophy of Astrology.* 3rd ed. Los Angeles: The Philosophical Research Society, Inc., 1970.

―――. *The Secret Teachings of All Ages.* Los Angeles: The Philosophical Research Society, Inc., 1978.

Heindel, Max. *The Rosicrucian Cosmo-Conception (Mystic Christianity).* 10th ed. Oceanside, Calif.: Rosicrucian Fellowship, 1925.

Heline, Corinne. *The Bible and the Tarot.* 4th ed. Marina del Rey, Calif.: DeVorss and Company, 1984.

Javane, Faith, and Dusty Bunker. *Numerology and the Divine Triangle.* 7th ed. Gloucester, Mass.: Para Research, 1985.

Kline, Morris. *Mathematics and the Search for Knowledge.* New York: Oxford University Press, 1985.

Kozminsky, Isadore. *Numbers, Their Meaning and Magic.* York Beach, Maine: Samuel Weiser, Inc., 1985.

Leadbeater, C.W. *The Chakras, a Monograph.* 2nd ed. Adyar, Madras, India: Theosophical Publishing House, 1938.

―――. *The Hidden Life in Freemasonry.* Adyar, Madras, India: Theosophical Publishing House, 1926.

―――. *The Hidden Side of Things.* 2nd ed. Adyar, Madras, India: Theosophical Publishing House, 1919.

Levi, Eliphas. *The Book of Splendours: The Inner Mysteries of Qabalism: Its Relationship to Freemasonry, Numerology and Tarot.* New York: Samuel Weiser, Inc. 1984.

Lewis, Robert C. *The Sacred Word and Its Creative Overtones: Relating Religion and Science Through Music.* Oceanside, Calif.: Rosicrucian Fellowship, 1986.

Logan, Robert. K. *The Alphabet Effect.* New York: William Morrow and Company, Inc., 1986.

Long, Max Freedom. *What Jesus Taught in Secret.* 2nd ed. Marina del Rey, Calif.: DeVorss and Company, 1985.

Lucas, Jerry and Del Washburn. *Theomatics.* Stein and Day Paperback Printing, 1986.

Manchester, Richard B. *The Mammoth Book of Fascinating Information.* New York: A&W Publishers, Inc., 1980.

Oliver, George. *The Pythagorean Triangle,* or *The Science of Numbers.* San Diego: Wizard's Bookshelf, 1984.

Pike, Albert F. *Morals and Dogma.* Richmond, Virginia: L.H. Jenkins, Inc., 1944.

Raleigh, A.S. *hermetic Science of Motion and Number. (A Course of Private Lessons).* Marina del Rey, Calif.: DeVorss and Company, 1981.

Reader's Digest Great Encyclopedic Dictionary. 10th ed. Pleasantville, New York: Funk and Wagnall's Publishing Co., Inc., 1975.

Regardie, Israel. *777 and Other Qabalistic Writings of Aleister Crowley.* 2nd ed. York Beach, Maine: Samuel Weiser, Inc., 1982.

River, Lindsay, and Sally Gillespie. *The Knot of Time: Astrology and the Female Experience.* New York: Harper and Row, 1987.

Roberts, J.M. *Antiquity Unveiled.* Philadelphia: Oriental Publishing Company, 1892.

Steiner, Rudolf. *Knowledge of the Higher Worlds and its Attainment.* 3rd ed. New York: Anthroposophic Press, Inc., 1984.

Stimpson, George W. *Why Do Some Shoes Squeak? And 568 Other Popular Questions Answered.* New York. Bell Publishing Co., 1984.

Taylor, Thomas. *The Theoretic Arithmetic of the Pythagoreans.* York Beach, Maine: Samuel Weiser, Inc., 1983.

Tomkins, Peter and Christopher Bird. *The Secret Life of Plants.* New York. Harper and Row, 1973.

Waite, Edward Arthur. *The Mysteries of Magic.* Mokelumne Hill, Calif.: Health Research., 1969.

Wang, Robert. *The Qabalistic Tarot.* 1st ed. York Beach, Maine: Samuel Weiser, Inc., 1987.

Weed, Joseph J. *The Wisdom of the Mystic Masters.* New York: Parker Publishing Company, Inc., 1968.

Wilson, Hazel. *A Guide to Cosmic Numbers.* Foibles Publications, 1982.

Special Sources

Development of letters from Hebrew to present:
American Heritage Dictionary of the English Language. New York: American Heritage Publishing Co., Inc., 1969.

Pronunciation of Hebrew letters:
Strong's Exhaustive Concordance of the Bible With Greek and Hebrew Dictionaries. Nashville, Tenn.: Royal Publishers, 1947.

Analyzed Words Index

Index

About the Author

Shirley Lawrence, Msc.D

has had a life-long interest in the study of philosophies, the pursuit of truth being her passion. Since completing the Science of Mind Practioner's course under Dr. Jack Ensign Addington in 1957, Lawrence continued to seek answers in the Bible, and found more than she expected in the study of numbers. With this information, she became a popular lecturer. In 1992 she graduated from the University of Metaphysics with a Doctor of Metaphysical Science and was on Dr. Paul Leon Masters' staff through June 2001. She then retired to pursue her research and writing.

Dr. Lawrence lives in Southern California with her husband, Jeff Lawrence. They have three grown children with families of their own.